Art Is My Life

ART IS

MY LIFE

The Autobiography of

WILLIAM ZORACH

The World Publishing Company

Cleveland and New York

Published by The World Publishing Company
2231 West 110th Street, Cleveland, Ohio 44102

Published simultaneously in Canada by Nelson, Foster & Scott Ltd.

First Printing 1967

Library of Congress Catalog Card Number: 67-12900

Printed in the United States of America

To Marguerite

LIST OF ILLUSTRATIONS

Art Is My Life

CHAPTER ONE

I REMEMBER THE LITTLE VILLAGE of Euberick in Lithuania where I was born. I remember our house, a low house with a slanting roof built into a bank in a river valley. It was made of logs and bricks and had a long dark hall where big black bears lay in wait for a little boy. There was an earthen floor and a huge brick oven with bunks over it where my mother tucked us in on cold nights.

Behind the house the land ran up the hillside, and my mother planted garden patches of beets and potatoes. At the top was a big barn in which flax was processed into rope. My father was a flaxmaker as was his father before him. My mother's people were farmers. She loved animals and growing things. When she was nineteen, her parents thought she had better be married or she would be a hopeless old maid. My father was brought around and they were married. She had never seen him before. My father owned a large barge, which he sailed and dragged with a tow rope up and down the Nieman River from Kovno to Konigsberg.

In the summers, we lived on the barge in a sort of poop deck on the stern. My mother's first child died when he was very small. I remember her saying he was a sweet child but fragile and could not stand living on the water. My oldest sister fell off the barge, but my father, who couldn't swim, caught hold of her long golden hair and saved her. I was the seventh child and the last one born in Russia; two more were born in America. All of us lived to a good age.

Recently my oldest brother who lives in Cleveland sent me a photograph of himself, his children, his grandchildren and various in-laws. My wife, Marguerite, looked at it and said, "That's not a family. That's a town."

I left Russia when I was four years old, but there are things I remember—the excitement of a fair and a little colt running beside a wagon galloping through the streets, of water being drawn from the village well by a long pole weighted with rocks, and trips to the village baker with my mother taking bread to be baked. One night there was a tapping on our windows, and my mother and father rushed out into the night. In the morning I saw hogs running about with scorched backs. Part of the village had burned in the night.

One incident stands out clearly in my memory; there was a beautiful castle outside the town surrounded by forests and a great, green meadow with grazing sheep. My brothers climbed the fence and began chasing the sheep. Suddenly soldiers with rifles strapped to their backs appeared and started chasing the boys. I was caught, impaled by my clothes on the spikes on top of the fence. I wept bitterly until a kind man came along and lifted me down.

I remember soldiers being billeted in our house—the Czar's troops. They spread their blankets on the floor of our big room and slept overnight. The soldiers all seemed to be very gay and everything was friendly. My mother asked them for a piece of pork fat. It was taboo in a Jewish house, so she hid it in the rafters and later tried it out for lard and rubbed it on us when we had sore throats.

Of the Russian language I remember only one word—the word for ice cream. And as for the trip to America I remember only the clanking of the chains at the German-Russian border as we slipped through in the night. We left because Jewish families had no rights and they dreaded having their sons drafted into the army. Too often, they never returned. I don't know that we suffered from persecution, but there was always terror of it in our minds. My father decided to go to America because his barge was confiscated, which meant the loss of his livelihood. He had been accused of smuggling a Bible into Russia—at least, that is the story. My father's brother had already gone to America, and my father and my oldest brother left to join him, leaving the rest of us behind.

Adjustment to American life was very difficult for my father. He had worked outdoors all his life and could not stand the confinement of a factory. My uncle, who had a store, fitted him up with a sixty-pound pack of notions, and he tramped from farm to farm, sleeping in barns and eating God knows how. Profits were terribly small, but he saved every cent so that he could send for his family in Europe. He had been in America three years, and he was walking down a country road thinking of my mother and the children in Russia and wondering if he could ever save enough to send for us when, behold—he saw five brand-new ten-dollar bills lying on the road before him—sent from heaven.

My mother landed in New York without one cent, only our tickets to Cleveland. On the train a man passed out boxes of candy and we children fell to. What a wonderful country! But when the man came around to collect payment there wasn't a cent. After much excitement, my mother sold a couple of silver spoons to a passenger and all was well.

We settled in Port Clinton, not far from Cleveland, in a house by the railroad tracks with fields and meadows on the other side. My family were totally Old World people. When they came here they had nothing, and they felt utterly lost in a completely strange country. In Russia they had inherited their house, all their copper utensils, their feather beds, their linens, silver, and pewter. Things like these were customarily handed down from generation to generation, and it was normal to be well supplied. They had their own land and their own garden. As average human beings in a low economic strata they were well off.

In America they started with nothing. My father and mother were very simple people, intelligent but without schooling. They could speak five languages but they could neither read nor write. Their education was traditionally Hebrew; they had learned the Bible by rote. They observed the Jewish holidays and traditions and said their prayers daily. My father was very much interested in the events of the world, but he was completely indifferent to commercial success. It was my mother who valued success—or perhaps it was security she wanted. Caring for a brood of children was an all-day and an all-night job. I remember getting up in the middle of the night and finding my mother scrubbing floors and washing clothes. My father drove around the country all day with a horse and wagon peddling notions. I can still see him sitting by lamplight in the kitchen, spreading out all the small change and counting the day's earnings.

My mother would argue with him and tell him he had started out with more money than he had come back with and ask, "Where is it?" And he would shout, "And how do I know?"

My mother was a handsome, outgoing woman, who made friends easily. I remember her trips to the docks to see fishermen. They would give her fish, and in return she would make gefilte fish and sweet and sour carp for them—things they had never heard of, and they found them delicious.

I started to go to school. When my teacher asked me my name I told her "Zorach."

"That's just too difficult to pronounce," she said. "We'll call you Willie." And William it has remained.

I did not adjust easily to life in America. The people I lived among were a mystery to me. School was a greater mystery. I was surrounded by unknown and often hostile forces and events, through which, with luck, I threaded my way but which I never quite understood. This was also true of my parents, and much of this must have been reflected in my childhood. At the same time I was exposed to the typical American boy's life. I remember sticking a pin in a bicycle tire to see what would happen and getting caught. And I remember getting into a row boat at the docks on Lake Erie and falling overboard. I was scared to death and soaking wet, but I never told anyone what I had done.

We sent for my cousins in Europe. When they arrived they were dressed in the clothes that children wore in Russia—long pants, boots, and gay overshirts with belts. My aunt was scandalized and ashamed of such greenhorns. She immediately stripped them of their clothing and dressed them in all new clothes from the store—Americanized them right away. My family had probably been Americanized in the same way.

We lived in Port Clinton three years. My older brothers were growing up and spending too much time around the docks. My parents decided to move to Cleveland, where the children could work and keep out of trouble. They felt they couldn't afford to send them to school when they could be wage earners. My father took the horse and wagon and went ahead. My mother with all the children followed a week later. After we were settled, my father found people he could talk to and trade with in the outlying districts—Poles, Litvaks, and Russians who worked in the blast furnaces. But they had no money to buy his wares. Maybe there was too much competition or the people didn't save the money to pay for things. He began exchanging merchandise for scrap iron and junk, which he seemed to be able to sell. I went with him to hold the horse and help. My father would start for the outlying districts and farms. He liked wandering from farm to farm; he liked farmers and they liked him. He seemed to be more interested in traveling places than in the money he could make when he got there. As I got older, this job that had been so exciting bored me and humiliated me.

My father had come to this country at forty-five. He never mastered the language. He remained a Russian, kept his beard, wore felt boots, and in winter he was enveloped in a huge black overcoat tied around the waist with a rope. He was a little man but tremendously strong, with powerful hands. I remember when two men tried to rob him and he held them by the lapels of their coats, yelling, "Police!" until they were arrested.

One time he found a huge piece of machinery for sale. The man wanted sixteen dollars for it. It was too big a deal for my father. He went back to Cleveland, got himself a partner, and they bought the thing. They were afraid to drive through the city, afraid of the cops who were always poking in their wagon, and afraid the machinery might have been stolen. So they had me, a little kid, drive the wagon home. They worked on this treasure with a sledge hammer for three days to separate the brass from the iron and finally made three dollars apiece on the deal.

One time I said to my father, "Those people down the street have a big pile of junk in their yard—why do they just pile it up? Why don't they sell it?"

My father said, "They keep it, and when the price goes up they sell it. That's how they get rich."

"Why don't you do that? Why do you sell it every night?"

He said, "Oh, for that you have to have a lot of money."

He had to sell his junk every night and make a few cents to make it possible for us to eat.

My childhood was spent in the slums of Cleveland. Images appear, vanish, and reappear like the detailed patterns in tapestry or colors spotted on a canvas in a correlated design. The eye and mind wander over the surface picking out details from the overall pattern—a wide street with clanking streetcars, trolly wires overhead; towards evening, crowds coming home from work, hanging like bees on the running boards of the trolleys. At dusk, wagons drawn by six galloping horses; smells, kids yelling "Ho, ho, honey dumpers." Woodland Avenue, once a beautiful, wide, tree-lined street with handsome houses—then a dilapidated slum, a market street where farmers lined their produce up along the sidewalks and cried their wares. Across the street, houses seemed a long way off, set in back of dried up lawns full of tall dried grass and weeds. A small boy seldom walked across the street.

Those were the days of a saloon on every corner, and livery stables; kids would jump from upper windows into soft manure piles. Of our neighbors, some were colored, some were cooks, laborers, Italian vegetable men, and commission merchants.

I remember the agony of Hebrew lessons after school. On Sundays I would sit in torture reciting Hebrew while the Rabbi and his family ate a beautiful dinner.

The winters were crowded with snow storms, cold, sleet, slush; I suffered constantly from catarrh. I remember the dispensary and funerals, our neighbor dying of lockjaw. A little girl in my class who lived across the street died—just died—vanished out of life and was no more.

A little, wizened man, always well dressed and wearing a bowler hat, carrying a cane, and with a stogey in his mouth, was pursued by a gang of kids throwing stones and yelling, "Stogey, hey, Stogey." He always stopped and shook his fist at the kids.

Some people moved into a house across the street. Around five o'clock that evening we saw a disreputable woman sitting on the doorstep; a red light appeared in the window at night. Someone complained to the authorities. The house was raided and closed and the woman disappeared.

The Educational Alliance was further down the street. There was a Gymnasium, a playground, and a library where we could read books.

The little boy next door played the harmonica beautifully. I bought one and tried to learn, but I could only produce sounds—not music. A mother brought a little girl over to our house who sang popular songs such as, "Bill Bailey, won't you please come home." I was terribly impressed. A boy at a party would do fancy jigs to a tune. I wished I could jig. I tried but I was clumsy, my feet wouldn't move. I remember my frustration and thinking it was wonderful to sing and dance and play a mouth organ or a Jew's harp, but I couldn't seem to learn.

My mother was very enterprising. She was determined to own a house, a home of our own. She found a brick house in a run-down section of Cleveland, on Woodland Avenue. The street had been widened, the big trees cut down; the flower beds and lawns were black patches and ran to weeds. It was a good, substantial house owned by an old man named Peter Steers, an early-American type. He'd been captain of a steamboat going down the Ohio to New Orleans. Now he was retired. He didn't have much money left, and he was alone in the world. My mother made a deal with the old man. She borrowed 300 dollars to give him on the condition that he could stay with us in his house as long as he lived. Old Mr. Steers looked after us children like a nurse. He'd wash our heads and bathe us. This was the beginning of my emancipation from being Jewish —there was a non-Jew in the family and we had only known Jews before. When we'd talk Yiddish he'd say, "What are you chattering about? Talk United States."

He was an old Southern gentleman who slept with a loaded gun under his pillow and "God bless our home" over his door. He played the banjo and sang old Southern melodies and entertained us with tales of steamboating on the Mississippi, the Civil War, and philosophy. He was a Democrat and easily made a Democrat out of me. He took me to political rallies, where I heard Teddy Roosevelt hold forth and saw Bob LaFollette stride up and down the platform like a caged lion. He took me to Rigoletto and Sappho and to a vaudeville show, where I had such a hilarious time that he was embarrassed and said that he would never take me again.

My mother used to take in boarders and roomers to help out, and she rented the upstairs to an Italian family. The neighborhood was a mixed one—Italians, Irish, Russians, Jews, and all kinds of laborers and, later, colored people. There were street brawls, knifings, and gay times when the streets were turned into colorful Italian festivals. And there were always Jewish weddings. A Jewish wedding was a very festive occasion: it meant all kinds of marvelous food and gaiety. My father was very lively at these weddings. He danced the Kasotsky—a version of the classical Tartar dance, a whirling dance on bent knees. It is about the liveliest dance there is. My father would always end up with a somersault in the air, and everyone would applaud. Years later, when I began to dance in Greenwich Village, I found that, without any training, I, too, could dance this dance—but not like my father.

The street we lived on was used as a local produce market. Farmers lined the sidewalks with their vegetables and wares. There was no place for the horses. They were packed one alongside the other on the street with traffic jammed around them. My mother took them off the streets and tied them in our back yard. It took courage and skill. There were twenty or thirty horses in the yard at a time and sometimes the muck was up to our ankles, but my parents made a little money that way, ten or fifteen cents a horse.

There were beautiful spider webs in the sheds. I loved the spiders and loved watching them. I remember my father getting a broom to sweep them off. I was heartbroken and protested and he stopped, but the next morning the spiders were all gone.

I raised bantams in the back yard. I loved the gay-colored, cocky little fellows, but I never wanted anyone to eat the eggs. I imagine the family solved that problem as they had the one of the spider webs, without hurting me.

There were some fresh kids, living next door, who had a bulldog. One day he took a bite out of my sister's leg, and my mother insisted he be shot so that my sister wouldn't get hydrophobia. There was much ill feeling over this, and one day these kids set an old couch afire alongside our barn. The first thing we knew, the whole barn was in flames. My father got his horse out and ran into the street shouting, "Fire!" Everyone was coming home from work, the trolley cars were packed inside and out, and people thought it was a joke to see an old Jew running out waving his arms and shouting, "Fire!" But the fire engines came and put the fire out.

If our neighborhood had become very international, it also had become very tough. Once, when one of my brothers came home from work, he was attacked and beaten up by a bunch of rowdies. He said nothing, but when this began happening every night, he became more and more miserable and finally told my father. My father and a couple of my older brothers went out that night. They took crowbars and went after this gang. We heard the crowbars flying and clanking around the street. After that my brother had no more trouble.

My father used to be harassed and attacked and stoned. Boys yelled "Sheeny" at him on the streets. I remember some kids getting him into their yard to buy a sack of junk. It was supposed to be iron, but when he looked in, it was only rocks. When he wouldn't fall for it, they began pelting him with the rocks. He ran down the street yelling, with the kids after him. Everyone thought it was a joke. All this made me very self-conscious and embarrassed. I didn't know how to live with it, and I was miserable for my father and myself.

These were the days of Tom L. Johnson and the streetcar strikes. Johnson was a reform mayor. He promised the people a three-cent fare if he could take over the lines for the city. The strikes were terrific. Quantities of strike breakers were imported and it was war. Streets were littered with rubbish ten feet high, rails and streets were torn up; effigies labeled "scab" were strung on trolley wires. I remember a boy watering his horse yelled, "Scab!" at a motorman. The motorman stopped his car, chased the boy, and shot him dead. The company got the man released, and he ran cars in Cleveland for many years, but I would never set foot in his car: I remembered. During the strike a man gave me a bar of soap and told me to grease the tracks. I thought it would be fun, but my father saw me and yanked me off warning me I'd be killed if caught.

I was in the third grade when I started as a wage earner, selling papers and shining shoes. After school a bunch of us boys raced to the public square and fought for the late editions. We hopped street cars, yelled, "Extra!" and developed strong lungs and legs. Life as a newsboy meant having amazing contacts with the world of people—medicine men selling snake oil, corn doctors, socialist orators, and Negro evangelists predicting the end of the world. I remember a quack doctor riding through the streets in a carriage drawn by four beautiful horses and throwing handfuls of nickels to the crowds. I sold papers to Bob Fitzsimmons and Mark Hanna. I watched the sleigh races on Euclid Avenue on snowy winter Sundays. I ran errands and carried heavy bags for salesmen until I thought my arms would be pulled out of their sockets. But with it all, I was no businessman; I made very little money, and every cent I made I gave to my mother.

Some kids asked me one day, "How much do you rake off selling papers?" They told me they kept part of the money and never gave their mother all. I was horrified. I couldn't think of doing such a thing.

The day McKinley was shot, I was delivering my papers. Women rushed out into the streets, weeping. Boys were rushing about selling the latest editions, crying, "Extra! Extra!"

And I had to go right on with my paper route.

Sunday newspapers were two for a nickel, and you sold them for a nickel apiece. Once when I bought two from a kid and gave him a quarter, he lit out, hopped a car, and disappeared. I caught up with him on the public square and demanded my change. He denied I had given him a quarter. Finally I knocked him down on the sidewalk and began pommeling him. A man grabbed me, slammed my head against a lamppost till I saw stars, and handed me over to a policeman, who took me to jail.

I told the policeman, "This fellow cheated me; it is not my fault."

He said, "You were disturbing the peace."

They put me in jail in a cell with a little colored boy who had run away from school. He was weeping and I was weeping. Fortunately, an uncle of mine had been riding by on a streetcar and had seen the policeman taking me away.

As soon as my father heard what had happened, he rushed over to see Harry Bernstein, the wardheeler for the Republican party. "Czar Bernstein" organized the immigrants, got them citizen papers, got them out of trouble, and delivered the vote. Harry Bernstein called someone up, and I was let out.

I was very miserable. There was no justice in the world; a crime had been committed against me, and I was the one to suffer. My parents were very sympathetic. They knew I wouldn't do anything wrong. But when I went back to school and told my teacher why I had been absent, she made a scene and treated me as if I were a criminal. I had committed the unpardonable crime of getting arrested.

I had to go to court the next day. A man there told me to plead guilty. "Then they'll give you a lecture and let you off."

I did—and the judge gave me a long lecture on how I was starting a criminal career and dismissed me.

I used to get up at six in the morning to go on my paper route. One terribly stormy day my mother stopped me. "You can't go out on a day like this." I didn't go and somehow that seems to have been the end of my life as a newsboy.

School was a world I never understood and never seemed to fit into. In the lower grades some of my teachers were very nice girls, and gay. They had flirtations with the firemen in the next block and used to send me down with notes. We were happy with these teachers. After the fourth grade the teachers were older and more removed from the children. We did not understand them, nor did they know how to handle us. Discipline was lax both in school and out. The kids were uncontrolled. There were gang wars and lots of trouble. Kids would line up at either end of the block and throw rocks at each other, and any unprotected kid was jumped upon. I remember our principal walking some of the boys home because of the gangs waiting for them. Those of us who weren't in the gang had to run the gauntlet.

I used to love poetry and recitation. And I remember every poem, song, and recitation from those days—Sir Walter Scott, William Cullen Bryant, and Longfellow. The rest of school was a mystery to me, a morass through which I stumbled and fought my way. Arithmetic was a trap, grammar another. It was German grammar that absolutely defeated me—German was taught in the public schools in Cleveland at that time. I was never any good at examinations; my brain would cease to function the minute an examination paper was put in front of me.

My seventh grade teacher, Miss Alice Sterling, was nice and took a great interest in me because I drew. I used to make drawings for her and often went out to her house to help her with such things as taking down screens in the fall. She was no disciplinarian; the kids in her class were a pretty tough lot, and she simply couldn't control them. Despite Miss Sterling's interest in me, I was disturbed and unhappy. I'm not sure now whether I quit or whether the school gave me up as a hopeless case. Anyway I remember feeling that I was through with school, that my parents needed my help, and that I should go out and get a job.

I was shy and big for my age. I wandered around the streets of Cleveland from one end of town to the other. I hung around railroad tracks and shops. I'd see signs, "boy wanted," but was too shy to go in and ask for the job. Finally through other boys, I began to get jobs, the jobs nobody else wanted and jobs I was not fitted for. They never lasted more than a few days or a week, and I penetrated into almost all the lower branches of industry. I got a machine shop job; a boy told me, "Watch yourself. The last kid working that punch machine lost all his fingers on one hand." I stuck a bar into the machine and broke it. I was fired. I had a job in a hat factory and got bored to death dusting hats. There was a job in a brass factory working with buffing wheels in an atmosphere dense with metal dust, which filled the lungs and eyes and left one coated from head to foot with brass. My job was to dip the hot brass in benzine and roll it in sawdust. It was so painful to the hands that I was in agony. I quit.

After these experiences, school didn't look as black as it used to. I wrote a long letter to Miss Sterling and told her I wanted to come back. I don't know what I said but it touched her deeply. I went back to the seventh grade, which was very humiliating to me because most of the children were half my size. That year the class was made up of an entirely different breed of children; everything was peaceful and lovely. Miss Sterling kept me happy by letting me draw copies of Millet and other masters, and I covered the blackboards with drawings. She wasn't teaching drawing—just encouraging me.

At an early age my art took the form of woodcarving. I began working on back fences and barn walls. The kids in the neighborhood thought I was good, but at school there was a boy who was a whiz at drawing cowboys and Indians. I was much in awe of him but was also inspired. I decorated books, papers, blackboards, even the backs of my hands with Indians and such. No surface was safe from me. I even drew all over a geography book and was sent to the principal. She took one look and said, "You will have to pay for this book." I paid five cents, and they let me keep the book. It was the first book I ever owned, and I still have it.

When we bought our house there were psuedo-classical chromos on the walls. They were my introduction to art. A scene by Turner hung over my bed; I always looked at it. My family could not see keeping a potential wage earner in school. I must learn a trade. They knew nothing of art—this habit of mine of drawing was just something that got me into trouble. The eighth grade teacher agreed with them, but Miss Sterling thought otherwise. She persuaded the supervisor of art to write me a letter of introduction to the Morgan Lithograph shop.

I went down with my letter. The office boy said no boys were wanted, but by this time I recognized the brushoff.

I said, "I have an important letter for the superintendent."

He took me up to the foreman of the printing department, who looked at the letter and took me over to the Art Department and introduced me to George Groll, the head of the department—a little round fat man with a moon face and a bad limp. He chewed on a cigar and rolled it around in his mouth while he read the letter. He told me to come back and bring some of my drawings. I had nothing but kid stuff—drawings of battleships, Indians, and copies from Prang's textbooks. I rushed home and got my sister and brother to pose for me while I drew their profiles. I went into our stuffy, unused parlor and made two careful drawings of a couple of plaster Indian busts that sat on the mantel. I also made a copy of a picture of George Washington. I took this little folder of drawings down to Groll. He was impressed and told me to come back on Monday and go to work. He said he couldn't put me on as an apprentice because of the union but would give me a job as errand boy at three dollars a week.

There had been a fire in the shop, and I was set to clean out the debris. I worked very hard, swept floors, ran errands not only for Groll but for all the men in the shop. I was so happy to be around art and artists that I made myself invaluable. I was there before anyone, kept the place in order, mixed colors, collected bits of crayon and boiled them into a liquid to be used in lettering. I was never allowed to touch a stone, but I practiced on them in the early morning before anyone was around.

An apprentice worked six months for nothing, then six months for three dollars a week, and then he started getting six dollars a week. That was his salary until he was raised to nine dollars a week after he had been working three years.

When I was put on as an apprentice, the whole shop walked out on strike. According to union rules, I was one apprentice too many. The strike lasted a whole year and almost wrecked the firm. I never saw such a bunch of incompetents as were brought in as strikebreakers—old has-beens, drunks, and an anarchist from Italy who only wanted to talk. They just about ruined the company.

Lithography in those days was one of the legitimate ways of making a living for artists who couldn't make a go of it by painting alone. In his youth Arthur B. Davies had worked in this same shop. Many fine artists drifted in and out of lithograph shops. Some stayed on for the security. I worked with a fine, sensitive fellow named Lisle. I used to be heartbroken when he'd do a beautiful job and the foreman would come around and wreck it—dig in and prettify it, harden it and take all the art out of it.

I worked with old man Archibald Willard, who painted the famous "Spirit of '76," and with Bill Sommers, who was a fine artist all his life. From him I learned the difference between a real artist and a commercial artist.

Then there was Billy Crane, an old time commercial artist who was not so much of an artist himself but was determined to make me one. Billy Crane came from a family of actors and theatrical designers. He had been a very successful scenic artist. He had just left his wife, run away with a very beautiful redheaded girl, come to Cleveland, and gone to work in the lithograph shop. They were very proud to have him and gave him a private room. He took a great interest in me, and I spent a lot of time with him. I ran his errands, bought his cigars (he had expensive taste in cigars) and kept him supplied with Bromo Seltzer, to which I thought he was addicted as a substitute for drink. He was very difficult in lots of ways. It seemed to me as if he was always raping the cleaning women in the building, or at least chasing them around with rape in mind.

He would never pay his bills and would send me out to tell the people to whom he owed money that he would pay them next week. These things were very embarrassing to a kid and I'd revolt. I'd refuse to do it.

Then he'd kick me out of his room and run me down the stairs shouting, "You goddamned ungrateful Jew bastard, don't you come here again."

It was tough on a kid. I felt that he was my master, a man who was going to teach me how to be an artist. I felt like a lost soul.

One day he said to me, "While I am out to lunch, you paint a picture out of the window."

I used to see him take his brush, twirl it around in the color, and give the brush a swish. I thought this was the way it was done. I took the brush, put it in the paint, gave it a big backward swipe, and put the paint on the paper.

When he came back he said, "What the hell's going on here?"

The whole place was spattered with paint. "Isn't that the way you do it?" I asked.

He laughed and said, "Well, you don't have to do what I do."

He sent me out in the country on weekends to paint and draw. He'd say, "You come back with a picture, or I'll break your neck."

One time he saw me sketching in the park and came over to help me and talk to me about painting.

One day Crane said to me, "I need some carmine—has Groll got any downstairs?"

"Yes," I said, "he's got some nice colors in his desk."

He said, "Run down and get me some."

I was very innocent—after all the company was supplying him with colors and materials. I never questioned his right to them. I got the carmine.

Later Groll asked me, "Did you take a tube of carmine out of my desk?"

"Yes," I said, "Billy Crane wanted it."

He hit the ceiling. Did he bawl me out. Did he lay it on.

"That's an expensive color; you had no business giving it to Crane. Don't you ever do that again. Who the hell are you working for—me or him?"

I told Billy Crane and he rushed down and jumped on Groll—told him to shut up and mind his own business, if he didn't like what he was doing, he'd get out and leave him and his damned shop. I made myself scarce.

Some Cleveland businessmen got the bright idea of having a group of artists paint a series of pictures of the life of Christ. They commissioned five of the most famous American artists to paint scenes from the life of Christ, and they planned to send the pictures around the country as an exhibition and charge admission. Billy Crane was to paint Christ in the Garden of Gethsemane. He sent me out to find him a studio where he could paint this huge picture—about eight by twelve feet. Imagine this man sending a kid out to find a studio for him and taking whatever he found. I went all over town and told people I knew an artist who wanted a studio. They just looked at me. I knocked at doors and asked if they knew of a studio. Finally in a market section in an old tenement I saw a sign, "Floor to rent." I told Crane about it and he rented it—an apartment on the fourth floor.

Crane had his beautiful, red-haired girl pose for the head of Christ and had me pose for the figure.

He'd say, "You want to help me, Billy? Take this brush and paint a rock." This was a kind gesture to make me feel I had a real part in the picture. We worked every Saturday and Sunday. I swept the room, cleaned his palette, washed his brushes, and did endless little chores.

His Christ had no beard and he began to worry about it. So he sent me out to find a Jewish character with a beard. I went down the street in this Jewish neighborhood stopping every man with a beard, and I'd say, "A man I know is painting a head of Christ and needs a model. Will you pose for him?" I had a pretty hard time; people thought I was nuts. Finally I thought of my father. He had a fine head and a beard. My father went down and posed for the beard. Crane finished the picture, but the enterprise was a complete flop. The paintings finally ended up in the barn of a Mr. Wade, one of the sponsors, and then one day the barn burned down.

I was going to art school nights all this time and learning to use my natural ability for art. I was clever at drawing, and during the strike I was doing professional work in the shop—work that men were being well paid for. I had been working for a year when the strike was called and went right into doing the big jobs even though I was only paid as an apprentice. The union men came around to see me one time when I wasn't home.

Old man Steers said, "Billy, don't you pay any attention to those fellows. The minute the strike is over, they'll put you right out of the shop and you'll never get back in again—you'll just be drifting." Finally the men came back one by one and the strike was broken.

There came a time when I found it hard to concentrate on the work in the shop. My mind began to run in too many directions—art and daydreams. One of the workmen was quite a gay blade and always telling about his affairs with women. One day I asked him what he thought about when he worked on a stone. I expected an entertaining answer.

He jumped, "What the hell do you think I'm thinking about, you damn fool? I'm thinking about my work."

I thought that one over and tried it too.

I must have been eighteen the fall I went to New York to study art at the National Academy of Design. I had finished my apprenticeship and managed to save, after paying my mother room and board, one hundred sixty dollars. Abe Warshawsky, a neighbor who was already an artist, was going to Paris and suggested that I go to New York with him and he would find me a place to board with his cousins, the Benders.

Abe took me to his cousins on 116th Street, near the Academy. I gave Mrs. Bender my hundred sixty dollars. Later I found out she gave it to her brother, a saloon keeper, from whom she had borrowed money. Mr. Bender was a gambler and an unscrupulous character who left his family penniless most of the time. That winter I slept in a clothes closet. It seemed to be the only available space.

I would get up in the morning and little Jessie Bender, who was seven and an enchanting little black-eyed, black-haired sprite, would say, "Willie, there's nothing for breakfast."

I would say, "All right, just give me a piece of bread."

She'd say, "But there is no bread."

"Then give me a glass of water." And I would take a glass of water and go to art school on that.

To get away from the misery of this family and because of my absorption in art, I would take the morning classes, the afternoon classes, and the evening classes. Afterward, I'd come home to a meager supper and go to bed. On Friday evenings, Zadu, the old grandfather, would come up from the lower East Side and bring a big basket of food. That kept us from starving. I lived with this family for one whole winter. When I came home the following spring, my parents were shocked. I looked like a famine victim. I suppose I could have sent home for money and eaten at restaurants, but it never occurred to me. I just accepted the situation and did nothing about it. I was used to poverty. Besides my mother had told me never to eat in restaurants—the food was poison. I guess I accepted that, too.

I worked hard. I won a prize in drawing in the Men's Day Class and an honorable mention in painting. I was becoming a pretty good painter in my way. My instructor was E. M. Ward, a very old-time genre painter of blacksmith shops and such. Then there was Francis C. Jones, a prissy little man who minced around the studio, said everyone was doing nicely and rushed out. He was a well-to-do artist who owned big apartment houses and studios on Fifty-seventh Street.

Ward always came in, sat down, looked from side to side, and said, "Where's your plumb line?"

If a student said, "I don't have one," he would roar, "If you ain't got one, borrow one."

I wonder now how I ever learned anything about art from these instructors. Instruction in those days was a matter of anatomy and correction of drawing from the viewpoint of realism only. The halls of the Academy were lined with the most perfect and meticulous drawings from casts and from life made by prize students no one has ever heard from since.

I remember there were parties at the Academy. Sometimes I would stand and look in the door, but I would never go in. It wasn't just that I was immature and too serious minded. I just had no interest outside of art and drawing and going to museums.

After a winter at the Academy I went back to Cleveland and the lithograph shop. It worked out well. Summer is the season when the lithograph shops are busy making posters for the coming winter. I could work all summer, save my money, and go back to study art in the winter in New York.

I went back to the Academy the second year, and this time I rented a room and ate in restaurants. That year I met a man, a successful writer, who asked me if he could get a room in the same rooming house where I was. He said he wanted to get away from his friends, who were drinking too much, living too fast a life, and disturbing him so that he couldn't write. He rented this room and isolated himself. He was wonderful at cooking and I certainly enjoyed my meals with him. He liked my company because I was so unbelievably naive and I made no demands upon him. And I was a perfect audience for his stories. I was enthralled just listening to him. Calvin Johnson was a typical western type, looked like Bill Cody and wrote railroad stories for *The Saturday Evening Post* and the Street and Smith pulp magazines.

My second year at the Academy I also went to classes morning, afternoon, and night, but I began to branch out. I went to the Metropolitan Museum and copied old masters. I copied Franz Hals. I copied the Dutch masters and Rembrandt and Velasquez. I copied Raeburn and still have the picture. A man came up to me one time and asked if I would make some copies of Mauve for him—sheep pictures. I made six copies of these sheep for him, and he paid me twenty-five dollars apiece for them, which was quite something for me at that time. I was very embarrassed by people standing in back of me and watching me paint. There was a young man who took care of the students' locker room in the basement. I told him how much people disturbed me by watching over my shoulder.

He said, "Remember this, if you think you don't know anything, they know still less about what art is."

I was convinced of this when a man standing back of me said, "Is that the first coat?"

After that people watching me never disturbed me. That year for the first time I began to wander around the galleries and become familiar with what was going on in the art world of the day.

I sound like a desperately serious young man without a thought in my head but work. Years after in New York I met a young woman who said, "Why, you're the young man my friend in the Cleveland Library was so in love with."

I was completely astonished. To me at that time librarians were all old women.

"But I was just a baby," I said.

"Nonsense," she said. "You were eighteen and she was twenty. To her you were the most charming, delightful, and serious young man she had ever met and she never forgot you." I couldn't even remember her. But evidently my picture of myself isn't totally objective.

When I returned to Cleveland and the lithograph shop that summer, I found things had changed. The foreman, Frank Seamons, had married a woman with illusions of grandeur, one who wanted things—an expensive apartment, a gay social life. Seamons and another man had left and started a shop of their own. They decided to make posters for the movies. It was a new idea and as it turned out, a very profitable one. Frank Seamons had no children of his own and had always taken a fatherly interest in me.

Our foreman, Groll, when I came back to the shop offered me a dollar raise. One day he came over to my stone and seemed much, much more friendly than usual. He had always been aloof and gruff.

I asked my friend, Elmer, "What's come over Groll?"

Elmer told me, "You know why he's nice to you, don't you? He's afraid you're going to go over to Seamons in that new shop and he'll lose you."

I was making ten dollars a week. Frank Seamons sent for me and said, "How much are they paying you, Willie?"

"I'm getting ten dollars a week," I said.

He said, "I'll give you fifteen if you'll come and work for me."

So I went to work for Seamons.

When Groll found out, he sent for me.

Groll kept going up and Seamons had offered to top any offer he made. In the end, I stayed with Seamons for thirty-two dollars a week. I guess I was worth it. I worked overtime and Saturdays and Sundays. I worked sixteen hours a day. Out of this I paid my mother fifteen a week for board and the rest I saved to go to Paris and study.

CHAPTER TWO

THAT SUMMER I SAVED TWELVE HUNDRED DOLLARS, and I felt I had enough to go to Paris. Bill Sommers advised me to go to Munich—Abe Warshawsky, who had just returned from Paris, was against it. Abe said Paris was then the art center of the world. Bill disagreed, saying that when he was a student everybody went to Munich, but Abe was undoubtedly right. I persuaded my best friend in the lithograph shop, Elmer Brubeck, a boy my own age, to go to Paris with me. He was more sophisticated than I but less outgoing. He was reserved and withdrawn, but we had more in common than the other boys. We took long walks, went sketching, and discussed life and art. He was interested in philosophy and talked to me about Plato and Socrates. I talked to him about art and becoming an artist. He was very clever at drawing and very inventive and discovered new and simple techniques in lithography that were very valuable. I thought anyone with his ability and talent would make a fine artist, but he did not have the drive or innate quality that makes an artist.

We sailed on the Holland-America Line in the fall of 1909, and for seven days we looked at the horizon and the ocean and wished we could die we were so sick. But finally there was an end to it. We landed in Cherbourg on a Sunday morning. Seeing Cherbourg was one of the most marvelous revelations of life that I have ever known. It was a strange fairyland that seemed not of this world. The houses, the people, the cobblestone streets, the hills, the streetcars drawn by tiny steam engines, the shabbily dressed people clattering along in wooden sabots stuffed with straw—a world drawn on a strange, small scale. The streets were crowded and bustling. I had the feeling I had been there before, as one sometimes does—as in a dream.

The United States Navy was making a tour of the world to show our strength. Theodore Roosevelt was waving the big stick. Our sailors had taken over Cherbourg, brawling and sightseeing. A young sailor asked us what we were doing there. We told him we were art students going to Paris. He was about our age and pleasant and said he'd take us around and show us the sights. We wandered around together. He took us up an alleyway and into a huge room. The room was lined with gaudy females sitting on sailors' laps. It was a scene from the life of Toulouse-Lautrec—a big hall filled with smoke and the smell of perspiring and perfumed females. The odor was revolting. We got out of there as fast as we could.

We had travelers checks but no money, and the banks were closed. It was Sunday. We asked for a hotel but no one understood us, and even if they had, we couldn't understand them. It had never occurred to us what it meant to land in a foreign country—that no one could understand anything we said. Always, after that, I have felt sympathetic towards foreigners in this country.

Abe Warshawsky had given me a letter to a young Frenchman. When we arrived in Paris, this young Frenchman took us over to the Café du Dôme and threw a big party for us and asked all his friends. They had a rousing good time with drinks and girls. I had never seen anything like this before. I was both intrigued and worried. I never drank and I never smoked. It was a matter of principle. Always as a youth I felt I wanted to make something of myself and that in order to do this I had to have a healthy mind in a healthy body. The early lessons I had received in public school on the evils of drinking and smoking were implanted in a lasting fashion (they carried through all my adult life). But I didn't want to act unfriendly or unsociable. So when they filled my glass I'd sip it and pour it behind me in the sawdust in the manner I had read of in a detective story. At the party was the model, Nina, who eventually married Leo Stein. She was already a famous character in the Latin Quarter. She was a good egg and used to pose and help the starving artists out in many ways.

This gala party wound up very late. The next day when I went around to the Café du Dôme, the waiter handed me a bill.

"What for?" I asked.

"You know," he said, "the party last night." Just the old routine to fleece the innocent.

Some time later one of the artists came to me and said this same Frenchman was broke and wanted to borrow fifty dollars. I was always a soft touch and still am, but I had stamina enough to say that I didn't have that kind of money and certainly not for him. After that he left me alone and looked for greener pastures.

Elmer and I took a room in an old house on the rue Servondoni near the Luxembourg Gardens. It was a stuffy French room not unlike a room in an old brownstone in New York, with an enormous high, curtained bed, a chair or two, and a fireplace. We cooked in the fireplace, but I don't remember what we cooked. I stayed in Paris that winter and studied in the various art schools. Elmer never went to any of them. He was restless and disturbed and wandered about the city, taking photographs, but he did not paint.

Finally Elmer went home. He felt that the precariousness of an artist's life was

1. William Zorach's family in Russia—taken about 1890. From left to right: William Zorach; his sister Mary; his mother, Toba Getal; his sister Rose; his brothers Otto and Abe; his sister Bertha, who is standing behind, tore her head off the photograph in embarrassment at showing it to an American friend.

2. William Zorach at six years of age. Taken in Cleveland, Ohio.

3. William Zorach at lithograph studio. *Ca.* 1908.

4. Zorach family taken in back yard of Cleveland, Ohio, home on Woodland Avenue in 1909. From left to right, top row: William Zorach; his father, Orchick; his mother, Toba; Peter Steers; his sister Mary. From left to right, bottom row: his brother Eddy; Fanny the dog; Jerry (Mary's child); his nephews Elmer and Bernie Brown.

5. Elmer Brubeck working on lithograph stone. 1908.

6. Left to right: Alex Warshawsky; Lascari; George Davidson; William Zorach. 1910.

7. Painting class at National Academy of Design in New York. 1907.

8. Marguerite and William Zorach. 1919.

9. Marguerite and Dahlov Zorach. Taken in 1918 at 10th Street studio.

10. Marguerite, William, Dahlov, and Tessim. Taken in 1919 at Plainfield, New Hampshire.

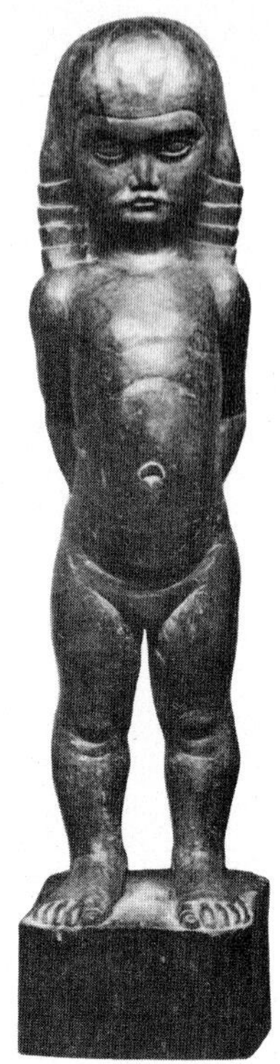

11. *Figure of a Child.* (Dahlov) 1921. Mahogany. 23″ high. Collection of Dr. Edward J. Kempf.

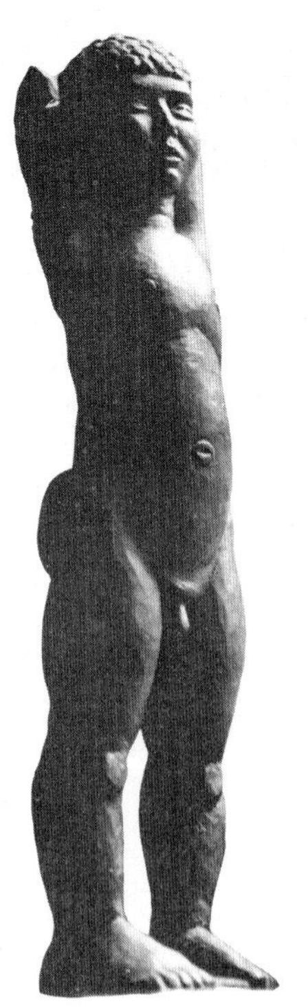

12. *The Young Boy.* (Tessim) 1921. Maplewood. 24″ high.

13. Marguerite Zorach in front of her mural *Land and Development of New England*. 1935.

14. *Interior and Exterior*. 1918. Oil. 36″ x 28″.

15. *Spring*. 1913. Oil. 40″ x 46″. The Downtown Gallery, New York City.

16. *Summer*. 1913. Oil.

17. William Zorach at Robinhood Farm. 1925.

something he could not face. He had a terrible feeling of insecurity—didn't see how he could make a living, and making a living was very important to him. I was worried and insecure, too, but the desire to become an artist and find my life and expression through art was more powerful than any sense of insecurity.

A pay check coming in every week can be an insidious thing. To be an artist you have to learn to live without security. You have to take the big chance. You have to gamble on yourself. Even today I lecture young people on this point. "You have to realize that your income is going to be uncertain and irregular. You have to adapt yourself to uncertainty, and at the same time you have to learn to make a living out of your work. It is difficult but not impossible. You can't dissipate your mind and energies in two directions—one, art, and the other, another way of making a living. Art is a hard mistress; she demands all you are capable of giving. You can't compromise your integrity. You have to create as fine a work of art as you possibly can with no thought of whether it will sell or even whether anybody will like it. You have to believe in yourself, and you have to be a dedicated person."

I had this belief in myself when I was a kid. I used to go out sketching on Saturdays and Sundays. I had what I called a guardian angel to whom I used to pray. I said a prayer every time I went sketching, that I hoped I would become a fine artist and make something of my life, that I should be able to paint nature as beautiful as she is—the pattern of leaves above me, the intricate patterns on tree trunks, the delicacy of ferns and flowers, and the lovely shapes and colors of sky and clouds.

In Paris I was studying seriously, interested in every phase of art, learning all I possibly could about art in the short time I would be there. I went to art schools—not just to one but to several. A young man took me to a school to study under a very fine draughtsman. I liked his drawings, but when I saw his salon pictures, silly nudes sprawling over couches, and painted like the females on cigar box covers, I was disgusted.

At the Academy in New York it had been all old masters. Impressionism didn't exist, although I was vaguely conscious of it. Sargent was the God. Whistler was admired by the more sophisticated students. Most of us worshipped Velasquez, Goya, and Franz Hals. El Greco was something quite strange. Today I wonder how anybody can not be interested in El Greco.

I was most interested in the drawings of Holbein and Ingres. The last year at the Academy I went to the Art Students League and studied for a month with Bridgman—that was all I could afford. One day I was in the Lenox Library making studies of Holbein when I met Bridgman looking up studies of hands. He said he was giving a lecture on hands that night. He told me the kind of drawing I did was beyond the student stage and I shouldn't be studying. I should get out on my own.

In Paris I was still eager to learn all there was to learn, but criticism in French was very unsatisfactory. The professor would talk and talk.

The student interpreter would say, "Pay no attention to him—he's just an old fogy."

"But what did he say?" I insisted.

I found I was getting the interpreter's opinion of the criticism—never the criticism itself. He was probably right, but I wanted to hear what the Master said and evaluate it myself.

I began to seek out schools where the criticism was in English and tried a school where Richard Miller taught. He was an important artist in America at that time. I wound up studying in a school called La Palette run by a Scotch artist, John Duncan Ferguson. Here Jacques-Émile Blanche criticized in English. He came in twice a week, an impressive, beautifully mannered Frenchman, a very successful portrait painter—with almost nothing to say—a few words, "Too short, too tall, a bit more here, a bit less there, not bad, keep right on."

I had never before seen a school where the students paid no attention whatever to the Master, disregarded him completely, and went their own ways. I was painting from the model, but I began to be conscious of the various modern influences that were invading the art world. Impressionism began to influence my painting.

I remember a young artist just arrived from Chicago. He came into the Café du Dôme.

"My god," he cried. "Have you seen what they are doing in the schools? It's absolutely crazy. It's insane."

I was disturbed and confused, and yet I felt that I was a very young man entering a new age. The forces creating modern art seemed more alive than anything I had known or anything being done in America. There the schools and the exhibitions were totally untouched by—utterly unconscious of—this new spirit. Yet in Paris it was already a powerful force, a highly developed direction though still in an early and dynamic state of evolution. Cubism at that time was a mystery to me. I was more fascinated by the bold and brilliant use of color by Van Gogh and Gauguin and the new conception of form through Cézanne. After all they were the true innovators.

I was very simple and naive as a young artist in Paris. I couldn't understand people socializing in tea rooms or spending time in bars and restaurants. When I was invited to tea by two nice old ladies I didn't know what to make of it; how and why should people spend an afternoon chatting and sipping tea? I did not know what it was to get up and offer a lady a chair. When a nice Frenchman and his wife gave me a card with their address and phone number and asked me to call them and come over and visit, I thought it very strange. A couple of nice American ladies asked Elmer and me over for a visit one evening. I was most uneasy and disturbed. It never occurred to me they had been glad to meet two

American boys who had come to Paris to study art and wanted to make them feel at home.

It was at La Palette that I met Marguerite Thompson, the girl who was to be my wife, companion, and fellow artist for the rest of my life. Marguerite was sharing a studio with Jessie Dismor, an English girl. Dismor worked mornings at La Palette and Marguerite afternoons, alternating with their own studio. As Marguerite tells it, Dismor talked so much about the new American boy in the class at La Palette that she decided she'd better see this student Dismor was so interested in. So they switched classes. Marguerite looked me over and found me not unattractive and said to herself, "When the model rests I'll go over and talk to him and find out what he's like." The model rested.

Six girls dropped their brushes and rushed over to me. "How do you like what I'm doing?" "Is this better?" "Is this color all right?"

Marguerite said to herself, "Another ladies' man! He'll have to come over and talk to me."

The next day I went over to her easel. She was painting a pink and yellow nude with a bold blue outline.

"Do you know what you are doing?" I asked. "And why you are doing it?"

She knew—and that was the beginning. But I just couldn't understand why such a nice girl would paint such wild pictures.

I remember Marguerite didn't look just like everyone else or dress like everyone else. Even then she made her own clothes. She wore a black silk turban on the back of her head with an enormous red rose in the center—a fascinating hat. She looked like an awfully nice girl who had always been protected and had never worked for a living. She was shy but sure of herself and gave the impression of character. I was shy about pursuing her and was very disturbed and jealous whenever I saw her with other boys. I remember one time she was walking down the street ahead of me and Lee Simonson who was also in the class gave me a shove and said, "Go ahead, walk along with her." And I did. The next day I was having lunch in a little restaurant, Henriette's. It was late and I was alone in the room. Marguerite came in, saw me, and came over and sat down with me.

"Have you had your lunch?" she asked.

"Yes," I said. "I'm waiting for dessert."

The waiter appeared with a plate of fried potatoes. My face fell. My few words of French had let me down. Marguerite laughed. We both laughed and Marguerite called the waiter and saw that I got the baked apple I thought I had ordered.

Marguerite had said to herself when she met me, "Watch your step. This young man is going to fall for you and things may get difficult. He's too nice a boy to get hurt." It never occurred to her she might fall for me.

I went out to Versailles with Marguerite. We wandered about the woods, and I was delighted that she was interested in nature and loved trees and flowers and landscape. We walked along the Seine at night and sat on the damp stones and discussed life and art.

Marguerite was living in her Aunt Addie's apartment. Aunt Addie was a very little woman, a New England spinster with a stern sense of duty and an invincible integrity. She had brought up a family of nine children when her parents died and her life had been completely subordinated to them. She did her duty by them but without affection or sympathy. Only Marguerite, among her relatives, loved her. Aunt Addie was a retired school teacher, and she had gone to Paris for The World's Fair in 1903 and stayed there except when traveling. When I first knew Marguerite, Aunt Addie was in America. We used to make tea in her apartment and I recited Longfellow to her and "Thanatopsis"—most of the poetry I had learned in school.

We went to exhibitions together and Marguerite took me to one of Gertrude Stein's evenings. Gertrude and Aunt Addie had been friends as young girls in San Francisco and had gone to Christian Science Sunday School together. A very young Picasso was there looking extremely subdued and unhappy. Gertrude sat, heavy and masculine, in her big chair and talked. Alice B. Toklas drifted about, thin and exotic, dressed in a harem costume of gaudy colors, waving a long cigarette holder. She was my idea of a courtesan.

"Imagine her sitting in the middle of a green field," I said to Marguerite. "Did you bring me here to enjoy myself?"

To me it was an unreal world and very decadent. "These people need contact with the earth," I said.

We went to the Salon des Indépendants, a big sprawling affair in an enormous tent, and saw Matisse putting the final touches to his big painting, "The Red Interior," now owned by the Museum of Modern Art. He was a tall, bearded young man not so much older than myself. I remember Delaunay's "Eiffel Tower," a composition in shattered forms; a large Léger; and a painting by Rousseau—all very strange to me. It was a fantastic show ranging from the inept and childish, through the most dull and conservative, to the latest in wild experimentation.

I sent four of my southern France pictures to the Salon d'Automne. They were all accepted; two were hung on the line. This was unusual and my friends were amazed. They said it wasn't because of their merit but because the jury felt patriotic over the subject matter, which was after all only French landscape. Marguerite, too, had a picture hung. We went to the vernissage with Zadkine, who was a friend of hers. He took her over and acted as if I was an outsider, a mere acquaintance. I was very jealous and unpleasant. Marguerite was horrified at my behavior; it spoiled the day.

La Palette closed for the summer. Dismor and Marguerite were going sketching in the south of France. I was going to Munich. It was the end. Two nights later in

Avignon, Marguerite dreamt she wrote me a letter. It was so compelling that she got up, lit the lamp, and wrote the letter, with qualms but no hesitation. I don't remember what was in the letter and neither does she, but when I got the letter I forgot Munich and left for Avignon. It sounded so beautiful and it was wonderful to think that we would continue our friendship. I thought I might join the girls and we would all paint. We wrote letters from all places in southern France, but we never saw each other until we got back to Paris. Marguerite hoped we would meet accidentally, but Dismor was uncooperative and said if I came along it would spoil her trip. She just couldn't be a third wheel, and we'd all be miserable. So in all of southern France we were never together.

I spent five months in Avignon sketching. I rented a room under the Palace of the Popes on the Rhone in a place called Hotel de la Marina. I was a hard-working artist. I painted all day and had a room on the top floor and went to bed early. I never heard anything that went on below. I never went into the bar except to eat. I became acquainted with a French boy who worked in a bank. He wanted to practice English; I wanted to learn French.

"My God," he said. "You live in the worst dive in Avignon."

"What do you mean?" I said. "It seems like a very nice place to me."

"I'll show you. Stay up next Saturday night."

I stayed up and we went down and sat in the bar—bottles flew, fists flew, insults and obscene language flew, knives appeared, there were knock-down and drag-out fights. The police raided the place and closed the bar temporarily. But I stayed on undisturbed.

I used to go along the road and across the long bridge over the Rhone and sketch. One time I was sketching and a whole regiment of soldiers came by me. They carefully walked around me so as not to disturb me. I was impressed, but what I couldn't understand was that they all yelled "Allemand." I asked my friend what it was all about—we never saw soldiers in America in those days.

He said, "You know, one of these days we are going to have a war with Germany, and when we do I will gladly give my life to go." He clenched his fist and struck his chest.

I asked, "What did Germany do to you?"

"They took Alsace-Lorraine from France!"

"How long ago?" I asked.

"Fifty years ago."

I said, "Why not forget it? Fifty years ago is a long time."

To a boy of twenty, fifty years is a long time, but to me today it is only yesterday.

At this time I was painting mostly landscapes. Cubism I couldn't understand, Post-Impressionism had excited and stimulated me, but I had no personal approach—no bridge. But working out of doors in the hot sun, I noticed the vibrations of the atmosphere. I discovered that we were not really solid, we were translucent. Everything in the sunlight was vibrating, nothing was solid. I had realized impressionism. Everything was moving and translucent, color moved in and out, form disintegrated and rebuilt itself, everything was alive and vibrant. My pictures took on life and sun and color. I was a happy painter.

Marguerite had returned to Paris; her money had run out. She wrote an article each week on Paris and her travels, for the Fresno *Republican*, saved the money she earned, and took a trip each spring, returning when the money was gone. She was in Paris when I got back. Her Aunt Addie had returned from America. I had been warned that Aunt Addie did not have much use for the male sex and none at all for anyone of them in whom her niece showed an interest. But when I met Aunt Addie she was very sweet and friendly and at first appeared interested in me as an artist.

Aunt Addie had a very busy life for one so fragile, and there were always females of her own type coming and going on their way to Tibet to install drinking fountains for horses or to right some terrible situation in some far corner of the globe. She was an artist in her own right. We have a beautiful little painting of Leadville, Colorado, the town she used to teach in, done by her and a painting of kittens and dandelions that is most sensitive and exquisitely done. But she never had the time to devote to painting, and when she found she had a talented niece, she brought her to Paris to live with her and study.

Marguerite was right. Everything was lovely until Aunt Addie realized we were seriously involved with each other. She wept when we went out together and made scenes if we were not back at an early hour. Certainly she did not believe in *love* or *men.* She felt it was her duty to return Marguerite to her parents in California intact and was sure that a trip around the world would be fatal to any romance. We were helpless, neither of us had any money. Our plan was that Marguerite was to go around the world on her way back to California; and I was to go back to Cleveland, work in the shop, and save enough for us to start life as young artists in New York. She would join me there.

I saw Marguerite and Aunt Addie off. I remember Aunt Addie had her usual hassle with the taxi driver over the tip. I was very depressed; things seemed very dreary and lonesome without Marguerite. I couldn't stay in Paris any more.

I took what little money I had left and went to Munich. I felt very much at home, it was so much like America—the Germans, the houses, the life. I met American friends there and we visited museums and galleries. On the way back I stopped in Basle and Zurich. Switzerland was like a big park, so neat and well kept. Everybody looked comfortable and friendly. I liked it. I was overawed by the Alps—the first real mountains I had ever seen. I looked off into the sky and saw beautiful orange-colored clouds. But they had sharp edges, and suddenly I realized they were mountain tops suspended above me in the sky. It was one of those unbelievable things that happens once in a lifetime.

Shortly after the trip to Munich, I had no more money and had to go home.

When I got to New York the customs official examined my baggage as if I were smuggling diamonds. I had brought back a few cheap frames and some tubes of paint. They made me pay duty on these and took every cent I had. I told them I didn't have a cent to get back to Cleveland with, but they didn't care. I have never understood this; it was so utterly ridiculous. Fortunately Alex Warshawsky, Abe's brother, met me at the boat and loaned me the money to go to Cleveland.

When I arrived in New York I felt utterly miserable and depressed. America was so busy, so business-like, after the easy pace of Europe. Everyone was so well dressed and trim after the shabbiness of Europe. Art had not touched the world I had returned to. I got my job back at the lithograph shop and worked day and night. I felt like a slave.

In Europe life had been accomplishment and work one loved, a girl one loved, the excitement of the art world, the companionship of artists, the lovely colorful country of southern France. The return to American may have been a challenge, a return to reality, but it seemed more like plunging into an icy sea or like being engulfed in a morass. No depression I have ever suffered through was more desperate and more overwhelming than my return to America. It was not the lack of money—I could remedy that. It wasn't the absence of Marguerite—I knew I would see her before too long. It was the people, the country. It was most of all the complete lack of interest of all those around me in the world outside of their own interests. Now I knew why the artists who had painted big, exuberant pictures in Paris painted small, subdued pictures when they returned to America. The artists seemed to turn in upon themselves. This feeling passed in time after I found my way back into the world of art again.

When I was in Europe I bought and brought home a number of beautiful posters and took them to the shop to show the boss what wonderful work they did in Europe and what could be done in posters. He wasn't interested. He wasn't raising any standards; he was giving the customers what they wanted. I remember that I used to ride on the subways in New York and wonder why the commercial ads were so bad, and I was sure that some day they would improve as people became more art conscious. I gave up worrying about posters back in 1913, but when I look at them today in the subways, they are just as offensive.

I tried to paint on Sundays. I had an idea that I might set up a studio, get away from lithography, make contacts, and sell my work. Another young artist, Max Kalish, and I rented a studio in a nice section of town. We decorated the place and fixed it up. I made a large poster announcing the opening of our exhibition and the shop printed it for me. I knew nothing about publicity or press releases or social contacts. I thought art spoke for itself and the world would come to it. We placed the posters around in the drugstores in the neighborhood. The opening was a terrible disappointment; nobody showed up—nobody came. We kept on for a month or two and then gave up.

Breaking into the art field is a slow and painful process for the young artist, and it's complicated by the element of luck. It was a long time before I learned even the fundamentals. When I was a youngster I painted a picture of a Bible and a candlestick and a prayer shawl and showed it in an exhibition at the Educational Alliance. I was asked if I would sell this painting. I told them I didn't know what to ask for it; I'd have to ask my mother. My mother said to ask ten dollars. So I did and Mrs. Flora Schwab, the President of the Jewish Council of Women, gave me twenty dollars. That has never happened to me since. I've asked twenty and have been offered ten, many times. This was a great encouragement to me—someone valued what I painted.

We gave up the studio. I did have an exhibition that winter in a little gallery in a department store. I showed my southern France paintings and things I had done in Paris. I sold one painting. A man came in, the President of the Akron Rubber Co. He asked what the cheapest painting was; it was fifteen dollars, so he bought that one. Another came around to my house. He didn't want to buy through a dealer. I don't remember whether I sold him anything or not.

One day a Mr. Black, an influential man in Cleveland, called the shop to tell me that a visiting businessman from Berlin had seen my exhibition and wanted to meet me. Would I come down to the Hollander House (Cleveland's best hotel) and have lunch with him? I was paralyzed. I didn't know what to do, but I felt I had to do something to spruce up; so I went out and bought a new necktie.

When we met in the lobby he looked at me and said, "You're very young, aren't you? Somehow I expected a middle-aged man after seeing your pictures. Let's have lunch and then we'll go over to the gallery and select a few of your pictures. I'd like to take them back to Germany. I have quite a collection, Rembrandts, Franz Hals, mostly old masters."

The waiter handed me a menu. I panicked. I couldn't even see the menu. I didn't know what to order. This was not my world nor any world I had ever known. I was desperate and speechless. This man ordered oysters and a complete lunch. There I sat paralyzed.

Finally I said, "Let me have a dish of ice cream."

I felt so miserable and such a failure that when we walked out I said "Good-bye" and vanished, sick at heart. When I think of it now, I am appalled at how insensitive this man of the world was. He should have known how to handle the situation. Just a suggestion or two would have set everything right.

Later when another man called me, I went to a friend of mine in the shop and said, "I wish you'd go and see this man for me."

He said, "No, Bill you've got to learn to see these people yourself." So I met the second man. I don't remember whether he bought anything or not, but he was a much warmer and more understanding person.

Years later, Ernest Fiene told me that one day a man came to his studio and selected a painting and asked how much it was. Fiene was young, and to any young artist this is a painful question. He hasn't thought of his painting in connection with money.

Fiene said, "Take it home and see how you like it and send me a check for whatever you think it is worth."

The man took the picture home, wrote Fiene how much he liked it, how proud he was to own it, and enclosed a check for five dollars. We all have to live and learn.

CHAPTER THREE

MARGUERITE HAD TRAVELED all the way around the world and back to California. She had written me from Jerusalem and Egypt, from India and Burma and Singapore, and again from China and Japan, and finally from Hawaii. In her home in Fresno, California, she waited until I had once more saved twelve hundred dollars from the lithograph shop. She had an exhibition in Fresno and in Los Angeles. She, too, only sold one picture. She gave a talk on art before the Women's Club and made herself unpopular by saying that California roads couldn't compare with the roads in Europe and, sometimes, not even with those in Asia.

We arranged to meet in New York just before Christmas 1912. I waited for her in the Grand Central Station worrying for fear I wouldn't know her after all these months. I caught sight of a girl disappearing in the distance and ran after her. It was a stranger. I rushed back, and there was Marguerite worrying and wondering why I was not there. The first thing I did was to take her for a ride on the Fifth Avenue bus to see the town. She thought it very strange, but said nothing. We were married down in City Hall. My oldest friend in New York, Calvin Johnson, came with us as a witness. I have heard that they now have a chapel in City Hall, but when we were married it was in a little room in the basement. A crowd of people were sitting around on benches in the semi-darkness. A drunken judge got up, mumbled through the ceremony—"for better or for worse—man and wife. Next!" It was a disgusting shock to two idealistic young people. However, Calvin took us to Keene's Chop House, and, over an elegant dinner, we forgot what we had just been through.

We rented a top floor in a small building on Fifty-fifth Street and Sixth Avenue: one very large room with a fine big skylight and a bathroom—no kitchen. We got a little gas stove and cooked in the bathroom. We furnished the place with the help of the local junkshops and never spent more than a couple of dollars on any one piece. Any hideous piece of furniture became beautiful with paint and decoration. Our first purchase was an Italian chair for a quarter. We still have it. We bought unbleached muslin and painted a wild forest scene and hung it across one end of the room. It served to create a clothes closet, a hide-all for paints and canvases—and junk. It was our glory hole.

Marguerite had never run a house before, but she was a wonderful manager. She could make pennies turn corners. She remembers going down to the corner butcher shop and insisting on two lamb chops for ten cents. There was an argument but she got them. The next time she came in, the butcher looked her in the eye and said he had no meat.

We begrudged every minute not spent on painting or something related to art. We sketched all over the city—Central Park, along the waterfront, across the Hudson on the Palisades—and painted wild pictures at home from imagination. Instead of one sun, I painted three red suns. I painted Central Park in all wild colors, peopled with exotic nudes. One morning sketching in the park, I found fifteen dollars in small change under a bush. What a bonanza!

I could not adjust myself to a life of free and unrestricted time after life in a shop. I said to myself, "I've got to solve this problem; I've got to create a foreman inside myself." I planned a daily schedule. In the morning I would go out and sketch. In the afternoon, I would develop the sketches at home.

Marguerite was busy and creative and unworried, but I worried desperately about money. One day my old boss looked me up. He was opening a new lithograph shop in New Jersey and asked me to work for him at a salary that was fabulous compared to anything I had ever gotten before. It looked good to me. I wavered. But Marguerite spoke up and said, "No, we are artists, and some way we will find a way to live as artists. No more lithograph shop. That is past history."

I couldn't believe it, but she was firm. "After all," she said, "you lived a year and a half in Paris without money. We can live that long here, and we'll find ways to manage."

I made more posters and peddled them, still thinking I might do some commercial work on the side, for a living. People admired them but I could never sell one. Evidently I was not a salesman. Marguerite made some beautiful textile designs. No one would buy them. But during the First World War, when there was no way for the manufacturers to get designs from Europe, she won a number of first prizes on these designs, usually one hundred or two hundred dollars, and the prize designs were purchased by the big companies. But when I took Marguerite's designs around, no one would buy them. I was always told to come back later—you know what that means. They would take the designs into their office to "consider," show them to their designers, who would copy whatever they wanted to use, and return the designs to me but never buy one.

Finally I said to myself, "There must be something wrong with my method. I will try the power of thought on these people." I went around to the man who had seemed most interested in our designs, continually saying to myself, "He's got to buy them."

He looked them over and gave me the same old run-around.

So I said, "You've got to buy them! You've got to buy them!"

I must have been so desperate that he was frightened. He rushed back into his office and that was the end of it.

Finally I said, "To hell with all these people; this is not for me. I want to be an artist, I want to make my living by my art, and I'm going to do it. Instead of wasting my time trying to educate art editors and textile people, I'm going to try to educate the art dealers." So I went around and talked modern art to all the dealers and got to know them very well. They would ask me to bring my work around, but when they saw it they wouldn't touch it or consider it. It was just wild and crazy to them.

I remember while I was still studying at the Academy, everyone was concerned only with "local color," that is, the actual color of the object itself. The effect of light or sunlight on color was not taken into consideration. Brown was brown, blue was painted blue, and a yellow dish was yellow. My friend, Abe Warshawsky, came back from Paris with a palette of brilliant, impressionistic color. I remember a conversation he had with a little woman in Cleveland. "The Impressionists, are they really being taken seriously?"

"Oh yes," said Abe, "everyone is taking them seriously, even in New York." I was eighteen at the time, and it was the first time I had heard the word Impressionist. I wondered. Later, when I was in Paris, all my little studies in the schools were not school studies anymore; they were Impressionist paintings. The new technique was based upon the juxtaposition of the primary colors in the spectrum. Sunlight was warm, yellows, reds, and oranges; shadows were cold, made up of greens, blues, and purples, with a sprinkling of warm colors to give life and vibration. Black was eliminated and colors were mixed on the canvas, not on the palette. White was used to modify and create values and lightness and the strong heavy colors to establish depth. Artists used dots of varying sizes and lines according to their temperaments, sometimes pulling the spots together, sometimes separating them, often with the canvas showing between. Painting became atmosphere and lively vibration. Monet fascinated me with his handling of light and the wonder of change in landscape from hour to hour. Seurat was almost too scientific for me, but his marvelous sense of design and the relationship of space through color was also wonderful to me.

A person evolves and develops his art through contacts and influences. We are not born Cubists or Post-Impressionists or even avant-garde. Those of us with talent are born naive draughtsmen and colorists, like the primitive wagon painters and early American portrait painters. We would each have a certain innate originality in our sense of color and handling of space, but the method would not vary greatly or the results. But one cannot remain isolated in an age like this. One has to absorb influences and through them develop one's own expression. I could not accept Matisse's distortions or the poster look of his paintings, but I found his color and his freedom exciting. After I went to La Palette, where Marguerite was working, I became more intrigued by the bold surfaces patterned with black lines as well as with brilliant color. I, too, began to leave Impressionism as such behind and to paint in this freer manner.

In New York in order to free myself from my academic way of seeing the world about me, I reset my course. Instead of drawing with my right hand, I tried to draw with my untrained left. My right hand was too clever and patterned. The left hand had no habits to overcome; it was clumsy but free. Strange as it may seem, it is easier to free your brain than your hand. Instead of looking straight at a landscape, I'd lie on my back and look up at the trees; I was seeing a new world, new forms and movements unfolded. Where I would see red I would paint green. I remember one picture that caused quite a sensation. I called it "The Red Sea." I painted a vermilion ocean with green figures lying around the shore. Instead of one sun, I painted three.

I used to visit the Montross Gallery quite often. Mr. Montross was a kind person, a dealer who handled Ryder, Winslow Homer, and such American artists, but he couldn't see introducing modern French art to New York. Dealers have to be asked by the public for something before they will handle it. One time I brought a painting to Montross. He said, "What is it?"

I explained, "This is a revelation of a world of rocks and sea and bleak houses. I visited the people in these houses. I came to know the life and the people. This picture is of a mother and child in the interior of a house. It is a cubist conception where the mother's activities with her child are portrayed simultaneously. You are not looking at one scene; you are looking at life in various forms combined with the exterior and interior of a city close at hand. It is a mystical interpretation of the life." (This early conception was expanded and developed when I painted "Interior and Exterior" in 1918.)

He said, "It all sounds very nice and poetic, but why don't you say it in paint?"

I said, "Mr. Montross, you sit me down in your sanctum sanctorum with its red plush walls. You hang a picture in a gold-leaf frame, and you say to me, 'Now that picture is worth ten thousand dollars.' You talk to me about money, and you have me look at a picture. I have been trying to talk to you about the quality of art and the quality of expressiveness in a work of art. Why don't you rip all this plush off your walls, paint them white, let a little life and air into these rooms? Then you would see how muddy and depressing all these dull colors in all these pictures you have been showing me really are. Hang some pictures by Van Gogh, Matisse, and Gauguin—reds, blues, yellows, greens—and see how full of life and joy your place will be! One of these days these pictures I admire will be sold for a hundred thousand dollars."

He went to his assistant and said, "Will you please show this young man to the door." He thought I was crazy.

Two years later Montross had an exhibition of Matisse paintings. It was a sensation.

Through fellow artists, I learned of the great international exhibition that was to be held in 1913—the Armory Show. I think they took two paintings from Marguerite and me.

The show hit the art world like a bolt out of the blue and it astonished the American public. They were utterly unprepared for what they saw. I saw Teddy Roosevelt being escorted through the galleries by Arthur B. Davies. He rushed out waving his hands and shouting, "This is not art, this is lunacy."

I saw women rolling on the floor, in hysterics over the Cubists and Matisse. The show was packed with people all day, every day, for a whole month. Art was stirred up as it never had been before. From that period on, everything began to grow and develop. American art was never the same again.

When the Armory Show was revived at the Munson-Williams-Proctor Institute in Utica in 1963, we had no idea what had become of our paintings that were in the original show and could not include them.

The Armory Show came and went. My pictures were not mentioned in the reviews, but Marguerite's pictures were written up in all the papers. No one took the Armory Show painters seriously. Certainly no one bought any of our work. But in a way it was a sensation. We were among the advanced artists of that time and our paintings seemed really crazy to the public and to the critics. A group of ten or twelve advanced young artists put on a show at the MacDowell Club, a very fine show with well-chosen, important pictures. I put in a large picture, "Spring in Central Park"—of two nudes in the park. The show created quite a stir but there was no follow up as far as we were concerned. There were very few places where we could exhibit.

In Paris I had not understood or been interested in the Cubists. But after the Armory Show I began making my visual observation of nature into Cubist patterns. It was another revelation; that one was not confined to the small section of nature framed in the space of a canvas and seen from only one point of view but was free to use all the colors and directions of space and form that surround one. My painting took on a deeper and more mystical tone. My subject matter became imaginative and expressive. I tried to paint what I felt was the inner reality of life around me. I became very much interested in Maeterlinck and Ibsen and in the poetry of Blake and Whitman. I went to the Museum of Natural History and studied the carvings of the Eskimos, the Aztecs, and the Mayans. I felt here were fundamentals—an expression of life directly spiritual in the sense of being of a spirit unhampered by external values.

We had two problems in our studio on Fifty-fifth Street and Sixth Avenue. One was the rats that came up from the grocery below. We caught them in traps and then didn't know what to do with them. Sometimes Marguerite had fun dropping them into open limousines parked below. Our other problem was heat. Our landlord would buy coal, and when it ran out, he would wait a week before ordering another load. We decided we couldn't live through another winter like that; so the first time we were frozen out, we went out at night to look for a new studio. We heard of one on Washington Square. An old woman in extraordinary clothes opened the door. The room was full of tables piled high with slices of bread, each table covered by a cheese cloth. The bathtub sat on a platform under the stairs, and there was a gas plate under it for heating the bath water. The bread was for a parrot; he liked it dry. It was all very dark and very cluttered and very weird.

She sent us to a friend of hers, Mrs. Van Eaton, on Tenth Street across from the Jefferson Market Jail. Her place was equally cluttered—she had three sets of mission furniture in a room fifteen by fifteen and several sets of curtains over each window, with stuffed canary birds on the curtain rods. There was a large painting of the Hudson River school over the fireplace, which she said was an Inness. Mrs. Van Eaton was a marvelous photographer. She bought unopened trunks at auction, kept the contents all around the place and stowed in every corner. From the contents, she set up tables and place settings, made mud pies and cakes, took pictures of them, and sold them to the women's magazines and the Sunday supplements. Mrs. Van Eaton said, "Move into the studio and give me about three days to get together and move out of the apartment." There were four small rooms, a good small studio, and a real bathroom. Thirty dollars a month and you furnished your own heat. We moved in but Mrs. Van Eaton didn't move out. We finally realized that we were to pay the rent and she had no intention of moving out. I kept waiting but Marguerite got fed up and was firm. Mrs. Van Eaton moved.

We lived in this apartment for more than twenty years. It was over the bail-bond shyster lawyers and opposite the Jefferson Market Jail. We couldn't afford thirty dollars a month; so we rented one room for ten dollars, first to Helen Montgomery, a librarian who wrote poetry. Later we rented it to Aletha Comstock, who lived with us for many years.

Heat was a problem always. We had two coal stoves and never learned to run a coal fire; it was always a struggle and an exasperation. We managed on a dollar and thirty-five cents a week apiece for food. It took great ingenuity but both Marguerite and Aletha became expert cooks and managers and we ate well. We survived these years by never spending a cent on anything that was not essential. We indulged only in pleasures that did not cost money, and we saw that there was always money for materials. We bought good linen and made our own canvases. Paints and brushes we had brought from Paris. We used the stretchers over and over, rolling up the finished pictures. When desperate, we painted on both sides of the canvas. We both worked in the small studio, and since we didn't use models but worked from imagination and memory, there was room for both of us. I had a small Sunday class in the Educational Alliance on the East Side. At first, I took the class without pay, but later on I received two dollars an evening.

In the summer we sublet our place and went to the country. Bernard Gussow, an artist friend, and I looked for a place for the summer. We found a run-down estate in Chappaqua, but the owner wanted two hundred dollars a month for it.

"Well," said Marguerite, "we can't lose by trying." So she sat down and wrote him offering him twenty dollars a month—and he took it.

We had a wonderful summer. We planted a big garden. Marguerite had always had a garden in California. With a book in one hand, we planted endless vegetables and they all flourished. When we started, the farmers used to come and sit on the fence and watch us—city slickers planting a garden in April, with a book in one hand. But luck was with us, everything grew and produced. Gussow had a job, so he had no time to work on the garden. Suzanne Gussow had a small child, so she had no time. Marguerite, with what help I could give, did the entire big garden. But when the Gussows began to sit on the sidelines and watch her weed and said what a wonderful job she did and how nice everything grew, it was too much. One day she cut a set of stakes and divided every row into equal parts—theirs and ours. That she felt was fair and decent, but after the division they had no end of time to work on the weeding and cultivating, and then Marguerite was really mad. We had magnificent vegetables and giant squash, a fine strawberry bed—already there—and later grapes and fruit. We lived off the place. There was a pond above the house. I suppose it furnished water—we never questioned anything—but it furnished frogs. It was full of noisy frogs; we sat on the edge with sticks and had frogs' legs for dinner. A caretaker on a neighboring estate showed us edible mushrooms and wild greens. He brought us snapping turtles for soup and fish which he dynamited in neighboring ponds.

Troops of friends would traipse out from the city on weekends bringing food. We took down doors and used them as tables on sawhorses, and we slept a dozen in a bed crossways—boys in one bed, girls in another. There was a small grate in the floor for heat, and sometimes one of the guests would sit up all night to see what went on in the room below. One time we made the mistake of putting a girl in a room with five doors, and behind each door was a boy. She was furious with all of us in the morning. She had had a sleepless night; behind each of the five doors had been a hopeful male.

And every minute that summer, I painted. The country was a new world to me—every flower and every weed was a revelation of color and design. The richness of invention in nature was unbelievable—the fairylike delicacy of tiny weeds along the roads, the bold coarse leaves on heavy stems supporting fine purple flowerlets by the old barn. I made endless colored drawings on typewriting paper, very simple and sensitive notes. I made drawings of our visiting friends. The paintings that I did were decorative and full of imagination, the colors were gay and brilliant. They were poems of appreciation of life in the country and the beauty of nature around us. There were no problems in them, no gloomy forebodings, no literary solving of the world's ills, only a joyous awareness of the world about us. Flowers bloomed, wild life carried on, clouds floated, trees designed themselves in the landscapes. Nude figures lay around pools, played with children, made love, dreamed. They were our summer friends, but sufficiently abstract not to distress anyone. Our friend Georgia Duhig, who sang, was an inspiration. Her singing colored the landscape and produced immense exotic plants and flowers in my imagination.

One time when some ten of us were swimming nude, in a forest pool on a neighboring estate, we heard horns and foxhounds baying, and the hunt came through the woods. We dropped into the pool like frogs. After they passed we rose up, undiscovered, and proceeded to go about our cook-out and picnic.

That was the year Germany declared war on Russia and France. I remember going to New York on the train and seeing someone reading a newspaper with screaming headlines. I told myself, "This is impossible." I thought we were living in a civilized world. I couldn't understand how civilized people could declare war.

When we first came to New York we were young artists who knew almost no one and had very little money. But young artists without money and with the same urge to develop their art, gravitate to each other. There is great give and take. They drop in to dinner with each other at any hour, whether there is any dinner or not, and sit up all hours at night discussing art and life. In no time our studio was a very active place.

We lived and worked freely. I created an interest with these paintings. I got things into various exhibitions and the critics gave me much attention–most of it adverse of course.

In those days I sometimes became so depressed over the complete absence of money that it would make me ill, and I would go to bed for a day or two. Now it seems fantastic that we were able to get along on so little. Through it all, we never borrowed, a habit we have kept all our lives. In a world based on credit, we have always paid cash.

Since no gallery would show our work, we decided to have little exhibitions in our studio on Tenth Street, and in time it became a place of interest for people to see. We had decorated it and there was nothing like it in the country at the time. Our floors were red lead, our walls lemon yellow. We made our little hall into a garden of Eden with a life-sized Adam and Eve and a red and white snake draped around the trunk of a decorative tree, with tropical foliage surrounding it all. Critics and newspaper writers came around and wrote about us in the Sunday supplements and on the art pages. The real miracle was that people came to these exhibitions and there was sometimes a sale.

At one of these exhibitions a doctor's wife from the Bronx came in. She noticed

Marguerite was pregnant, and when she went home she said to her husband, "I don't believe those young people have a doctor or know what to do about a baby. We must help them." And they did.

Dr. Alfred and Tessie Raabe became our life-long friends and in a small way, our first patrons, buying little things and getting their friends to buy. They had us over to many wonderful dinners in the Bronx, gave us clothes to make over, and arranged with a hospital for the birth of our child. We waited for the baby to be born, but week after week went by and nothing happened. Everyone got terribly nervous.

One morning I woke up about five o'clock. There was a great commotion in the street and a fire engine was in front of our house. I saw the hose going in the window below us. I woke up Marguerite, who looked out and said, "I think we'd better go to the hospital."

We called Dr. Raabe and rode up on the Sixth Avenue elevated to 125th Street, where Dr. Raabe had arranged for a room in a small private hospital, leaving the firemen to save the house. At nine o'clock that night, on March 28, 1915, Marguerite gave birth to a nine-pound boy, Tessim Zorach. I can't even remember that this complicated our life. He slept in a corner of the studio, and when we had all-night parties, he never said a word.

Dr. Raabe had a friend, a Dr. Weichsel, a manual-training teacher in the public schools, who organized "The People's Art Guild." I don't know who the people were who were supposed to love art, but Dr. Weichsel loved art and artists. He had little money but he bought small things here and there and had nice dinners and evenings for the artists.

Through Dr. Weichsel I was asked to exhibit a large canvas, "Spring" (No. 1), done in Chappaqua of nude figures lying about in a bright, gay landscape. Marguerite exhibited two pictures, "The Magnificent Squash" and "Maternity." This was the Forum Exhibition at the Michael Kennedy Galleries in 1916, and it was one of the first modern exhibitions to command respect.

Later, in 1920, the Pennsylvania Academy in Philadelphia invited a group of younger modern artists including us to exhibit in a show called "The New Tendencies in Art." We all went down to the opening, and Dr. Barnes treated us royally, showed us his collection, and sat around all day talking with us. It was very hard after that to believe all the tales of his strange conduct and the continual insults he heaped upon artists until years later when we experienced it ourselves.

There was a man named Charles Daniel, whose father was a saloonkeeper. This young man revolted against his environment and dreamed of another kind of life. Sam Halpert, Ernest Lawson, and some of the other artists used to hang around his father's bar, and through them he became interested in art and then in opening an art gallery for the younger and more advanced artists. Daniel started with

Halpert and Lawson. Halpert was painting very broad and very handsome pictures; Lawson was expressing himself in a sort of American Impressionism. Sam Halpert introduced me to Daniel, and when he opened a gallery on Forty-seventh Street, he took on Marguerite and me and exhibited our work. Daniel had a great influence on American art. The artists he took up, showed, and promoted were the advanced and the unknown who had no reputation and no place in the world to exhibit. Anyone can take up unknown artists and promote them, but you can't make a good artist out of poor material with promotion—at least not for long. The "unknowns" that Daniel encouraged became some of the renowned among American artists. None of them were the unknowns that appear in great numbers in the art world and in a year or two disappear without leaving a ripple. Charles Daniel had little knowledge of art and no confidence in himself, but he had what was more important, an instinct for the real in art and a belief in artists. Practically all his men came through. The men who went through his hands were Sam Halpert, Man Ray, Charles Demuth, Preston Dickinson, Ernest Lawson, Karl Knaths, Thomas Benton, Stuart Davis, Rockwell Kent, Joseph Stella, Louis Bouché, Charles Sheeler, and the Zorachs. He also showed John Marin, Maurice Prendergast, McFee, and Marsden Hartley but did not discover them. Hartley and Marin he got through Stieglitz. When Daniel opened his gallery, Stieglitz said, "Well, if saloonkeepers are going into art, America is certainly waking up."

Daniel exhibited our work for four years. Once in a while he sold a little thing, but it was very hard to get the money out of him. I guess he always liked to hold on to a dollar no matter how many he had. We could only get our money a few dollars at a time; it was very painful. He had the rich man's incapacity to realize that anyone was living in this world without money or that the ten dollars he gave us from a sale was for bread and meat. He would seriously tell us what stocks to invest in. We didn't know what a stock was, and, while he may not have been rich, he didn't know what poverty was. In the summer he would send us wonderful boxes of food and delicacies to the country. This was exciting, but it was painful trying to collect for the rent from him.

We heard from Abraham Walkowitz that there was a rich collector very much interested in my exhibition at the Daniel Gallery and that he wanted to come over to my studio. We were told that he would probably buy something. One day there was a knock on the door. A big man in a sweat shirt with a market basket over his arm walked in and a young fellow after him. This was Hamilton Easter Field, artist and art patron, and the young man with him was his protégé, Robert Laurent.

I asked him what the basket was for, and Field said, tapping his basket, "You know I live on Columbia Heights in Brooklyn and take in boarders. I came over here to the Fulton Market because I can buy fish here for three cents a pound cheaper than I can in Brooklyn and I like to walk across the Brooklyn Bridge."

I said to myself, "Well, that's it. If he wants to save three cents a pound on fish, he isn't going to buy any of my work." And he never did.

But he asked us what we were doing for the summer. We didn't know.

He said, "I have a deserted farm in New Hampshire. I don't know what shape it is in, but you can go there for the summer. All I'd like in return would be for each of you to give me a picture from your summer work."

We were delighted but Daniel was unhappy. "There goes my sale," he said. And he never allowed Field to take the two pictures of ours, although we didn't learn that until much later.

Later we used to visit Field on Columbia Heights. He was a Quaker and lived with his mother in one of the two brownstone houses he owned overlooking the harbor. The other he rented as apartments to artists. In 1921 he founded the *Arts Magazine* and published an article of mine on "The New Tendencies in Art" the following year.

Hamilton Easter Field not only collected art; he collected farms. He couldn't resist putting down a few hundred dollars on a bargain, and that was the end of it. He never knew what to do with it afterwards. It was one of these farms where he let us spend the summer. It was a terrible trip to this place by train, all day and all night, with several changes and hours in ice-cold station waiting rooms in April with a two-month-old baby.

The house sat in a wilderness on a plateau surrounded by a range of mountains. It was decrepit, the roof leaked—we had to abandon the kitchen and set up a kitchen in the dining room. There were a few odds and ends of furniture, a couple of beds, a bureau or two. We made a table out of a door and used boxes for chairs. The baby slept in a bureau drawer. There was a stove, some firewood, which surprised us, and a deep well in the back kitchen. During the summer a Boston professor and his wife appeared. Field had also given them the place for the summer. But when they saw us living there they kindly said nothing and went elsewhere. I don't know how we got by. We had no money. As Marguerite was a good gardener, we raised vegetables, but it is hard to live off the land. We bought milk from our only neighbor on the hill and what supplies we could from a rural delivery service. We walked miles to and from the post office. One day I was exhausted carrying the baby such a distance and Marguerite took over. A car came by and a woman cried, "Look at that big hulk of a man making that poor woman carry that child."

"Give me that baby," I said. "I'm not going to be put in that class."

Our friend, Mary Boretz, a social worker and a dynamic personality, wrote us she was coming up to spend her vacation with us. We wrote her not to come, but she didn't get the letter. She came up and stayed all summer. Off and on that summer, friends wrote us they were coming up, and we quickly wrote them to stay home. We wanted to work and we had all we could handle without visitors.

There were lovely rocky pastures where Mary posed nude and Tessim lay in the sun; there was a wild mountain stream circling the plateau, and we had picnics and fished and climbed among the rocks. And always there were the mountains towering over us, changing with every hour, snow trimmed when we came and all greens and granite in mid-summer, and a New England radiance of color in the fall. We loved the magenta of fireweed and the unbelievable sight of three men mowing a tremendous field with scythes, each in his row above and behind the other. All day they mowed, always keeping pace and rhythm. Marguerite made an embroidery of them and also one of us seated in front of the house in the White Mountains.

At first it was hard to keep warm in that empty, drafty house but when it was summer, we slept out under the stars. One morning I heard two shots at daybreak. When I went up to our neighbor's for milk I said jokingly, "Did you get him, Elmer?"

"Did you see me?" he said. "Come around tonight and I'll give you a roast."

The next day Marguerite had the roast in the oven, when I looked out and saw two men in khaki uniform out under our tree where the deer was shot. There was a $500 fine or jail. I was scared. We didn't want to be caught with the roast and we couldn't think where to hide it, so we put it in the fire. Then I went out and talked to the men. They were inspecting apple trees for gypsy moths! I rushed back and got the roast out of the fire. It was a bit overdone on the outside but delicious.

That summer we painted. The pictures had greater depth, a sense of relation with the universe and with the lives of people. Unfortunately most of this work was ruined. Hamilton Easter Field was supposed to be an authority on the composition of paint and on preparing canvases. He gave us a formula which we carefully followed, for we prepared our own canvases. This formula did not work. The canvases flaked, the paint degenerated and fell off in powder, the surface crumbled, and almost everything was ruined. Only a very few paintings survived. When we returned, we had a show at the Daniel Gallery. Daniel thought we would be a great success. There was great interest but no sales; this was hard on him as well as on us. Nevertheless, a Chicago lawyer, Arthur Jerome Eddy, was so interested that he arranged for a show at the O'Brien Gallery in Chicago. The actor, William Gillette, bought two pictures—my first real sale. I don't know what he paid for them—probably one hundred and fifty dollars apiece. It was so long before Daniel finished paying us for them that we lost track.

After the show at the O'Brien Gallery, Arthur Jerome Eddy, the lawyer and collector, looked us up on Tenth Street. He was kindled with enthusiasm and selected fifteen pictures from both of us and asked how much I wanted for them. For a minute I felt like a millionaire. Fifteen pictures. I figured I should get one hundred dollars a picture, so I said fifteen hundred dollars. He said, "I'll give you two hundred dollars for the lot."

It was an awful shock to me. I said, "Mr. Eddy, I am not starving—there is a loaf of bread in the kitchen. Any one picture is worth more than you are offering me." Later he told me that he bought a batch of paintings from a deaf mute girl studying at the Art Students League for the two hundred dollars.

There was another man, a Fifth Avenue dealer by the name of Kilgore, who looked me up. He said he had heard I had some paintings I had made of the south of France. He looked at them casually and said, "I'll give you fifteen dollars apiece for the lot."

I asked him why he wanted them; it seemed a bit fishy.

He said, "You know that's the country Corot painted. I have a man who can take the compositions and turn them into good Corots. Of course, if you'd like to do the job for me yourself, I will pay you well for it."

Years afterwards, when I saw Kilgore uptown at parties and a bit drunk, he would always welcome me gleefully and say, "Friends, here is the artist that threw me out of his studio and kicked me down the stairs when all I wanted was to buy his pictures."

We were active in most of the independent shows that took place after the Armory Show. Some were held in vacant ground-floor stores which we rented, some in the Grand Central Palace, and some on the roof of the old Waldorf-Astoria. Many of these were huge events hung with every kind of good, bad, and indifferent painting and sculpture. I remember especially one of the first ones held on the ground floor of a building on Forty-second Street west of Sixth Avenue in about 1915. I painted two large decorations on either side of the entrance. I decorated a white suit and umbrella in vivid cubistic colors and hired a man to parade up and down Forty-second Street in this suit. He was stopped by the police. I painted a huge sign on the sidewalk and was informed that this too was against the law. A critic from the Philadelphia papers came in to review the show and went around the exhibition saying the East Side Jews were running and ruining American art.

I said, "Who do you mean? John Sloan, Rockwell Kent, Stuart Davis, Gaston Lachaise?"

It was quite something to set up an independent exhibition. We had to build stands, arrange for catalogues and publicity, and do all the hanging and odd jobs ourselves. But we were young.

One artist who profited by the independent show was Eilshemius. He was an odd fellow who painted strange, imaginative pictures. He was sort of a misfit in the art world—perhaps in any world—there was a touch of chromo in his work and one of real expression. Valentine Dudensing, the dealer, had showed an Eilshemius to Matisse and Matisse said, "That man is a good painter!" Then Dudensing promptly rushed over to where Eilshemius lived and bought most of his paintings for one thousand dollars. After that he began to promote him, at first selling his paintings for very little and finally for more and more until he was getting good prices.

We met Eilshemius for the first time at an independent show. He told us that he was asking ten thousand dollars for the painting in the show. He admitted that nobody would buy it at that price but that everybody would look twice.

Eilshemius and his brother lived on Fifty-seventh Street in a crumbling brick house. When I saw it, it looked as if it hadn't been dusted for the last sixty years. The brothers lived in a world of their own, in dire poverty, the house falling down around them. When Eilshemius died I heard that he was buried in a pauper's grave. The house was sold and later turned into a beautiful gallery for Chinese art.

CHAPTER FOUR

SOME TIME LATE IN 1915, a woman by the name of Myra Carr and an actor by the name of Freddie Burt started a school of Modern Art on Washington Square South. They asked me to be an instructor. There were few pupils and little money but much hope and enthusiasm. I taught there all winter, and in the spring Mrs. Carr said she was opening a school in Provincetown for the summer and wanted me to go there and teach. But when we got there, we found that Mrs. Carr had also engaged another artist, Nordfeldt, to teach. This was very embarrassing for both of us. Since he was already established in the school, I stepped out. It was not as much of a problem as we thought; there were no pupils.

We rented a fish loft on the shore in the town banker's back yard. There were steep stairs and no door. Tessim was a year old and we worried about the stairs. But after he rolled down them twice and survived, we relaxed a bit. Marguerite shocked Provincetown by wheeling Tessim up and down Main Street and letting him play on the beach naked. She said it was much easier to wash a baby than to wash his clothes, and besides he was handsome to look at and draw.

We had become expert swimmers, thanks to our New York roomer, Aletha Comstock, who was a professional swimmer and had taught us in the New York pools. We used to swim out to the boats at night, remove our suits, put them in a fisherman's dory, and swim naked through the harbor—a wonderful way to swim. Fortunately we were always able to find the boat where we had parked our suits.

I went out with the fishermen in the early morning before sunrise to the weirs. I painted the black figures against the tremendous red sun of the morning rising from the horizon, pulling in their nets. I felt as if I were on another planet seeing for the first time a new pattern of life. I painted a little boat floating in the translucency of color—suspended between the sea and sky, throwing a shadow into the depths and the schools of fishes weaving in and out of the light, and I painted the Zorach family sailing in the harbor in bright and lively colors. I exhibited these paintings in the local exhibitions and later in New York. They were shown with all the conventional pictures. People and the other artists as well thought we were crazy.

That summer we became fascinated by the Provincetown Players. A group of unknown playwrights were producing their plays on an old wharf. They asked Marguerite and me if we would design and paint scenery for them. It was their first experience with the theatre and ours too, but we had no hesitation. We were full of ideas and eager to use them.

Eugene O'Neill had come to Provincetown and was living in a little shack on the beach beyond the town with the anarchists, Terry and young Becky Edelson. Three beachcombers! He was a very withdrawn, very young man who swam long distances daily with beautiful style. He was shy and shunned everyone but a few cronies.

John Reed had just come back from Mexico where he had been covering the Mexican revolution for the Hearst papers. Louise Bryant had left her husband on the West Coast and followed him here. They had a pleasant big house in Provincetown with much extra room for guests. Hippolyte Havel, the anarchist, cooked for them. He was a superb cook. Jack Reed invited everyone to visit him. The house was always full of artists and writers. He fed them and made them happy and so welcome that they never thought of leaving. In desperation Jack rented a room over Francis' General Store, where he tried to go and work.

One day Jack said to me, "You've got to help me, I'm desperate. I can't work, I can't earn any money, I can't keep all these people. Marsden Hartley has been here a month. He doesn't even contribute anything intellectually and I don't really like him, but how can we move him out without offending him?"

I forget what strategy we worked out—but Hartley moved. Afterwards Hartley said to me, "You know, Jack has asked a number of people to leave. I'm so glad I moved out before this happened. I would have been humiliated if it had happened to me."

Louise Bryant fell in love with Eugene O'Neill and helped him with his plays about the sea. She was an inspiration, a taskmaster, and she had complete faith in his genius.

Gene's *Bound East for Cardiff* series were among the first plays put on by the Provincetown Players. I never made a set for an O'Neill play. Gene insisted everything had to be factual. If the play called for a stove, it couldn't be a painted box. It had to be an honest-to-goodness stove. If there was a sink, it had to be a real sink. I used to try to make him understand that a stage is a work of art like a painting. It is a world in itself or at least an illusion of a world. You cannot, for instance, have a real tree or a real ocean. There, at least, you have to accept the illusion. I could make no impression on him.

Louise Bryant had written a little English morality play called *The Game.* It was not much in itself, but she wanted to produce it and thought an exciting stage set might put it over. I must confess that we were as determined to do things our way as the playwrights were to do them theirs. Louise said we could do whatever we wished with her play and even asked me to act in it. We were delighted with the opportunity to put on a play and ruthlessly turned an English morality play into a sort of Egyptian pantomime. The backdrop was a decorative and abstract pattern of the sea, trees, the moon, and the moon path in the water designed by Marguerite. The Provincetown Players used this as a decoration in front of the theater in New York for years after we were no longer with them. The costumes were slight and abstract and the movements were worked out in a flat plane in pantomime. It made a hit. When the Provincetown Players went to New York, this was the first play they put on.

I worked with the Provincetown Players for four years. I was fascinated but at the same time I resented having allowed myself to be roped into this absorbing activity. Yet it was a great education to me; reading plays, making decisions, influencing people, rehearsing, painting scenery, and planning sets. I got to know the theater as well as I got to know painting and sculpture. I produced some of the first modern and abstract plays ever put on in New York. Marguerite and I designed them. We did Alfred Kreymborg's *Lima Beans.* I was the huckster who is heard but not seen. It was a lively production using colors in planes and angles with patterns of remarkable vegetables. The acting was gay and subtle and especially well handled.

The Provincetown Players had no professional actors. Most of the plays were written by the players themselves and almost everyone did some acting. Edna St. Vincent Millay and I could put on a real show at the first reading of a play if it was one that appealed to us. Everyone would get excited and say the play must be put on and we must act in it. But as rehearsals went on we lost our spirit and interest. Finally, everyone would begin to feel it was all a mistake and it usually was.

One of the most interesting things Marguerite and I did was Alfred Kreymborg's *Jack's House*—I think it was the first Cubist play ever produced in New York. We designed and painted the scenery, made the costumes, and produced the play. I doubt if anyone remembers it now, but it was a major accomplishment. The critics were excited over *Jack's House*. There was much publicity and the scenes and sets were reproduced in color in the Sunday supplements. But the public was indifferent. They found it confusing and it meant nothing to them. It certainly was not a success as far as the public went, and the theater has to have a public.

On the same bill we put on a school-girlish play by Edna St. Vincent Millay, *Two Slatterns and a King*. We had to do this in order to get Edna to act in *Jack's House*. It wasn't much of a play but it was fun. I played the king and wore a robe of purple and ermine made by Marguerite. Instead of a modest crown, I made one twenty inches high and a magnificent scepter from a bed post covered with tinsel and designed with colored papers. The Cubist painter Gleizes was visiting here and was so fascinated with my scepter that he took it back to Paris with him.

Gig Cook was the one who held the Provincetown Players together through all their quarrels and difficulties. Sober, he was dull and commonplace and plodding, but drunk—and fortunately he was more often drunk than sober—he became a dynamic and intelligent person. He thought clearly and creatively, and luckily he was a good executive. His wife, Susan Glaspell, the writer, was a marvelous actress. Acting played a minor part in her life, but she had that rare power and quality inherent in great actresses. She had only to be on the stage and the play and the audience came alive.

Eugene O'Neill was the solid backbone of the Provincetown Players; his plays put over the project and held it together. I used to gripe at his literal realism, but whatever he did was true theater. Gene never acted but he directed. We thought him terribly conservative. One day his father, the actor James O'Neill, came and gave Gene a criticism on one of his plays. Gene slumped down in his seat.

"That old fogy!" he said when he left.

In Provincetown Gene stayed aloof. He seemed to like to have strange, defeated, and frustrated intellectuals and derelicts surround him. He was living then in a house on the dunes with his second wife, Agnes, and their two small children. Occasionally, we visited them. One night when we were there, we decided to go to a dance in Provincetown. Gene insisted Agnes wear a brooch that had been his mother's. She was worried about wearing it; perhaps she had had bad experiences before.

At the dance Gene, who was thoroughly drunk, walked up to Agnes and said, "What do you mean by wearing my mother's pin?" and knocked her down on the dance floor.

Normally he was a shy, quiet man and sweet with his children, but he was a heavy drinker and one of those mean drunks. All the black Irish welled up in him.

I made a drawing of Eugene O'Neill for *Scribner's Magazine* and one of Edna St. Vincent Millay. They are now in the Museum of the City of New York. Edna was quite a personality; a tiny little female, self-centered, adventurous where men were concerned, flirtatious and gay. A poet and not a playwright nor an actress, except in real life. In a group she was always a dominant personality. She was a prima donna who never kept an appointment, was never on time, and made everyone wait on her.

It was hard to give up the fascination of the theater but one has only one life and one cannot divide it between two gods. I found myself torn between art and the Provincetown Players and I began to feel terribly frustrated. The theater had been a good education, but art was my medium of expression. I had to make a decision. I gave up the theater.

It was the summer of 1917 and again we had no place to go. We met Mrs. Henry Fitz Taylor, Bishop Potter's daughter, a little old lady active in art circles. Her husband was one of the first abstract artists in this country. He had been on the committee that ran the Armory Show. He was a fine painter but a shy man. He had no dealer, no one exhibited his work—even after he died. His art died with him, as art often does. Mrs. Taylor had a lovely home in Cornish, New

Hampshire, and she also had an abandoned farm in the hills back of Plainfield, which she offered to us for the summer. Cornish was an old settlement. Many successful academic artists and writers lived there. St. Gaudens' studio was there, and there also were Herbert Adams, Kenyon Cox, Maxfield Parrish, and the writer, Winston Churchill. They all had beautiful homes. Mrs. Taylor wanted to give us Echo Farm but I was too simple a person to know how to go about taking such a gift. Later she offered it to another artist, who said, "wonderful, make me out a deed." And she did. He spent two summers there, then abandoned it for Santa Fe.

We had a delightful summer at Echo Farm. As I look back, all our summers were wonderful. We had a vegetable garden, raised a pig which we sold in the fall, rented a cow for the summer for twenty-five dollars and bought a horse and buggy for another twenty-five dollars. There was only one door and it was in the kitchen, a big room with a beautiful beech floor. There was a stove but no furniture; however, we were used to that problem. We had shipped our bed and bedding by American Express. They did not arrive until fall when we were leaving. We were ingenious at making a place livable.

We were living in a wilderness. I had to learn to milk the rented cow. It was a painful problem in the beginning and my hands got so numb I could hardly use them. We bought the horse and buggy so we could go to town for supplies. Our horse was a handsome old beast but windbroken. We felt so sorry for him going up hills that we would get out and walk. The farmers said, "What a nice boy that is. He walks up the hill to save his horse."

In return for the use of the farm, we were supposed to cut the hay. I bought a scythe and cut the whole field without sharpening it. It never occurred to me that it wasn't sharp when I bought it. We asked a farmer to help us. He looked at the field and said, "What did you chew that off with?" So he came down with a pair of magnificent, brown-eyed oxen to mow our hay. At night he put them in the corral. It was a lovely moonlight evening. No sooner was he gone than, zip—the oxen it seemed leapt over the stone wall right into our garden and started eating our cabbages and lettuce. I didn't know how to handle them; they didn't shoo but rolled their eyes and shook their sharp horns at me. I harnessed the horse and Marguerite went to get the farmer while I tried to protect our food supply. When he arrived he just crooned at the critters and they followed him like puppies.

"They're just like kittens," he said, "don't be afraid of them." And he put them in the barn. "But," he said, "if you want a wife, don't let her drive that horse and buggy. She raced that horse downhill. You don't do that, you race him uphill."

"But," I said, "we can't race him uphill, he's windbroken. The only way we can get him anywhere is to race him downhill."

Marguerite said, "In a way he's right but I notice the farmers are scared to death of horses, I'm not."

All day the country was serene and silent, but at night, when we were securely in our beds, it was rampant with wild life. The mosquitoes roared like the sea against our window netting; heavy animals clumped and coughed and growled and bumped into the house. A "bear" or a "wolf" would follow us along the road through the bushes when we drove home late and the horse would be terrified. When we first came to Echo Farm, the porcupines had eaten up the steps and half the porch. I made new steps and every night the varmints would come back and chew on them. One night I got mad. I got up stark naked, grabbed a lamp in one hand and an ax in the other. There he was. I chopped his head off with one blow of the ax and went back to bed. In the morning the whole place was littered with quills, but not one had touched me. Just luck! It took us two days to pick them up. We didn't dare let Tessim go outside till there wasn't one left. We had read that the Indians prized porcupines as food and we could have used a little meat, but we couldn't quite take him. We buried the culprit instead. Deer ate our garden every night. We were more hopeful about them. I borrowed a rifle and sat up three nights waiting but they never came back. Before we got the gun we could look out any moonlight night and see them enjoying our peas.

I did shoot a raccoon. A farmer came over and said he had treed one and asked if I would shoot him. I don't know where I got this reputation as a hunter–I had never fired a gun in my life. I took one shot and down he came. He was young and made a delicious roast.

This was a transition period for us in art. We found it difficult to work. We had to dig into ourselves for material and had to build the material we found into new forms until it evolved a life of its own. I worked most of the summer on a large painting, doing it over and over, always unhappy with it, until I could no longer see it and threw it away. Marguerite felt bad about it; she liked it. I also painted a large picture of a figure with a scythe–the scythe is a beautiful form. I feel that this picture is unusual in its color and conception. Marguerite painted a lovely little picture called "Whippoorwills," which the William Kents have. It was of the New Hampshire country at dusk with birds flying. She also painted a picture of a fascinating swamp we passed on the way to town, and one of a deserted mill, which many years later we gave to Bob and Diana Folley when they got married. Marguerite did a series of watercolors of the woods, pictures that analyzed the colors and forms around her and built them into new combinations, yet retained the beauty of the woods.

It was here at Echo Farm that I made my first carving. We found two small butternut panels, the fronts of small bureau drawers. We each started to carve a woodcut, but I got so fascinated carving that I didn't stop with a woodcut. I developed a fine and most original bas-relief which I afterwards sold to Adele Wolman of Baltimore. I don't remember what happened to Marguerite's effort.

We stayed very late at the farm until the winter shadows closed in on our valley and the sun only sat above the hills for a few hours in the middle of the day. We were waiting for our second baby to be born, and things were off schedule. Every time I drove into town, the farm wives all rushed to the windows and said, "There they go. What'd you bet, a boy or a girl?" And every day all three of us returned and they said, "Well, what do you know—not yet!" Finally one night just before the first snow, we drove into Plainfield at midnight, where the doctor met us and took Marguerite to Windsor, Vermont, while I returned to the farm. We had left Tessim sleeping alone and when I got back he was still asleep and the squirrels were noisily rolling butternuts around the attic. Our daughter, Dahlov, was born November 12th, 1917, in Windsor, Vermont, and I had to go back to New York with Tessim and leave Marguerite and the baby, to come down alone when she was able to. It was pretty grim. The berth on the train that the doctor had reserved for her was not available, and she had to sit up half the night. The baby howled, the passengers swore, but not one person would give her a berth. In the morning Tessim and I met them at the station, weak, exhausted and miserable.

The next summer Mrs. Taylor lent us a magnificent house in the village of Plainfield with so many rooms that we shut off half of them and never went into them. There was such an enormous studio that a billiard table looked like a postage stamp in it. This was the Fuller House and was supposed to be in such poor condition that no one could live there, at least not the kind of people that would rent a house that grand. Nothing was supposed to work—the plumbing, the water system, the swimming pool hadn't worked for years. We started things and there was water. We filled the swimming pool and enjoyed it all summer without a bit of algae to corrupt it. Everything was so grandiose and luxurious that we just couldn't work. I made endless drawings but I painted only one small picture. Marguerite had an order for two embroidered bedspreads from Mrs. Nathan Miller, Max Weber's patron. She worked on these all summer. This mansion, the Fuller Place, belonged to a friend of Mrs. Taylor's and had stood unoccupied for years because it was too run down to interest any possible tenant. We never used the beautiful living rooms, but we read books from the library and enjoyed the swimming pool. We had lots of guests. Mo Moskowitz, a young Australian pianist, spent weeks with us. He played beautifully on the grand piano and wrecked our garden by digging up all the vegetables and replanting them in mathematically correct rows. The plants couldn't take it, and neither could we. In the end it didn't matter as we had a killing frost the first of June and another the first of September.

That summer Mrs. Taylor brought up a man named Applegate, a potter. He built a kiln out of an old stove and some fire brick, and we all played with ceramics. I did my first modeling—several decorated pots and some small figures. We sat up all night firing the kiln, cooking hotdogs, singing songs, and stoking the fire. It was wild and exciting. Awful things happened; our work blew up from not being properly dried, bricks blew up and wrecked the kiln and everything in it. Something always went wrong. We had a lot of fun and experience but only one or two pieces survived. One of them, of Dahlov just learning to walk and balance herself before taking off, was broken but I managed to restore it and make a cast from it in bronze. "First Steps" has all the sense of form and accomplishment that is in my later work. This was the first piece of sculpture in the round that I did. It was in the year 1918.

Then that summer there was Nettie May. Applegate asked Mrs. Taylor to have her up, and Mrs. Taylor suggested she stay with us. Nettie May helped with the children and Mo Moskowitz was to help with the dishes. Mo never got up in the morning and he found it easy to forget the dishes after meals, but he was good company and played beautifully. Nettie May wasn't beautiful. She was sensitive and charming and delightful and a little fey. There was something rare and out of this world about her. And she was very young. I think she was a student of Applegate's. He had fallen in love with her and was looking forward to an affair with her away from the eyes of his family. Nettie May was not in love with Applegate but wondered if she should have an affair with him. We were horrified. He looked like a very old man to us; he must have been forty-five and had a wife and children in New Jersey. Men fell for Nettie May. Mo Moskowitz was so intrigued he couldn't be persuaded to leave. An artist friend staying in the village haunted our swimming pool. I was very intrigued myself, being always susceptible to feminine charms. But it is a little complicated when the charmer lives in the house with you and your family and is pursued by various males. I found myself in the position of protector from the wolves, for I sensed there was a sensitivity there and a fragility that could not stand up to temporary romance. Yet she had her own method of protection: she thought she was in love with an artist in New York, a protégé of Arthur B. Davies. Davies thought this young man was a genius. He was a strange, attractive, talented fellow, but unstable and erratic.

Nettie May had no money. Her father was a poor minister. She was capable of doing all sorts of artistic work but hers was a very minor talent. She just wanted a not too difficult life and love. She came back to town with us that fall and stayed with us off and on while she tried to work at various things and find a niche where she fitted. She pursued her strange romance with her young artist, writing him letters, and he wrote and encouraged her to the point that she was going to marry him. It was off and on, off and on. Finally his brother came to see us and then Nettie May. He told us it was hopeless. There was something wrong with his brother. He could never marry anyone. He said this was a tragedy and it was. Nettie May disappeared.

Two weeks later she appeared at our door. I almost fainted. She was in a wild state of excitement and did not even know us. She had worn the shoes off her feet wandering about the city. We kept her with difficulty and called her father. She had to be strapped to a stretcher and carried away. Ten days later she was dead. It was a terrible thing that haunted us for years.

CHAPTER FIVE

WHEN WE RETURNED FROM PROVINCETOWN in the fall of 1916, our apartment was still rented and we had to move in with Jack Reed, who later wrote "Ten Days That Shook the World." We found ourselves so busy with the theater that we needed someone to take care of Tessim. Through Louise Bryant's maid, we found Ella Madison. Ella was an old minstrel singer who lived in a broken-down tenement over a ragpicker on Third Street. Her mother had been a slave and in her youth Ella had played the role of "Topsy" in the early productions of *Uncle Tom's Cabin.* She had appeared to be utterly down and out and offered to take Tessim to the park daily and sit with him at the house for three dollars a week. We were astonished the next day to see her arrive dressed up in a lace cap and a voluminous starched white apron, the conventional mammy. She promptly put Tessim into his best clothes and took him out to Washington Square for air. They returned at five o'clock, black from head to foot, covered with dirt and mud. Marguerite was horrified but realized that dirt wouldn't do Tessim any real harm and he'd probably had a good time.

Ella Madison loved babies and was very proud of looking after our children. She stayed with us for fifteen years off and on, doing housework and caring for the children. She never cooked and we could never take her to the country with us. She would beg to go and twice we tried it. But she was desperate and miserable and frightened to death. She barricaded her windows at night and saw wolves and bears in every thicket. The rat-ta-tat of a woodpecker, drilling for his grub, was an army of soldiers invading our woods. All her good nature congealed and she became ugly and mean. We had to send her home. When I heard that she once went to Asbury Park and couldn't stand it—it was too much country for her—I realize what the wild places we took her to must have meant. She missed the rumble of the elevated under her window on Third Street.

She was a powerful character. She sang and danced and taught me spirituals. She would perform for our guests. She took the children to movies, sending them

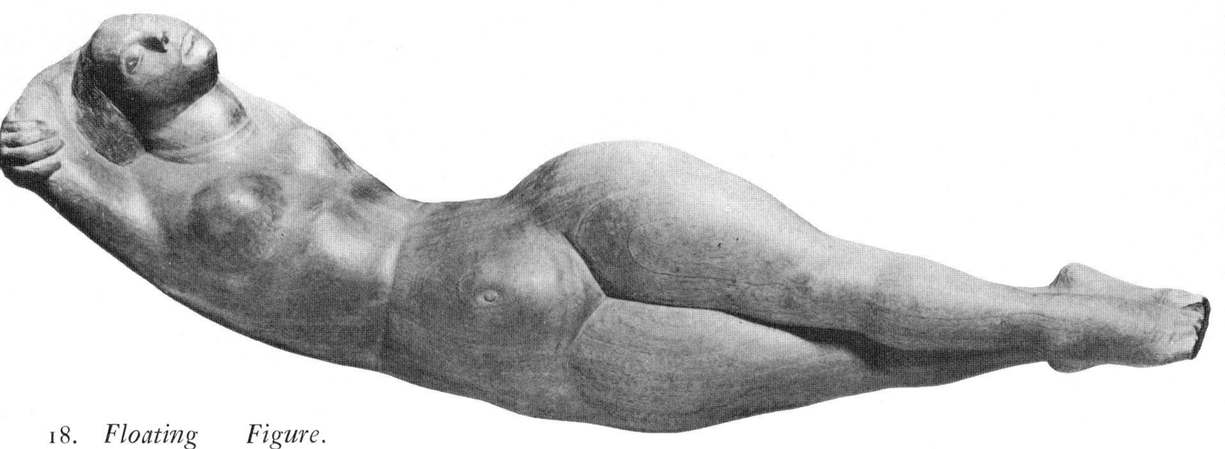

18. *Floating Figure.* 1922. African mahogany. 33¼″ long. Albright-Knox Art Gallery, Buffalo, New York.

19. *Two Children.* 1922. Mahogany. 36″ high. Collection of Theodore Frost.

20. *Artist's Daughter—Dahlov.* 1923. Italian marble. Collection of Mrs. Robert Wheelwright.

21. *The Artist's Wife*. 1924. Tennessee marble. 18″ high. Collection of the Zorach children.

22. *Pegasus*. 1925. Walnut. 15″ high. Whitney Museum of American Art, New York City.

23. *Two Figures.* 1929. Crayon and pencil. 29¼″ x 20″.

24. *Dahlov.* 1935. Ink. 23⅜″ x 18⅜″. The Downtown Gallery, New York City.

25. *Football Player.* 1930. Swedish granite. *Ca.* 4′ high. Bowdoin College, Brunswick, Maine.

26. *Bathing Girl.* 1930. Mahogany. *Ca.* 3′ high. Collection of Mr. and Mrs. J. Marin, Jr.

27. *Cat.* 1931. Green Maine boulder. Collection of Mrs. John D. Rockefeller, Jr.

28. *Child on Pony*. 1934. York fossil marble. 25″ high. The Downtown Gallery, New York City.

29. *Mother and Child.* 1927–30. Detail of early stage of roughing.

30. *Mother and Child.* 1930. Spanish florida rosa marble. 65″ high. Metropolitan Museum of Art, New York City.

in ahead and when people began to be disturbed over these two lost tots, she would bustle in and claim them dramatically. She would take them to Coney Island, wait at the gate and collect tickets from people going out, and then take them in and they would do the rounds. We never knew this till long afterwards; we thought our children were taking the air in Washington Square. Out in the park, within earshot of all the white maids, she'd coach Tessim to, "Call me black nigger." And then in a loud voice, "If you ever call me nigger, I'll lay you out!" Dahlov would never cooperate. One day on the elevated, Dahlov saw a big poster of Aunt Jemima. "You, la," she cried so loud that the whole train could hear. Ella went into her act and was simply delighted.

Years later Ella got a part in the original production of *Porgy and Bess.* While she was given an important part, she made her role twice as important. She was a huge woman, and in pink satin was startling. She sang her own songs, danced her own dances, and did as she pleased with the dialogue. Ella went to Europe with the play, where it was a great success. But after the European tour she returned to America to slip back into the old life on Third Street, over the ragpicker, without any money and without a future. Eventually, she became too old to work and we managed to get her into an old-folks home in Harlem, run by her church. At first they treated her beautifully; she had a little money, but gradually they moved her from the first floor to the attic. The caretakers drank and consequently they neglected and starved their charges. Ella was not one to take anything of that kind meekly. One Sunday morning she stood on the front steps and yelled—and Ella had a voice—"I'm hungry." She stopped the clock and things were changed for the better in the old-folks home.

We lived at 123 West Tenth Street in Greenwich Village for twenty years, a part and yet not a part of the life there. We didn't eat at restaurants or sit at bars or frequent night spots. We simply had no money and we did have two small children. There was never a cent for anything beyond bare necessities in all these early years. We spent absolutely nothing for extras, carfares, newspapers, or movies. Our one extravagance was Ella Madison for three dollars a week. But neither of us could bear to spend the afternoon in the park when there was so much to do and we were so desperate to get to it. People were very good to us; they gave us clothes and materials and would often drop in at mealtimes, bringing food. Marguerite was very clever and made almost everything we wore except shoes and my suits. She made delightful and charming clothes for the children, which old timers in the village still remember. How shocked she was when my underwear wore out. She couldn't believe it possible—and how were we going to replace it?

Marguerite was a wonderful cook. She could make nothing into something delectable at a moment's notice. We had gay parties and sings, and Tessim and Dahlov slept peacefully through it all in a corner of the studio. We enjoyed all the things that didn't cost money. We took ferries over to the Palisades and sketched and had picnics among the rocks and trees. We took walks in Central Park, and along Riverside Drive, and on the waterfronts; and everywhere we sketched. We didn't sit around and chit chat, we didn't play games or cards. We drew each other and our friends. "Hold that pose," was a constant cry. We evolved visions into forms. We experimented with techniques for the fun of it and enjoyed the unexpected results. We played with combinations of form. We discussed life and ideas and philosophy and people and art and money. None of us had any money. Problems were immediate at Tenth Street, life was a constant struggle, but it was also gay and rewarding.

We went to the Liberal Club dances and the Kit Kat balls and the Webster Hall balls, often getting home just as the children were waking up in the morning. Marguerite made exotic imaginative costumes for these balls. Sometimes we decorated Webster Hall. I remember a Mississippi steamboat ball run by Egmont Arens where I designed all the decorations—backdrops, curtains, banners, and streamers. Various people helped enlarge and paint them using the cheapest showcard colors on the cheapest unbleached muslin. Frank Crowninshield, the editor of *Vanity Fair*, thought it was tremendous. "Must have cost a lot of money," he said. "Just fifteen dollars," I said. I don't think he believed it. Of course none of the workers were paid. In all the things of this kind we did—and we worked days and weeks on them—we never thought of being paid for anything—none of us.

We acquired quite a few pieces of furniture on the streets in the early morning. People would move and put things out that they no longer wanted or no longer had room for. Some pieces just helped out for a few years; some we still have and cherish—a dining room table, a large chest of drawers, some chairs, and an antique desk we got in Provincetown for five dollars. Once Marguerite rushed home to tell me there was a fine bureau thrown out on the sidewalk in the next block. But when I hurried down I met a young man walking off with it on his shoulder. He had beaten me to it.

Every summer we went to the country with just a few dollars, never more than a hundred, spent the whole summer, and came back penniless. When we left we looked around at our friends and wondered if they would still be around in the fall. And every fall they were still alive—no one had starved to death—and, a miracle, everyone had lots of new work. Some of them also had new wives; there were always a certain number of casualties in human relationships over a summer. The only way we could keep the Tenth Street place was to sublet it, always to such nice people. They would move in with bouquets of flowers and baskets of fruit and were delighted with the colors and decorations, even the furniture. Sometimes they paid the rent, but too often they left owing at least part of it. They broke the furniture. "After all it was worth nothing." True, but it was all we had. One girl tenant we had gave it all away to her boy friend, and we had a hard time locating it. The boy friend was very embarrassed. "I thought of course it belonged to Gladys," he said. They left our kitchen full of dozens of empty beer bottles and milk bottles with various amounts of spoiled milk in them, and our bureau drawers full of mouldy peaches. They cut up our books and took those that they wanted. One fall we returned to find the door unlocked, the place abandoned and infested with bedbugs.

There were grim moments when suddenly there would be absolutely no money—not one cent for anything. It could be pretty terrifying. Marguerite said, "We'll have to establish credit for these emergencies, somewhere somehow, so we won't be caught helpless in a crisis. The next time we have money we will borrow two hundred dollars, put it aside, and in six months return it. In that way we will have established credit." When we had enough money for this, she persuaded me to go the Kraushaar Galleries, where I then exhibited, and borrow two hundred dollars. Mr. Kraushaar wasn't very happy about it and neither was I—in fact I was so unhappy that two days later I took the money back to him. Marguerite gave up, but she went out and opened a charge account at the corner grocer. It came in handy.

In those days we knew lots of young poets, and they spent much of their time with us. They would meet at our place to discuss poetry and what could be done with it. They would plan little magazines and publicity and places to get poetry published. We would all read poems and discuss them; Alfred Kreymborg, whose plays we produced, William Carlos Williams, Marianne Moore, Maxwell Bodenheim, Lola Ridge, Wallace Stevens, and Orrick Johns, who rented our place one summer and left it a wreck—he used to take off his wooden leg when he came home and hop around the room. Our furniture was too weak to support him.

Marguerite and I both wrote poetry. Ever since I was married and especially when we later visited the Yosemite Valley, which carried me beyond myself, I wrote poetry. I never considered myself a poet. I just sat down and wrote what I felt when I was deeply moved, and the modern young poets liked what I wrote. They liked the naiveté, the simplicity, and the direct expression of a mood. They published some of our poems in *Others*—a booklet they got out. Egmont Arens published some in *Playboy* and I even had poetry published in *Poetry*. I was amazed when I received a check from them. When I became more proficient and began editing and shifting words and working over my poems, the poets lost interest. The element of surprise and glamor was gone for them. Bodenheim objected to my using the words "purple" and "tiny"—yet they were favorite words of his. They all objected to anyone using the word "beauty," but I was stubborn and still wrote poetry as I felt it, but I stopped publishing it. I became self-conscious about expressing myself in too many art forms. I couldn't bear that people should say, "Oh, Zorach, he just does everything." I did do everything. I loved every form of art expression and I could project myself into any one of these forms to some extent, but I had begun to realize that I could no longer dissipate myself in too many directions. It had all been an education and a realization and broadening of awareness, but now I had to concentrate on what I wanted to do most. In time, I realized that sculpture—not painting—would have to become my life work and sculpture was a time-devouring master. I could not take it or leave it; I had to see it through. It consumed me, and I lived it.

Marguerite was frustrated at not having any uninterrupted time for painting, and uninterrupted time was a necessity for the kind of painting she did in oil. It was not something she could turn off and on; it was something she built up in a creative conception and had to see through. To be distracted or torn away at a crucial moment was very destructive to her. There was no uninterrupted time with caring for two small children, cooking, and running a house; and running a house came hard for her. I helped but it didn't come easy to me either. We would get up in the morning, have breakfast, leave everything and start working. When I was working in wood the place was full of chips; I often sat on the bed and the bed would be full of chips. Marguerite had little piles of wools and odd skeins for her embroidered tapestries everywhere. The place would be a mess. We were never conscious of it until someone came in. If I knew someone was coming I could clean up and have everything in order in nothing flat—the chips under the bed instead of on it, the dishes in the sink instead of on the table, odds and ends pushed into corners. Still I am afraid we had a bad reputation as housekeepers in those days. It was a long time before we could bring ourselves to get up from the table, wash the dishes, make the bed, and establish order before we got to work.

When we had begun to use brilliant color, Marguerite had been fascinated by the brilliancy and range of color in woolen yarns—beyond anything in paint. She had never embroidered anything in her life or been slightly interested in it, but she was unhappy over a picture she had painted of an Indian wedding and redid it in wool;—with all the pinks and reds and cerises, the blues and greens and yellows, of Jaipur, India. She found she could pick the work up at odd moments and lay it down any time. The picture she kept in her head, it was only possible to do such work a little at a time—as one works at sculpture. These embroidered tapestries soon ceased to be paintings in embroidery but took on an art form of their own unlike anything ever done before. I became excited over them and worked on some of the early ones with her, but I soon saw that she was much more expert and inventive than I. I was clumsy with the needle and could only make one stitch—over and under. She varied her stitches amazingly. She began to create and vary them to develop the forms—the animals, birds, people, objects. Her embroideries looked like tapestries and that is what they were, embroidered tapestries. At that time they seemed to be like nothing else done in this world. People were fascinated by them; the art critics devoted columns to them in *The New York Times* and other papers. They took forever to do, but she felt she had all the time in the world and it was a creative joy to work on them. When she had a show of them at the Montross Gallery women came and raved.

Before this we had exhibited about five of them—the first ones at the Daniel Gallery together with our paintings. We had met Bill and Lucy L'Engle in Provincetown. They brought her brother, Lathrop Brown, and his wife, Helen, to our show. They were so delighted with the embroideries that they bought all but one that were in the exhibition. We just couldn't believe it. We were to get all of twelve hundred dollars.

Prendergast, who was also one of Daniel's artists, took me aside and told me seriously, "You had better insist on getting your money. There is a war on, and the first thing you know Daniel won't have any gallery and you won't have any money. He owes just everybody."

I thought how hard and humiliating it was to beg for every penny owed me from Daniel. But anyway Marguerite insisted that I get the money and I did. Daniel was furious.

He said, "If you don't want to invest in my business, I'm not going to invest in you."

He didn't show our work any more. I was sorry it ended that way. I liked Daniel and he did much for American art and artists. This was the first real money we ever had. It lasted a long time and things were never quite so hard for us again.

The Lathrop Browns still own most of the early tapestries. The mistress of the Governor of Sumatra bought the "Waterfall." Later it was stolen from her apartment. It has never turned up or been reported seen by anyone—which is very curious. A small but delightful one of the circus, based on Marguerite's large circus picture, is in the collection of Judge Untermeyer. She made one of our home and life in Maine which was bought by Mrs. David Levy. Marguerite had meant to keep this for herself but she weakened. Mrs. Levy had meant to give it to the Museum of Modern Art but they said it didn't fit into any category that they knew of.

Suddenly aware that our children would have none of these unique works of art, Marguerite in later years made one for each of them. They were young and had babies and their kitchens were gay and bursting with life and activity. They now each have a portrait of activities in their kitchens. Then she made one of her home and life in California for us to enjoy.

Max Weber's patron, Mrs. Nathan Miller, as I previously mentioned, commissioned Marguerite to make her two bedspreads; designs on heavy linen of whatever she pleased and with much linen exposed, on the order of the Bayeux Tapestries. These she worked on all summer, designing delightful groups of people, mothers and children, and animals. The centers were a man and woman with flower forms. This was at the Fuller House in Plainfield, and she finished them that winter in New York.

Marguerite did a tapestry embroidery of our life in Plainfield. All the activities of the kitchen—all of us eating at the table, the animals, the patterns of curtains, dishes, linoleum—all interwoven, appearing and reappearing on different planes in different color patterns. A very modern and abstract work of art—with the village of Plainfield in the background; the trees and church and hills, all done in browns and blues and reds—not brilliant colors but strong. She called it "Family Evening" and considers it her masterpiece.

I like equally well her one of New York City with all the activities of the city woven into a pattern and interwoven—Greenwich Village, Fifth Avenue, a ball game, a Greek temple of a bank, the ferries, Central Park, the Zoo—all surrounded by the waters around the city and the activities on these waters. Both of these are owned by the Lathrop Browns. They were very happy with our work, and we were so glad they liked it and wanted to own it. At first we sold these tapestries for very little, but later we could get anything we cared to ask. Marguerite began to realize just how long it took to do the work and set her price accordingly. For many years they were really our main source of income and brought us unexpected security and gave us money to carry on our painting and sculpture. The work she did because she loved it. She ignored the time element, and when someone bought something it just meant that we had money to live on and time to devote to our work.

In the year 1919 we looked in *The New York Times* and saw an ad: "Five room cottage on private beach, hand woven blankets, wood supplied, also a vegetable garden. $90 for the season." We got off the steamer at Stonington, Maine, on a cold gray morning in May. A number of old men were sitting around the wharf and a decrepit taxi was waiting. We asked if anyone could tell us where Maggie McGuffy lived. Each man looked at the next man and shook his head. We waited.

Finally the taxi driver said, "Get in—I'll see if we can find her."

We headed for the wilderness. Finally I saw a farmhouse and insisted we stop and ask. He did and came back, "Never heard of her." And we continued right along down the island; a wilderness of rock and scrub pine with glimpses of water. An hour later he stopped in Maggie McGuffy's dooryard. Maggie had lived there all her life and her parents before her. Everyone on the island knew her, but like true state of Mainers no one was going to commit himself.

The garden was a pocket handkerchief, the house was minute—not one of the five rooms bigger than eight by ten—but the woodpile was enormous, much bigger than the house, and we burned every stick of it. The next day we went into Stonington for supplies and the first person we saw was John Marin. "I saw an ad in *The New York Times*," he said. He lived in the town of Stonington. We saw quite a lot of him that summer.

It was a very fruitful summer. Maggie let us use her front porch as a studio. I was entering a new world, the world of the imagination, but the ideas were assimilated intuitively, not so much intellectually. As long as it was a subconscious growth I was comfortable and happy. When painting began to have intellectual overtones in it, it began to have an ill effect on me. There were severe states of depression. I felt that I was digging down into my inner soul, bringing out new and beautiful treasures, and the world would not see them or want them. My development took an inner, mystical turn; I felt that I had to express something beyond the surface reality. I knew there was a deeper reality which I must put into my work. My reactions have always been poetical and emotional rather than intellectual. I approach depth through emotion not intellect. Sophistication has always repelled me, never attracted me. That summer I painted several compositions of ships with interlacing colors and planes—figures and landscapes transformed into abstract compositions.

Maggie was having foundation work done on her house, and the workmen were using a beautiful piece of cedar to hold up the corner. I kept my eye on it and when they finished I took it home. It was a trunk with three branches and I carved three figures in it with a pen knife—quite primitive and quite modern. In fun we called it "The Man with Two Wives." This was my real introduction to sculpture—but I was still a painter. To my astonishment, Mrs. Nathan Miller bought this piece when I came back to the city. This was very encouraging to me.

That winter we went to California. Marguerite was born there and her parents lived in Fresno. They were old and we thought they should see their grandchildren. We talked it over with John Marin, and he thought it was something we should do. Like most parents we thought our children were very special. I suppose it was a sentimental impulse. I don't think it meant as much to the grandparents as we thought it would.

I arranged to give a lecture in Cleveland on the way out to help pay expenses. It was the winter of the great flu epidemic. Marguerite had just gotten over a case of flu in New York. That night in Cleveland she went to the lecture with me. On the way back there was a terrific snow storm and blizzard. It was bitter cold; we couldn't get a cab and waited for hours for a street car. Marguerite was desperate. I didn't realize at all how sick she was. When we got home she collapsed in a coma. She was rushed to a hospital in the storm and was there for over two months. People were dying all around her but she finally pulled through.

It was a harrowing time. There I was with two babies; we were staying with my sister and she was anxious to get us out of the house. She was terrified her baby would get the flu. I moved over to my mother's house. When Marguerite came home she was still too weak to travel. And then Tessim got blood poisoning from a cut on his finger and abcess after abcess under his arm had to be operated on and drained. Finally we got away from Cleveland and arrived in California in April.

We stayed in California almost a year. It was cold when we arrived, and the air seemed thin and chill like air on mountain tops; yet we were in the San Joaquin Valley. No one living there felt this chill; they were all very comfortable.

Marguerite had a sort of relapse and was still weak and sick, but she insisted that I go up to the Yosemite, set up a camp for us, and sketch, and she would follow with the children as soon as she was able. Her parents weren't used to small children in the house. Her mother loved pretty golden-haired little girls—her own two girls had been a great disappointment to her—she thought Dahlov was wonderful. She couldn't stand little boys. She thought Tessim was a little monster and predicted a criminal career for him. A change came over Tessim in Fresno. From a delightful little boy full of imagination and purpose and fun, he became obnoxious and disagreeable. Later, when we visited Aunt Addie in San Diego, Tessim became his gay and charming self. Aunt Addie loved him and was just as nice to him as she was to Dahlov.

What a struggle Marguerite had to get away and join us in the Yosemite. Every time she was ready to leave, her father had a heart attack and she felt she couldn't leave a dying father. Finally I got desperate and wrote "Come or else" and she came. The "dying father" followed within a week and set up camp next to us and kept us in trout all summer.

I spent five months in the Yosemite Valley sketching, drawing, painting, and doing watercolors. Every now and then in life we have an experience that moves us so deeply, that holds us with such sheer, transcendent beauty, that it takes us completely out of this world. It is this feeling that only an artist can convey in his art. It is a journey into infinity. This has happened to me twice in my life. The first time came after seven days on the endless expanse of the Atlantic Ocean with nothing in sight but the constellations in the heavens, the sun's rising on the horizon in the early dawn, and the evening sunset's magnificent splendor. After seven days of this great expanse of emptiness, at dawn on Sunday morning I behold the harbor of Cherbourg, France. It was a dream world, a vision captured from childhood's imagination.

The other vision was the Yosemite. Never had I dreamed of such awe-inspiring magnitude, such beauty and grandeur of forms. The tremendous waterfalls dropping from the blue sky thousands of feet into the valley, the domes and mountains of granite, the silent lakes, the rushing streams, the giant sequoias with their delicate fern-like needles and tremendous slabs of bark. I climbed all over the mountains, with a sixty-pound pack of sketching materials and blankets on my back, and slept out under the stars, naively undressing at night and putting on my pajamas and freezing until I had to get up and build a fire. The loneliness and vastness were overpowering. This was the garden of Eden, God's paradise. I sketched and painted in ecstasy.

One day as I was walking along a rippling stream in the valley, the most magnificent goddess-like creature I had ever seen came walking toward me. Our eyes met and we knew that we had always known each other. Wherever I went I saw Doris but we didn't speak. She was nineteen, tall, with beautiful eyes, long black hair, and a magnificent carriage. An elderly woman seemed to chaperone her everywhere. A goddess of another world, a dream of beauty existed here in this paradise.

Finally one morning we met alone. We walked up a mountain path and sat on the edge of a cliff above a waterfall. We said very little. We stayed there a while and walked back. In the evening I'd see Doris at the dances in the valley but I never asked her to dance. I just watched her. I wanted to have the floor to myself and dance with her in the clouds that drifted over the moonlit mountains. I saw Doris in her riding habit riding with an escort. She asked me if I rode and if I would come riding with her some day, but I never did. Then one day she was no longer in the valley. I received a letter from her saying she was getting married. I was in the valley alone then, camping, and I would write her poems.

For ten years we wrote letters. It was a very romantic affair. In my life I have had three or four of these very abstract romantic affairs; quite different from the other women with whom I became intrigued, for I was always appreciative of the female sex. One day Doris wrote me that she and her husband were coming to New York and asked if I would meet her at the Plaza. I met her but the spell had lost its magic—the goddess was gone. She came to our place on Tenth Street and met Marguerite. She wore a corsage of purple orchids and she was very distraught. She was beautiful, but the beauty had an artificial quality. She was no longer real. I walked with her in Washington Square, and I walked with her one evening in Central Park. She seemed very unhappy. I met her husband, a pleasant, handsome young fellow.

He told me, "Doris is incurably romantic. I hope you don't take her seriously. But I suspect you are incurably romantic too."

She had two beautiful children, an understanding husband, money, a gay life—but she could never be happy with anything, anywhere. Drink and illness, I suspect, mostly imaginary illness, made an invalid of her. She is still alive—occasionally she calls me long distance, but she never leaves her bed and sees no one. Once in a while I send her orchids. I hope it makes a bright moment for her.

We had rented a tent and set up camp on the Merced River. We fished for trout, hiked through the trails, and sketched everywhere, while the grandparents took care of the children. Bears roamed around the camp at night; we slept outdoors and didn't like the bear tracks around our children's beds. We rented a burro and with the two children packed back into the high Sierras to a lovely, deep blue lake set in white granite above the timber line. We wanted to go swimming but some instinct held us back. The water was such a blue-black and there was no outlet or intake to the lake. We threw a stick into the water; it disappeared as if by magic. We tried a log and that too vanished. We stayed out of that lake. Both children rode the burro. When Tessim got on, the burro would kick up his heels and throw Tessim over his head but Tessim would climb right back on and insisted on sitting on his back until supper was ready when we had stopped for the night. I had no experience with burros so I staked him out in a nice grassy meadow for the night. In the morning he was wound up like a cocoon in the rope and his hocks were cut and raw. When we got back we were told that burros never eat green grass, that we should have turned him loose at night to fend for himself. When it came to going back, we went home or else—that burro wouldn't even stand for a side excursion—he was going home. I still don't believe in that "turn him loose" theory.

I almost lost my life in the valley. Ansel Adams, our finest photographic artist, was a young man of nineteen and in charge of the valley library. He was quite a mountain climber and a member of the Sierra Club. He asked me to go with him to climb Grizzly Peak, a cone-shaped mass of rock rising about three thousand feet above the valley floor. It took all day to climb to the top, winding around and back and forth on the trail and fighting our way up when the trail ended. He took a rope and I took my sketching materials. We had to climb by throwing the rope over rocks and pulling ourselves up. I had never climbed any sort of mountain before. From the peak of the cone we looked down a sheer three thousand feet to the valley floor below. The place where we stood was so small and the sheer drop of granite around us so perpendicular that we felt like two specks on the head of a pin. Around us was the panorama of the whole Sierra Nevada range. I made some sketches and Ansel Adams took some pictures. He put a record for the Sierra Club in a capsule wedged in the top and removed the file that was there. Only one man had ever climbed this peak before and it was his file we removed. It was getting late. It was already dusk in the valley, only the peaks were in the sun. Ansel said we'd be all night getting down the way we came, "I don't like to try it in the dark—but if we go straight down we can do it in an hour." I knew nothing about mountain climbing so I trusted Ansel implicitly. It was a sheer cliff as if you were climbing down an egg and at times it was undercut. We swung over space on the rope and caught the mountain on the rebound. Everything went; watercolors, paints, brushes flew into space—my sketches and portfolio I had left at top—I hadn't even tried to take them. Everything began to slide away from us; we picked up momentum, I especially. We snatched at every twig and bit of brush and fought for every crevice. I clawed and worked my way back to where Ansel was. He had discarded the rope and was working his way down by crevices. He knew how to maneuver in and out of every crevice. We wormed our way down to the shale slides and then along them as best we could. We were both scared to death but we got down to the valley floor in nothing flat. There wasn't a stitch of clothes on either of us. Our shoes were gone; we were smeared black and red with blood; we were torn and bruised and exhausted. I dropped in the camp and lay flat on my back and couldn't move for a week. It was a terrible and terrifying experience. It was a miracle either of us survived.

We left Fresno in the fall. I was glad to get away from the great heat of the summer, but I loved the magnificent foliage and the gardens full of all marvelous colors and shapes of plants and flowers. And the fruit. All sorts of fruit grew in the Thompson's yard. I couldn't believe it—oranges, grapefruits, lemons, all kinds of grapes, apricots, guavas, and pomegranates.

We went to San Diego to visit Aunt Addie, who had given up wandering to far away places. She had crossed on the Siberian railroad when it was rough going and food was something to be fought over; she had traversed the Andes and seen the land of the midnight sun when such trips were an ordeal as well as a pleasure. She was a sea captain's daughter, and the sea and the need for faraway places were in her blood. She had settled on San Diego as about as perfect a climate as the world offered. She built herself a large house overlooking the bay; she meant this to be a home for herself and her sisters, whom she was sure would outlive their husbands—and she was right. Aunt Addie loved the children and they were happy there.

In San Diego I was asked to give a talk and exhibit my watercolors done in the Yosemite before a society of ladies interested in art. They were full of enthusiasm and bought six watercolors. I was very naive. I thought I should take the whole group of watercolors back with me to the East Coast and exhibit them first. The ladies were willing. It never occurred to me to get a down payment or that they would renege on their purchases. We were dead broke and had only our fare back to New York, but we felt very comfortable with this money ahead of us. When we reached home we began to receive letters. One of the ladies needed a new fur coat, another's father was ill, another was planning a trip to the Orient, and one of them didn't think she should indulge herself. Not one of those ladies came through with her purchase.

On the train coming back we met a young woman, Grace Wells, on her way to London to meet her fiancé, Don Parkinson. We developed a friendship that has lasted all these years. She was sweet with our children and we had fun on the train. Life overlaps in strange ways—she knew Doris well. Back in New York she came over to our Tenth Street place and helped us clean and paint and redecorate. It was no clean and easy job but she worked right along with us.

Some years later when Grace Wells was married to Don Parkinson, I almost got the commission to do a frieze for the Los Angeles City Hall. Don was the son of one of the most influential architects on the West Coast. They were building the City Hall and asked me to design a frieze ninety feet long by nine feet high to go over the entrance. It was decided the theme was to be the history of California, using simple art forms—none of the conventional academic conceptions of a frieze, but modern as of that time, for what is modern today is no longer modern tomorrow. Art has to have an eternal quality that transcends fashions and periods. I was very aware of this. I used highly simplified forms—from primitive life, to man today. They were mostly nude and not in costume. I spent much time and thought creating as fine a design as I possibly could.

I still have the design. It was never executed. The depression put an end to spending—especially for art. The empty panel is still across the face of the Los Angeles City Hall. I exhibited the design in New York. Edwin Alden Jewell, the art critic of *The New York Times* said it was the finest frieze since the Parthenon. The design was reproduced across the entire page of *The Times* Art section, and an analysis and description covered three columns.

Contrary to the general idea, the conception of the idea and putting it into its form is the really creative work—the most difficult, time-consuming, painful, exhilarating, and exciting part of any work of art. After that, the rest is work, though satisfying work for the artist in that he is perfecting and putting into permanent form his conception. But the real act of creation is in the design. The artist is seldom paid anything for this. It is considered a sketch—to be altered, turned down, or accepted with reservations. I will always be sorry when I look at the Los Angeles City Hall and see that great blank space, but I will always have the satisfaction of having solved this problem; of having created a, to me, magnificent design.

CHAPTER SIX

IN PARIS I had realized the design quality of Japanese prints. It was a new point of view. Gauguin fascinated me, not only with his color but by his painting of a picture that had its own life. He saw with an inner vision of reality and not with an optic vision or a camera eye. Van Gogh and Cézanne I felt were basically realists—more like scientists exploring the development of new aspects of their surroundings. Gauguin took me into a mysterious inner world of the spirit. Picasso did, too, in his blue period and later on when he moved into Cubism. Braque had, for me, the same kind of expressiveness in his development of Cubism. I was stirred by Matisse's command of color but felt that he never quite rose above the ground when form was involved.

In time, I began to realize that my painting was two dimensional. Painting is essentially a two-dimensional art, but it can be enhanced and developed, in the way Cézanne has, to give the illusion of a third dimension. My painting had begun to take on a three-dimensional quality, and I realized I must carry it over into the true three-dimensional art—that of sculpture.

I stopped painting altogether and devoted myself to sculpture. I had found my true medium of expression. I have continued to paint watercolors all my life. Their spontaneity gives me a certain release and satisfies my love of color. After all, painting was my training and my world for all my early years, and I will always see the world in color as well as in form. But sculpture is my natural medium. Once at a lecture a student asked me why I did watercolors when I was a sculptor, and I said, "I guess I am a dual personality."

All art is correlated; all stems from the great creative impulse. There is no reason why sculptors shouldn't paint and painters sculpt.

I had been carving little things with a penknife. My carvings were simple, rather primitive. I had never had any training in sculpture but I had been thoroughly trained in art—and very thoroughly trained in painting. I was full of habits and ideas from which it was a tremendous effort to free myself. In sculpture I was free. I approached sculpture directly without inhibitions but with the skill and knowledge of a mature artist. I felt free working within the limitations of the medium.

I was interested in primitive art. When we first came to New York I had seen the sculpture of the Aztecs and the Mayans and the carving of the Eskimos in the Museum of Natural History. At "291," Stieglitz's gallery, I saw De Zayas' exhibition of African sculpture. It had an extraordinary magic and spiritual quality that is unequaled; it showed the spirit of man in all his terror and awe of the forces of the universe; it transcended the flesh; and it had almost unbelievable power, versatility, and imagination. Charles Sheeler made a marvelous set of photographs of this sculpture. I could at least have them through Sheeler's book. It cost fifty dollars. I could barely scrape the money together but I bought the book. This was later. First I was carried away by doing sculpture. Later I was excited by seeing what had been done in sculpture by all peoples of all times.

In Provincetown I bought two pieces of mahogany, each of them about twenty inches high, which a sea captain had brought back from Africa many years ago. Dahlov was three and a half and Tessim six. I carved a figure of each child standing, chunky and compact figures in positions no one had ever used before. I had no facilities for work. I held the wood between my knees and used small carpenter chisels and a penknife. The children played around the room nude so I could study them and watch the forms move. Dahlov picked up one of the chisels and began to play with it. I was afraid she might cut herself and kept my eye on her instead of on my work. My tool slipped, ran into my wrist, and almost severed the tendon of my left index finger. I ran to the doctor, who promptly poured alcohol into the cut, and I passed out. He couldn't decide whether to try to sew up the tendon or not and in the end took a chance that the injury wasn't too bad. The tendon was so badly injured that I have had limited use of that finger ever since. For a long time it always got in the way and was very annoying, but one finally adjusts to these things. Fortunately it was my left hand.

The little figures of the children were unusual and they delighted me. Dr. Kempf, the psychologist, saw the one of Dahlov in the Kraushaar Galleries window years later and bought it. The one of Tessim I never sold but gave to him.

We spent two more summers in Provincetown before we bought our home in Maine. Once or twice I got involved in producing a play, but my world had narrowed down to painting and sculpture. There didn't seem to be time for other things or the urge to go into them. In 1922 I did get roped into producing *Don Juan*, a play by Harry Kemp. It was a very ordinary play, in fact, a pretty bad one. But I had fun, I really went to town. I got all the surrealist stuff longings—what one calls "cool" or "in" today—out of my system. I created benches and trees out of boxes, hung up a dishpan with a light in it for a moon, strung all manner of "found" objects to create constellations in the heavens, painted a wild curtain, used objects in planes and moved them in fantastic ways. It was fun but it was the last time I attempted anything on the stage. As I think of it now, I'm reminded of the show of "pop" art held recently at the Modern Museum, which, after all, is something which belongs in show business.

Our last summer in Provincetown we rented a small house from John Francis, owner of the General Store. It had an attached studio with a fine light. Here, I carved the "*Floating Figure*" now in the Albright-Knox Art Gallery in Buffalo. This, too, was carved in a piece of Borneo mahogany, and it was done from my deep feeling of pleasure in the sea. It was here that I painted my last picture in oil—a large three-dimensional "Mother and Child" inspired from a drawing I had made several years before of Nettie May holding Dahlov.

I don't know what this house had been originally, the one that we rented that last year—certainly it was not a house. Downstairs must have been a meeting place of some kind; upstairs were lots of small inadequate bedrooms. In the front yard was a small round pool complete with algae and tadpoles. The children fished for turtles and tadpoles and we worried lest they fall in. In the fall men came with iron scoops and fished a dozen or so big snapping turtles out of the pool and shipped them off to market to be sold for turtle soup. We were indignant that we had been harboring these monsters and hadn't had turtle soup ourselves. And we were horrified at the danger in which our children had lived all summer.

That summer the Provincetown Art Association asked me to give a lecture on the modern point of view in art. Modern art was a mystery to them and an irritation. They wanted at least to find out what I thought it was about. I got very serious about this lecture. I made color charts analyzing Picasso and other modern painters and tried to explain the inner workings and evolvement of a work of art. A number of people said it sounded good but the pictures still had no meaning for them. The lecture was published as I mentioned earlier in the *Arts Magazine*. Rereading this article today, I find it still holds up. I am surprised how contemporary these thoughts are. It seems to me that, in the course and development of an artist, our first youthful enthusiasms and ideas are basically a part of us. We change very little. We grow, we mature, but life is an ever expanding circle—not a broken pattern. Some people think that progress is constantly going ahead and ahead and following the bandwagon of change and novelty. But progress is not so much going ahead as it is expanding the powers that are within us all.

I am at home in cutting wood or stone—form reveals itself to me and I can weigh the relationships between what could be there and what is there and make the continual adjustments that arise as the surplus material is removed. The more I work on a thing, the more the volume grows and the power of expression deepens. That is how I know I am a true sculptor. I am not one who deals with surfaces and quick results. I find my expression in the depth and union of emotional content with the sculptural integrity of form slowly evolved. I have never considered time or effort. No time is too long if I am evolving a work of art—no effort too great if I am putting into the rock my deepest and truest vision of life and form.

After carving in wood, I wanted terribly to carve in stone. In Boston I picked up a piece of Tennessee marble and a piece of white Vermont. I felt perfectly at ease carving stone because of my experience with wood. Stone seemed natural to me. I liked it better than wood. I liked the effort, the hard resistance. I liked the time it required; one could dream and organize while the stone slowly took form and life. There was no place for haste, no quick and easy results. I knew nothing about tools beyond a point, a chisel, and a hammer. I talked with a tombstone cutter. He told me his father used files and rasps and small flat chisels, and the weight and balance of the hammer was important. But he knew very little about it. He said a man no longer carved a tombstone, he sold tombstones. The various stages were done by different workmen with different skills, and it was all handled by big companies in an assembly line technique. These companies supplied tombstones to sales outlets throughout the country.

Some sculpture is completely rough-hewn, and some is enhanced by polishing to bring out the beauty and color of the stone, and the delicacy, warmth, and subtleties of form and expression. There is a lot more to sculpture than chiseling —than just using a rasp and a file for finishing. Eventually I learned about every kind of carborundum and hone and the importance of the sequence in using these stones to get a highly polished surface.

I took the large block of white marble and carved an over-life-sized head of Dahlov, a warm and expressive work of art, which Ellen Du Pont Wheelwright has in her home in Wilmington. Everyone including myself was astonished that I could carve this directly in stone without preparation. The tombstone cutter whose advice I had asked couldn't believe I had never carved stone before.

"Why," he said, "it takes an apprenticeship of at least seven years to be able to carve a piece like that."

In the other stone, I carved the head of a young woman but not as a portrait. I used only the forms of her head because I considered her very sculptural. This is in the Newark Museum.

In these early carvings in stone I was probably influenced to a certain extent by the sculpture of Gaston Lachaise, who was at that time a friend of mine. Lachaise had been delighted with my woodcarvings. He expressed interest in my direct carving in wood and felt that it was real sculpture. He felt my carving had a primitive strength and freshness and he liked it. Lachaise encouraged me greatly and even brought around Albert Gallatin, who bought one of my small wooden figures carved in the Yosemite. Later he put this figure up for auction and I bought it back. I don't know why Gallatin lost interest in it. Afterwards I enlarged it to life size.

I finished the two stone carvings in Provincetown, and when I came back to New York with them, I was eager to show them to Lachaise. He looked at them and was very scornful. He said I had no business carving stone—it was perfectly all right to do wood carving but not stone sculpture. I suppose he felt I was a painter and as long as sculpture was a hobby with me it was all right, but when I began to work seriously at sculpture he resented it. Perhaps I was just too enthusiastic over carving and it offended him to see me going wholeheartedly into this field of art—his field. To him I must have seemed an amateur moving in. And when I actually got a commission he was through with me and for a long time wouldn't even speak to me on the street. It was hard to understand. I had great admiration for him as an artist and he had been a valued friend. After all, I wasn't the only one in the world doing sculpture besides himself. Certainly I was no rival. I was just a beginner and he already had an assured position in art. He recovered from his antagonism, and there were times when we were good friends—then suddenly I would be a stranger to him. At first I was deeply hurt. I had thought a great deal of him. But finally I got tired of this and just plain forgot about him. But Marguerite and Isabel Lachaise always remained friends, and after Lachaise's death I renewed my friendship with her. I felt very bad when Lachaise died. After a long struggle he was just beginning to be successful financially, and had he lived he would have been considered one of the most important of the very advanced sculptors, for he was always doing provocative and controversial sculpture, advancing with the more advanced sculpture of Europe. But I doubt if he would have been very happy with the direction sculpture has taken today.

Another sculptor I saw a lot of was Hunt Diederich. Hunt was a vibrant, unscrupulous, disorganized person of great talent. He was always doing wild, impulsive things such as putting his "Running Hounds" on a pedestal in Central Park at night and basking in the scandal over it. He was always exchanging art with me. Then at some unexpected moment he would rush in saying, "I think I have a customer for that piece," and be gone with it before I could say hello. I never got the piece back, and I never got back the piece I had given him in exchange for it. One day he came over and said, "I just left Maruska and the children in Woodstock without a cent for food or anything and here I've just gotten a check for two hundred dollars. I'll send it to them. Won't they be happy."

"Wonderful," I said. "Here's a pen. Sign it over to them and we'll take it out and mail it." I stood over him while he reluctantly signed it and put it into an envelope. We mailed it, and half an hour later I met a friend. "I just saw Hunt," he said. "He was running to catch the boat to Woodstock; someone must have built a fire under him." I suspect he got there before the check.

One day in the winter of 1920 I met Gifford Beal in the Kraushaar Galleries. He introduced me to Kraushaar. Kraushaar asked me if I would bring some of my work around and show it to him, which I did. He kept it around and later gave me an exhibition. I think I had three exhibitions at Kraushaar's. When I was still a painter I had been asked to exhibit at the Whitney Club, a place Mrs. Harry Payne Whitney had established to give young artists a chance to exhibit. She sometimes bought their work and even supported certain ones she thought worthwhile. I was very happy to be invited but when I went to the opening I found my painting hanging behind the door. I was indignant and took it down and took it home.

Mrs. Force, who ran the Club, was insulted. I think she said, "Never darken my door again."

I didn't but when I had my first show at Kraushaar's, Mrs. Force bought two pieces of mine, a wood carving called "Pegasus" and a small panel relief. After that we were friends and comfortable with one another again.

Once during the war, Mrs. Whitney had furnished canvas and paint and invited several artists to paint their ideas about war. I refused, I said I couldn't paint to order. It seemed a phony idea to me. Now it seems to me I was a little stuffy about it. Mrs. Whitney thought something profound would come out of the artists if she furnished the materials and let them express themselves freely. But when each artist faced one of those blank canvases on the walls of the Club, not one of them had an idea. All they could do was paint the same kind of picture they always painted in their own studio. The difference with me was that I knew I couldn't come up with an idea.

I did do a huge poster for a Red Cross parade on Fifth Avenue. We all thought this showing of modern art sponsored by the Red Cross would put Modern Art on the map. Walt Kuhn organized the parade, with the artists riding papier-mâché hobby horses that had been made for one of the Kit Kat balls. Max Weber and Pop Hart, the watercolorist, were so elated they danced all the way up Fifth Avenue from Washington Square to Fifty-ninth Street to the music of the band. The police were on hand to see that the artists didn't dance on the sidewalks. Kuhn warned the society ladies who were sponsoring the affair not to criticize anything because Max Weber would create a scene and quit. At Fifty-ninth Street there was a terrible downpour that wrecked the parade. The banners and costumes were a sticky mess in minutes; everyone fled. With the rain and the public indifference, the millennium was slow in coming. It is here now but how long it will last no one can say. But one thing we do know—art will never be the same again. The inflated and promoted names will vanish into oblivion and the real artists will emerge and make art history. Who these will be no one knows.

I went down to the docks one day and came home with a large piece of mahogany. It was wet and green. It should have gone to pieces when carved but it never developed a crack or check. It was thirty-six inches by twenty-four by twenty-two. I carved a mother and child in it—my first sculptured mother and child—a theme I have always found new inspiration in all my life. I fitted it compactly into the block and developed it so that it functioned from all sides.

The Lathrop Browns thought they wanted it and talked of buying it, but I never had the facility for culminating sales. They left for California without it. It was another appallingly low period for us financially. I did not know where to turn; the worry made me ill. Marguerite sat down and wrote the Lathrop Browns asking if they really wanted to buy this piece and mentioned the price. They wrote back they had meant to buy it and were glad she had written and enclosed a check. We were saved again. It was really a turning point in our lives. From then on things began to happen for us in sales and commissions. We had other low moments financially but never again so many nor so low.

In those days I loved people and those who were involved in the creative arts. The academic world and the business world were outside my life. I hardly realized their existence. The artists we knew best, besides Lachaise and Hunt Diederich, were Max Weber and Walkowitz, Hartley, and to a lesser degree Marin.

Egmont Arens lived on the corner top floor across from us. He ran the Washington Square book shop and was always full of wonderful ideas. He created a little magazine called *Playboy* to which we contributed work. It was quite a special little magazine, a lively gay publication and very good while it lasted. "Eggie" was quite a special person, to poets and artists and young writers.

We knew the Reverend Percy Grant of the Church of the Ascension on Fifth Avenue and Tenth Street. An extraordinary man, big, broadminded–intensely interested in people and art and life.

We were good friends of our patrons, the Lathrop Browns. I remember they invited us to dinner and Lathrop's sister, Lucy L'Engle warned us, "You'll have to wear a dinner jacket."

I didn't know what a dinner jacket was. I was completely oblivious to clothes. At the time I had only one suit. I still remember my horror when a suit wore out. Marsden Hartley was always so well dressed and well groomed, I asked him how in the world he kept his clothes so nice. He said, "You know, Bill, I'm going to tell you. When you come into the house and undress, don't just throw your clothes on a chair or on the floor. Hang them up neatly on a hanger and brush them, then they stay neat." That was news to me. When I see some of my photographs taken at that time, I notice that the pants are all wrinkled. That was my first lesson on how to treat clothes. I had never been interested in clothes; they were just something between me and the world and still are. I was uninterested in anything that hadn't to do with art. I was untouched by the world outside.

It is usually the rich who buy art or at least talk about buying art. We found the rich very strange. They would come and rave and say how much they would like to buy certain things but would always leave without buying. And they always wanted bargains. Now a few dollars more or less can make a lot of difference to a poor person, but it can't possibly mean anything to a rich person unless he has a "poor" psychology. A woman in a sable coat would sit an hour in front of a watercolor and say how desperate she was to own it, if she could only afford it–it was priced at one hundred dollars, yet she did not buy it. Another haggled over an oil of Marguerite's. It was priced at a hundred and fifty dollars. She finally got it down to ninety-five. And that night she gave a dinner at a night club that cost her five hundred dollars if it cost her a cent. And then there were the rich who felt that spending a few dollars for art was self-indulgence–they were the most annoying of all. Unless it was the people who came over, "bought" a picture or pictures–one time four–but for some reason didn't take them along, and we would never hear from them again.

There was Frank Harris living on Washington Square, whom I enjoyed visiting. I always found him in bed dictating to his secretary, a handsome redhead. He gave me a set of his *Life of Oscar Wilde.* I never got a chance to read it, it was lifted from our bookcase so quickly. I remember Frank Harris going into Jefferson Market Court and exposing detectives who enticed young girls, often innocent ones, and then arrested them for prostitution. We faced the Jefferson Market Jail door where the wagons brought in the night's haul, and below us would be the bail-bond lawyers waiting to bail them out. We used to see a manhole cover just outside the jail lift up. A man would stick his head out and whistle and a boy would rush a bucket of beer over from the corner saloon. This went on for years, and then one day a prisoner escaped through the manhole and that stopped the flow of beer. One snowy day we saw snow gathering on an invisible wire running from the jail to the apartment of the bail-bond lawyer next door. Another time Cushman, our landlord, accused us of tapping his electricity. We couldn't believe it. There was an investigation. The lawyers had run a wire through our place into Cushman's line, and he was furnishing them with electricity.

Around election time the lawyers would suddenly notice our presence; was there anything they could do for us, did we have any trouble with anyone they could fix up? We had been unable to get the phone company to put in a phone; they took care of that for us. Another time they asked me if I would paint a portrait of Judge Mancuso for them. They wanted to put it up where the judge would see it every time he came out of court. I thought it would be fun. They stretched a big canvas in Patchin Place and set up ladders. I gave the judge a nice spotted tie to liven things up. When I finished one of them said, "My God, you've made him look just like a white slaver." Another spat, "That's just what he is." While we were all looking at it, a gust of wind came down the alley, ripped the poster from the wall and the ladder went right through it. That was the end of that.

When I was in Yosemite Valley I met Caroline Pratt, the director and founder of The City and Country School, the first progressive school in New York City, then in MacDougal Alley. She saw Dahlov riding on a burro and said to me, "I wish you'd bring her to our school. I'd love to have her." Dahlov was still too young but I took Tessim to her school and a year later Dahlov also went there. In exchange for tuition I went to the school for a few hours twice a week to watch and guide the children in art work. This led to my working with children in other progressive schools—Walden, Birch Wathen, and Rosemary Hall in Greenwich. I wrote and lectured on the art of children. I was paid very little but it did not take too much time and it helped. I was eager to work with children and was fascinated by their lack of inhibitions, by the freshness of their imagination and the freedom and spontaneity in their handling of form and color. I learned as much from them as they ever learned from me.

I was the first person in this country, to my knowledge, to give children large sheets of paper and showcard colors. The results were encouraging, to me as well as everyone else. I feel that much of the art work in schools is due to my pioneering—to my letting children express themselves and develop, without superimposing grownup ideas upon them. I don't mean by freedom that I just let them muddle around. It was rather a method of subtle and intelligent guidance. I would look at their work as I would look at an artist's work and we would discuss things as if we were all artists. Children have a keen instinct—just your presence, your quality as a human being is felt by them. They are aware when the person who is guiding them knows what he is doing and what he is talking about. Words are not necessary.

When I came up against a teacher who knew nothing about art and was telling the children what to do, I'd say, "Say nothing to them. Every time you open your mouth you say the wrong thing. Unless you know and sense what art is, don't try to tell children what to do. They will do all right if you say nothing; otherwise you stifle their creative efforts." I'm afraid I found most teachers ignorant of art. But when you do find a teacher who is an art-conscious human being, it is wonderful. I had my own growing children and I learned from them. It gave me a more intense insight than I might otherwise have had, a sort of inner knowledge.

The lovely free creativity of spirit lasts for children until adolescence. Then, the outside world moves in. Suddenly, they want to conform. They are overwhelmed by the low grade "Art" that bombards them from all sides—magazines, books, shops, comics—all with such authority.They cannot discriminate; that has to come later with maturity. Only a very few remain uncontaminated, because the inner creative force is so powerful or their sense of real values is supported by knowledge and sensitivity.

I am appalled nowadays when I see how these ideas about teaching children have been stereotyped and made into formulas, just as the old teaching had been ridden with formulas. At the time I was teaching, a modern artist's whole idea was to free himself from the academic point of view, to see the world with a view as primitive and unsophisticated as a child and then go on from there to build his own art forms and see color with a new vision. That's what Matisse was doing and what the modern artists were all doing. They were beginning a new world. We were barnacled with the junk of ages both in our children's schools and in our art schools. We were so loaded down with tradition that we had to fight to get air into our lungs. The real contribution an artist can make is to exploit his personal reaction to life around him and to expose the innermost thoughts of man.

In 1929 I became an instructor at the Art Students League. This meant a great deal to me. It gave me status and it meant a dependable income of two thousand a year where I had never had anything before. It was a great moment. I taught the afternoon sculpture class for thirty years, one afternoon a week. It brought me in touch with all kinds of wonderful young people. I wish I could mention all the students who studied there and who have gone on to become fine artists in their own right. I took the students very seriously and gave them everything I had. I was terribly let down when they would be there one week and gone the next, or when they drifted off into other lives than art. Later on I came to accept this as one of the inescapable hazards of teaching.

All my life I was eager to learn. I had great respect for my elders and for all those whom I felt possessed knowledge. I do not think it was because I had had no formal education but was something fundamental in myself. I would listen and take them seriously to a fault until I, myself, began to teach. Then I realized that you cannot do in art what someone else thinks is good and right. It is wrong for you unless you can see it. You not only have to develop in your own way but you have to develop a confidence in yourself. You must listen and then make your own decisions as to what is right for you. I had to teach myself this as well as my students. A student who has not developed a sense of discrimination, knowledge, and taste doesn't know when he has done something fine and expressive. Art expression is in the collaboration of the artist and his medium, whether clay, stone, wood, or paint. There is a metaphysical collaboration between the artist and his medium. This is only possible when we are receptive and our consciousness is sensitized. I have often said that the artist is the antenna. He catches the vibration of emotional vision. He is attuned to seeing with the inner eye the eternal, and he works at his sculpture until he gives back in permanent form that vision. Art, like all creative effort, stems from vision and from love—love of the revelation of the beauty that surrounds us in life. No one can teach us this. It is an innate and rare quality. It cannot be arrived at by imitation. A student can learn to copy; it is always easy to do what someone else has envisioned and put it into concrete form. But the inner life will be lacking—all he will have is a piece of craftsmanship. Some students of the dance asked Isadora Duncan to see them dance, and when the dance was over they said, "Isn't it wonderful, Miss Duncan, what you have done for modern dancing and what has come of your teaching?"

She shuddered, "I think it's horrible."

I have reached the point today where I have a great respect and interest in the past accomplishments of mankind. But you have to be able to discriminate between true values and the dead wood of tradition, and you have to do what is infinitely more difficult, evaluate the real and the trivial, the sensational and the creative in the art that is being produced today. This can come through intuition, but certainly it should be realized with maturity. Here am I who, in sixty years, have gone through so many phases of art, who have seen so much and have done so much, who am so familiar with the forms art has taken both in the past and in the present; yet I am utterly amazed at how people can take seriously infantile work exhibited by men of sixty. The power of self-deception and self-hypnotism of the human race is beyond belief. Yet I can't discount illusion, it is always with us. It is logical to get excited and fascinated by the daubs and splashes of a four-year-old, but when a man of sixty does the same thing and exhibits it, to me it is retarded development. In the past we spent a lifetime perfecting the outer image of art, losing track of the inner meaning. Today the pendulum has swung the other way. We encourage the most infantile efforts in ourselves and admire them. We are afraid knowledge and skill will nullify expression.

Only one in a thousand art students is an original artist, yet each student has the potential of being that one; that is why we have no right to discourage him. Newton was not just an ordinary man watching an apple drop. All manner of men have seen apples drop in all the ages. He was a scientist with a background of knowledge, and suddenly an apple dropped and a door opened in his mind. You can never see the thing that opens a door unless you are prepared by knowledge as well as intuition to see.

CHAPTER SEVEN

WHEN I WAS TEACHING art at the Walden School I met Mrs. Nathan Krass. Her husband was the Rabbi at Temple Emanu-El on Fifth Avenue and their two little girls went to Walden. She was an unusual and beautiful woman, intense in her interests and outstanding in any gathering. We found we both came from Cleveland and knew some of the same people. Her two little daughters were very young and very shy. I took a great interest in them. I am always fond of little girls, especially shy, attractive little things. My friendship with Eda and Nathan Krass lasted as long as they lived and continues into this younger generation.

One day Mrs. Krass came over to our place and brought Ruth Jonas, then about fifteen and very anxious to study art. She was a serious girl with fuzzy hair, frightfully intense and enthusiastic. I said I could not give her lessons but I would criticize her work and watch it develop if she would bring it over once a week. I find it is always better to require some effort from students. Then if they are unwilling to go out of their way to learn, that ends it. It is a very sound process of elimination. The world is full of young people who think they want to be artists but to whom any effort or sacrifice is too much.

Ralph Jonas, Ruth's father, was very important in the financial world at that time. He insisted on paying me for the criticisms. Ruth was a very talented girl but desperately temperamental. I used to have her go around to the galleries to become acquainted with art. One day she told me she had taken her mother around to the galleries and that she had bought two pictures. I said to Ruth, "Here I am a well-known artist giving you lessons. Why don't you bring your mother around here to look at pictures?" She did and her mother selected a number of things and had me bring them over to their house. They had a tremendous house with expensive furniture but not one picture on the walls. The only thing they had on the wall was a calendar. Now the house has been sold and many families live in it. It is just around the corner from where we now live in Brooklyn

Heights. In those days when we went from Tenth Street in the Village to visit the Jonases we felt we were going to the ends of the earth.

We tried the pictures on the walls and the rooms came to life. The Jonases were delighted. They bought several oils and two batiks of Marguerite's. Later they bought two woodcarvings of mine, one a carving of our two children in mahogany about thirty-six inches high. Ralph Jonas commissioned me to carve a large walnut panel for over the mantel about five by six feet, of figures and horses.

Mrs. Jonas was a wonderful woman, warm and generous, and very absorbed in her children and friends. The tremendous wealth that had come to her was a little overpowering. I tried to get them interested in other artists but they were more interested in us and our work. They invited us to their parties and dinners and to many of the musicals they gave. They were seriously interested in young musicians and eager to help them. Ralph Jonas was always sponsoring musical and other cultural activities. They too were our close friends as long as they lived or rather as long as Mrs. Jonas lived. After her death Ralph remarried and went into an entirely different kind of life. We never saw him. I believe that he also separated himself from his children. Mrs. Jonas had ordered an embroidered tapestry from Marguerite. It was to be four by five feet and was to hang at the entrance to the stairway. She never asked to see a sketch or what the price would be. She left Marguerite absolutely free to do anything she wanted. Marguerite made a lovely tapestry abstractly representing the Jonas family, on a large scale compared to her other pieces. We understood that it was to have been left to Ruth but Ralph Jonas would never give it to her. Later he sold it.

In 1928 everyone was making money right and left in the stock market. At the Jonases' parties Eddie Cantor would get up and say how wonderful Ralph was and how much money he had made for him.

One evening Mrs. Jonas said, "You ought to let Ralph invest that money you got for the tapestry. He could make quite a lot of money for you."

I said it would be very kind of him. Neither of us knew anything about the stock market or finance.

When we saw Mrs. Jonas the next time, she said, "Ralph has already made quite a bit of money for you."

This sounded strange to me, for we still had the money in the bank. I asked Ralph if I shouldn't give him this money.

He said, "You just leave it in the bank and I will let you know when to give it to me."

We went away for the summer in the country. When we came back I called Ralph's secretary and asked what to do with the money.

She said, "Mr. Jonas says you should leave it in the bank."

Two weeks later the stock market crashed and the Jonas investments were worth nothing. I always thought he saw it coming and left us out of it, and I thought it was quite wonderful of him because, if things had gone on building up and not falling down, he would have given me the gains. But he did not let me share the loss. That money held us over the worst of the depression.

We were at the theater one evening. The girl in the seat next to us couldn't sit still—she was frantic—she kept saying, "They told me to take my money out and I couldn't get to the bank in time. They said it will be too late tomorrow." She kept running out to telephone. Finally she came back white as a sheet and collapsed.

"It's all over," she said. "The Bank of the United States is gone." We wondered what it was all about.

It was the great crash. There was the Bank Holiday when no one could get money from any bank or even open a safety deposit box. No one knew what to do. It was very terrifying. The regular peacefully functioning world had fallen apart. The basis of our civilization is money. Suddenly money ceased to exist. Everyone was terrified. Anyone who had cash and could, turned it into gold. Then gold was called in and outlawed, then gold certificates were called in. No one knew what to do. But the ordinary little people, even if they lost everything, did not jump out of windows or put a pistol to their heads. They went on living in a changed world. Twice as a child Marguerite had seen financial panics and banks close their doors and not reopen them. She remembered people standing in the streets day after day unable to believe—unable to give up hope. Her father lost a fortune in a bank panic in Leadville, Colorado. He never made another.

Later one fall when we came back from Maine I was amazed to see the bread lines along Greenwich and Seventh avenues. And the hundreds of men just sleeping in Washington Square on newspapers. There were empty lots over toward the west side of town where men built "Hoovervilles"; they dug themselves underground and made shelters out of old sheets of tin and worn-out lumber and rags. They lived and cooked in these holes in the ground all winter with snow all around. We were lucky. We were not without money during the depression.

In the early twenties a young woman, Ilonka Karasz, was one of the outstanding personalities of the Village. She had great talent and great beauty of a very extraordinary kind. It was the period of Wiener Werkstätte design in furniture, colorful and original textiles, and astonishing interior decoration from Austria. Ilonka belonged to this movement. She had such talent and ability that I think she could have done almost anything in the way of creative art but this is what she chose to do. There was a large exposition in New York in 1925 to promote and feature silk. Ilonka introduced me to Robert Schwarzenbach, one of the big silk manufacturers. He wanted something very unusual in the way of art for his exhibit, and after we had talked it over, it was decided that I would do a life-sized, seated Bodhisattva and twelve Chinese heads to be put on pedestals and draped with silk. I was to get five hundred dollars for the whole thing. I spent months working on this project and made a work of art out of what was to be just a commercial job. Then I helped at Grand Central Palace with the arrangement.

Schwarzenbach took a real liking for me. When he wanted some carved doors for the entrance to his house, his architect, Kenneth Noské, suggested that I do them. Noské had only seen the two small butternut panels that I had carved in New Hampshire but he had imagination enough to know from looking at them that I could design and carve doors. This is a rare experience. So few people realize a man can do something he has never done before and would be willing to take a chance on it. Noské ordered the panels of Brazilian walnut to be kiln dried, and I set to work on the designs. That summer I did two sets of designs for the doors, full-sized complete cartoons. Schwarzenbach kept them for weeks but said nothing.

Finally he called me over to his office and said he had decided not to go through with it because this was the entrance to his home. "Suppose after the panels are carved and installed," he said, "I do not like them. I would have to go through these doors every day and I would be very unhappy."

He told me to forget them. He would buy something else from me instead. It was a shock because it had been quite an undertaking. I went home and told Marguerite; she was stunned. After all, we had planned to live on that money for the next year or two. She told me he couldn't do that to me and to go back and tell him so.

I went back to him and said, "After all, Mr. Schwarzenbach, we have the designs and we have the wood ordered and kiln dried. I tell you what I will do. You select the design, and I will carve the panels on my own and put them up in your vestibule and you can see if you like them. If you don't, I'll exhibit them and try to sell them. All it will cost you is the money for the wood you ordered."

He agreed and I worked all winter carving the two panels. In the spring we put them up in the vestibule of his home. Schwarzenbach came in after lunch, and from two until six he paced back and forth in the vestibule undecided.

Suddenly his wife came in and said, "Robert, we have a dinner engagement. You must decide one way or the other and get dressed."

"All right," he said. "I'll take them. Go ahead and have the doors made."

After that I had a lot to do with Robert Schwarzenbach. He was a medieval baron at heart, but he was a fine person and seriously interested in and appreciative of art. He would have us for dinner at his home. He lived in a grand style and had beautiful tapestries and old masters on his walls. I had never been in such a house before nor had had such magnificent dinners with liveried servants waiting on us hand and foot. We had the Schwarzenbachs to dinner at our place, and he was embarrassed that he had worn evening clothes and we were so informal.

He was Swiss and had a Swiss's love of wood carving and trick figures. He wanted a carved clock for the front of his building on Fourth Avenue with the figure of a man and a girl, "The Spirit of Silk," to appear on the hour. He had McKim, Mead and White design this clock for him and he hated it. Then he asked me to design it. It was a terrible ordeal. He drove me crazy fussing over these designs. That summer in Maine I had a model made full size in plywood and painted it to look like bronze, shipped it down, and hung it on his building. Schwarzenbach came down from his office, took one look, said, "That's not what I want," and disappeared. I felt utterly defeated. But I went ahead and carved the little figures in wood anyway. I took them to Noské's office, and when Schwarzenbach came in he seemed rather pleased with them.

He said, "I've got to leave for South America tomorrow; so go ahead with the figures and the clock."

Schwarzenbach was my first contact with the temperamental businessman. I had been brought up on the myth of the sober, hard-boiled, calculating, efficient businessman as opposed to the happy-go-lucky, unreliable, temperamental artist. It didn't take me long to find out that the temperamental artist can't hold a candle to the temperamental businessman.

Schwarzenbach wanted a symbol for his silks and asked me to design him one.

I said, "You know, I wouldn't be too good at that but Marguerite makes beautiful designs. If you would like to commission her to make one, I'm sure she'd be glad to."

This he did. But when he saw the design he wouldn't have it. I looked at his desk. It was covered with designs and he was cutting them up and putting them together in all sorts of patterns, having fun. He had asked almost every designer in town to make him a design and he was cutting them up and reassembling them like a little child. Since he had ordered the design from Marguerite I sent him a bill for it.

He was furious and said, "I thought this was included in your work."

I told him, "My wife is an artist in her own right. Her work cannot be included in my fee."

He had Noské send her a check and said to me, "Don't ever say a word to Marguerite about the fuss I made."

Someone had sold him the idea of having a bronze panel of the silk industry in each of his street windows. The project had never been consummated—I could guess the reason. One day he asked me if I would consider going ahead with this and arranged for me to go out to his factories and make sketches and studies of the making of silk. I finished two panels and had them cast in bronze. He seemed pleased and paid me for them. When the next two were finished and delivered I sent him a bill for them.

He hit the ceiling and raved, "What do you mean by asking me for money this time of year when business is slow? I paid you for the first panels."

I said, "That's what we've been living on all winter. We were planning on this check to see us through the summer."

He kept on raving, saying he never wanted the panels anyway, that I had made him order them. I was shocked.

I said quietly, "Look here, Mr. Schwarzenbach, when I was eighteen years old I made more money as a lithographer than I am making now. I gave that up to be an artist of sincerity and integrity, but I find people like you don't want sincerity and integrity. You want to get stuck. You fall for some phony with a line and get stuck and like it."

I had hit the nail on the head—like so many rich people he was always being taken in by clever phonies, and then he became suspicious of even the most honest and sincere people.

When I finished my speech he called his secretary and said, "Give him his check."

I thought I'd never hear from him again, but in the fall he called me up and asked me to have lunch with him and the President of Antioch College and suggested that I go out there to teach art. But I did not want to teach art. I wanted to create art and I didn't think it wise to leave New York.

Schwarzenbach would call me in and bring up projects; one of them was a pair of wrought-iron gates for his Long Island estates. I made a handsome design, but when the usual vacillating over it began, I just dropped it. I had a block of yellow Kesota limestone and I made sketches of his head; his form was very clear and sculptural. This, and because of all that had gone on between us, led me to carve his head in this stone. I meant to give it to him, but he hated it and said I made him look Jewish and did I think he was "yellow" that I did him in a yellow stone? That summer I got a wire from Noské, Robert Schwarzenbach was dead. I felt very bad for I had developed a real affection for him. I offered the stone head to his son but he did not want it. After all his conflicts over the carved doors, Schwarzenbach had enjoyed them greatly and was very proud of them. He was delighted to see them reproduced in *The New York Times* and magazines and was proud when people asked him if he was the Schwarzenbach of the carved doors. After his death the house on Sixty-first Street was sold to a Whist Club, and when they moved they took the doors with them.

Between my commissions and Marguerite's embroideries, we were no longer hard up. There were long periods still with no income, but these were less long and the income was much greater. We got substantial sums at times and when this happened we bought something. We took care of any major need we had put off while waiting until we had the money. We never borrowed money and we never bought anything on time. We couldn't because we could never count on being able to meet payments since we had no salary and our income was completely irregular. Nor did we ever save money for a specific purpose or need. Money came to us in lump sums at unforeseen intervals. Each time we acquired a real sum we bought a supply of materials for work, and if it was sufficiently large, we bought something important—a house in Maine, a new coat, a suit, a bed, something for the children, and finally a car, an ancient Maxwell.

After our last summer in Provincetown with John Francis' broken-down furniture, decrepit cooking utensils, and miserable cottage, we had resolved never to rent another summer cottage. We would buy a place of our own somehow, somewhere. One day that summer Bertram and Gusta Hartman came by on their way to visit Isabel Lachaise, who had just bought a place in Maine, and they asked Marguerite to go with them. Marguerite will go anywhere at the drop of a hat. Off she went.

Maine was beautiful. To show what city slickers will do—after supper Bertram and Marguerite walked down to the shore, got into a boat they found there, and rowed into the cove. It was dark and starlight. Suddenly they saw a wall of water bearing down upon them. They turned and rowed like mad for shore. It was a small bore from the Goose Rock whirlpools and very dangerous waters for anyone unfamiliar with it.

Isabel Lachaise took Marguerite for a walk through the woods. She said, "I want to show you a house and I want you to pretend that you are considering buying it. It is full of beautiful antiques and old Mrs. Baker only sells them to me on the condition that I sell this house for her. She owns two houses—the Baker house she lives in and the John Riggs place." It was a sea captain's house of thirteen rooms set back above Robinhood Cove and surrounded by a sea of alders front and back—you could hardly see the water. Marguerite hadn't the faintest intention of buying it. She had in mind some small place with beautiful woods and a brook. She was also determined upon a place with gravity water. This place sat in a clearing between two stone ledges; there were magnificent woods and lots of shore but no brook and very little water on the island. But the day before she left, she saw it from the water and realized it was lovely.

In the spring of 1923 we had about two thousand dollars with which we could pay for a house in the country. We drove up to Maine to look at a place Marguerite had seen the year before. I might as well say here that everything we ever owned has been over my dead body. I am always opposed to owning anything—a house, a car, a studio, even a refrigerator or hiring a servant; but we always end up owning these things, and once we get them I am delighted and proud.

The John Riggs house was in the woods set back above Robinhood Cove about half a mile from the town road. It had been unoccupied for thirty years but was in excellent condition. All together there were four Riggs houses in the village and the place was called Riggsville—later on, a man named Williams had the post office name changed to Robinhood after an Indian called Chief Robinhood by the early English settlers.

We arranged to buy the John Riggs place in two installments—first the house and then within two years the land around it, which included wood lots and pasture. But we found Carrie Baker was arranging to sell the woods behind our backs to a lumber company, so we were forced to buy everything at once. We didn't have that much money. Our kind friends and relatives who had always said, "If you ever find a place you want to buy, we'll be glad to lend you the money," froze cold at the suggestion. The local bank considered Maine property worth nothing and could hardly bring themselves to give us a five-hundred-dollar mortgage. Then suddenly we got a letter from Lucy L'Engle with a check. She said she had heard we were buying a farm and was afraid we might be short of money. We were deeply touched. With this and the small bank mortgage we were able to manage. We had no money for repairs but none were really necessary that year.

Between the house and the water and in the field behind the house was a forest of alders. We had to hire a man with a team of horses to pull them out. I never saw anything as persistent as an alder. Every year they would try to grow back and caused us no end of trouble. No Riggs had ever planted a flower or even a lilac bush. The house stood completely stark and barren. This is hard to believe when you come today and see Marguerite's beautiful gardens, the grass mowed down to the water, and the bronze "Spirit of the Dance" on a rock ledge overlooking the waters of Robinhood Cove.

We found the nice white paint on the outside was thin whitewash and the new paint on the floors vanished when we walked on them. The well was some distance below the house but without a pump. All water had to be lugged. All light was from kerosene lamps and we never did get very proficient in handling them. Heat came from the fireplaces, which had all been closed off and which we reopened. We cooked on an ancient wood stove left in the kitchen. We built an old-fashioned privy in the little pine grove in back of the house. We lived this way very happily and very comfortably for twenty years. There were always students who wanted to come to Maine and study with me and these furnished a source of income for our summers. There were times when we had from four to eight students living and working with us. And a cook, William Holly.

William came to us at the age of seventeen. After a few days I said, "William, we'll have to let you go, you just can't cook."

He said, "Mr. Zorach, if you'll give me a little time and help I think I can learn."

I said, "We will try. Mrs. Zorach is a wonderful cook; she will tell you just how to do things."

He became a fine cook. He took over our house and our life. He kept track of appointments, invited our friends to dinner, did our housekeeping, and in the summer cooked for the students and took care of them—even advising them on their love life. He was fascinating to look at, like a piece of Khmer sculpture. We expected to have him with us all the days of our life; he was so much younger than we were. But at the age of thirty-three he had heart failure and died. We never tried to replace him. We knew we just couldn't.

Later on we bought the second farm above us from Carrie Baker—now we had over one hundred acres, mostly woods, beautiful woods and stone hills and pastures. We bought a horse and a cow and we put up hay. Marguerite loved to garden; we had flower gardens and bountiful vegetable gardens with more wonderful vegetables than we could ever eat. We made hay for the winter; all in the old-fashioned way with a one-horse mowing machine, hand rakes, bull rakes, a hay wagon painted blue with vermilion trim. I will never forget the shorn fields like colored carpets before the heavy green woods and the great white clouds hurrying across the blue sky and how we hurried to load the hay wagon when suddenly the sky turned black with threatening rain. Marguerite used to drive us crazy—every blade of grass had to be cured perfectly in hay cocks and shaken out to air in the morning. The children loved it too. We all worked. Now that everything is mechanized she doesn't feel the same way about haying. The excitement and pleasure is gone. Sometimes we filled both barns with hay—forty tons of hay. We were amazed that one or two cows and a horse could eat so much hay in a winter. Years later farmers would come around asking to buy hay, and we found that in the winter our hired hand was selling the hay that we had worked so hard over in the heat of July and that he was pocketing the money.

My greatest adventure was in 1927 when I bought a three-ton block of marble from a stone yard in Astoria and had it shipped to Maine. I set it up on beams in my small studio and started to carve my "Mother and Child." Facing this huge block I started in with chisels and hammer to create the conception of the "Mother and Child" that was evolving in my brain. It was one of those rare periods when I was free from financial worries. I spent three years completing the work. For the "Mother and Child" I did what I had never done before. I made a small sketch in clay to establish my directions—in and out and around. The whole thing worked on a spiral; you could look at it from all sides, and look down on it and look up at it. It functioned as a unit, flowing in and out and around.

I made a silhouette or template of my small sketch and enlarged it on the stone. I used a very primitive and simple way of doing this. It was purely an approach of my own and very simple. I took the clay sketch and put it on a table in a dark room. I made a little hole in a piece of paper, put a light behind it, and threw a shadow on a large piece of paper tacked on the wall. By moving the table back and forth I could establish the exact dimensions of the figure in the stone. Then I traced the four sides of the silhouette on the stone and cut away to within an inch or so of the outline. In doing this I kept away from the surface of the form, allowing myself room to carve. This gave a volume one could never get by using a pointing machine. It was a fine simple approach. When you work in this way, the stone is actually collaborating with you. The sketch only gives you direc-

31. The artist's studio in Hicks Street, Brooklyn. Forefront figures: *Conflict*. 1935. Plaster. 7½′ high. Sculpture far left: *Builders of the Future*. Center sculpture between *Conflict* figures: *Youth*. 1935. Borneo mahogany. 51″ high. Painting, far left: *Land and Development of New England* by Marguerite Zorach. Painting behind *Youth*: *Ella and Dahlov* by Marguerite Zorach. Painting, far right: *Screen* by Dahlov Ipcar.

32. *Spirit of the Dance.* 1932. (Picture 1.) Plaster model for aluminum casting. 78″ high. Radio City Music Hall. (Picture 2.) Aluminum. 78″ high. Radio City Music Hall.

33. *The Artist's Daughter.* 1930. Georgia marble. 25½″ high. Replica of damaged original, done in 1946, is at the Whitney Museum of American Art, New York City.

34. *The Embrace.* 1933.
Plaster cast. 66″ high.

35. *The Embrace.* 1933.
Bronze. 66″ high. The Brooklyn Museum, New York City.

36. *Lenin Memorial.* 1934. Plaster. 3′ model.

37. *Memorial to the Pioneer Woman.* 1936. Plaster model. Finally executed in bronze. 8′ high. Columbia Savings and Loan Assn., Denver, Colorado.

38. *Youth.* 1936–39. Front view. Botticini marble. 47″ long. Norton Gallery and School of Art, West Palm Beach, Florida.

39. *Youth.* 1936–39. Back view. Botticini marble. 47″ long. Norton Gallery and School of Art, West Palm Beach, Florida.

40. *Artist's Daughter*. 1936. Maine granite. 18″ high. Collection of Des Moines Art Center, Des Moines, Iowa.

41. *Seated Cat*. 1937. Swedish granite. 17¾″ high. The Metropolitan Museum of Art, New York City.

42. *Benjamin Franklin.* 1936–37. Pink Tennessee marble. 90″ high. Post Office Department, Wash., D.C.

43. *Builders of the Future.* 1939. Plaster. *Ca.* 16′ high. Back view. New York World's Fair, 1939–40.

44. *Builders of the Future.* 1939. Plaster. *Ca.* 16′ high. Front view. New York World's Fair, 1939–40.

45. *Faith of This Nation.* 1939–42. Georgia white marble. 28″ long. Collection of Wright Ludington.

tions—it is not something to be copied. You are free to develop your forms in any direction. In direct carving you retain the volume and the form expands. The power and strength that exists in the stone reveals itself to you. But you have to recognize it, you have to be in tune. You have got to be equipped to see what is going on in the stone, what is unfolding, what the stone is revealing to you as you chip away. Someone, I think it was Michelangelo, said there is a piece of sculpture in every stone. All you have to do is cut away the superfluous material. A student not aware of what is revealing itself to him can chip the whole stone away and make a lot of gravel for the road. You have to have an artist's awareness and vision. There is another saying of Michelangelo's, "As the stone shrinks, the volume expands." In carving stone you are continually cutting away and the sculpture seems to grow thicker and thicker and shorter and shorter. In making a template you have to elongate the template both up and down leaving excess space at both top and bottom and in the middle before you start carving.

There is a strange paradox here. In cutting stone you are continually cutting away and the sculpture grows larger. In modeling you are constantly adding clay and the form shrinks. You can never seem to get on enough clay. That is because there is no inner volume.

I finished this carving after a period of three years. One of the satisfying things about carving in the country is that you work all summer and then put it away for the winter and go back to the city, where you work on other things. Then when you come back in the spring you start fresh with a clear mind. You feel as if the stone has been roughed out for you. You forget what hard work you put into it the year before. Problems seem to have resolved themselves; you can go right ahead. This is true of any work of art. You should never work on it too constantly, because the minute you are really tired, your brain doesn't function and your subconscious isn't functioning. All the creativeness that goes into a work of art goes in through the subconscious working in collaboration with the brain. If you are uncertain or exhausted, leave the work alone for a while. Give your inner forces time to pull themselves together. Come back when you are fresh. I have always tried to impress this point on students, because after a certain point of realization they begin just working. They have gone as far as they are capable of going at the moment; they are now tearing down, not building. I try to tell them, "When you don't know what to do, don't do it. Rest, relax, try something else, clear your brain."

I feel my "Mother and Child" is my finest piece of sculpture. Every artist throughout history has expressed himself through a life motif. I have chosen the mother and child—not consciously, but because this is basically a part of me and my life. It is the embodiment and expression of the love of man for his family, which is an overpowering tie in his life and in his background. My aim plastically and sculpturally was to achieve a unity, a sculptural relationship of mass and form. Instead of portraying any one person, I have attempted to portray the more universal aspect of the mother and child. Through the expansion of forms and planes and through the rhythmic relationships of the various units, I feel I have created a living flow of forms—similar to what one might attain in the dance—and fused it into a permanent and solid rock pulsating with an inner life. This is what I feel I have attained. A farmer in the country was watching me one day. "Why do you carve a mother and child?" he asked. "Why don't you do a real subject like war and peace?"

I said, "Without a mother and child there would be neither war nor peace."

The problems of making this sculpture were tremendous, but the problems of handling it after it was done were even more so—for me at least. I bought chain blocks and dollies, propped up floors and built up huge beams to hold it and move it. I crated it myself. All this business of handling and moving stone I learned by just using my brain. I had people fixing barns, fixing foundations, repairing buildings. It was all new to me but I worked right along with them and learned. I learned by watching stonecutters and axe carpenters. I had a moving van back up to my studio and rolled the sculpture into it. I rode down with the truck. At Boston we shifted it to another van and delivered it to the door at Tenth Street. We rolled it into the ground floor store which I had rented under our apartment. There are always complications no matter how well you plan. A two-ton marble in a crate, a narrow street at just that moment being repaired, and only one man on the truck. It was an impossible situation but we accomplished the impossible. I drilled a hole in the ceiling, fastened a cable around a beam, and with a block and tackle set the stone upright. Our place at Tenth Street was part of the original Cushman Bakery. There was a big sign, "Founded in 1860." It was a three-story brick building painted to simulate marble; old Mr. Cushman was very proud of his marble front. The odor of fresh bread was always with us and very pleasant. The bakery mice were also with us and not so pleasant; however, we always had a cat. First we had the top floor; then we took over the second floor for the children; and when the downstairs laundry moved out, I took it over for a studio and moved in with my "Mother and Child." I worried about the floor with two and a half tons of marble on it, all in one place.

One morning I went out to get the paper. People were frantically running about the streets. A man shouted, "Remember the little French coffee shop across the street? It's gone! The whole building is gone and all the people are killed!" It had fallen into the huge hole which a construction company was excavating to build a big apartment house. Part of the family had arrived the day before from France. There were no survivors. No one ever heard anything more about it. The family and the coffee business had just vanished. I got terribly frightened; our building too was over a hundred years old and the bricks were put together with lime mortar not cement. I rushed out where they were repairing the street and got some beams and timbers and shored up the ground floor under my big stone. I was terrified that this building too might collapse.

I worked all winter on my "Mother and Child" and in the spring exhibited it in the Downtown Gallery on Thirteenth Street. I built a dolly strong enough to hold it and at five o'clock on a Sunday morning, when all good cops were asleep or at mass, I rolled it down the street from Tenth to Sixth Avenue to Thirteenth Street. Not a soul saw us. Down two steps on a ramp, through the front gallery, up three steps on a ramp, and into the garden gallery. We made it through the doors without an inch to spare. We set it on a base Edith Halpert had ready for it in the center of the room under the skylight. All this with the help of Tessim and two art students.

CHAPTER EIGHT

IT WAS in 1930 that I had my first sculpture exhibit at Edith Halpert's new gallery on Thirteenth Street. The depression had not yet settled down over the country. I had known Edith Halpert back in 1915. She was an attractive young thing working at Macy's to help support her widowed mother and studying art nights in Leon Kroll's class at the National Academy. Sam Halpert fell in love with Edith, and although he was a man twenty years older than she, Edith, being very young and very much impressed with art and artists, married him. Sam's art was too modern for his time and there was only the Daniel Gallery to show his work. Edith went to work every day—she was then an efficiency expert at Strauss's bank. Sam stayed home and painted. He seldom sold a picture. Edith got the idea that she could sell paintings if she tried. Through friends she arranged an exhibition in a hotel lobby. It was no place for an exhibition, but she did sell a few paintings and this encouraged her. That was in 1930.

The next summer Edith and Sam went to Ogunquit, Maine. This was quite an art colony in those days—not so many summer people but lots of artists and lots of antique shops. All of us were picking up early-American furniture and antiques. Not only were they more beautiful than the regular manufactured products but they were much cheaper, and a lot of us had acquired houses and had very little to furnish them with. Hunting antiques was great sport and lots of excitement. Edith got the idea of picking up antiques and opening a little shop in New York with Bea Goldsmith, a sister of Leon Kroll's. They bought an old house on Thirteenth Street—I think Bea put up most of the money. They converted the basement into a shop and gallery. They hung Sam Halpert's pictures and Marguerite and I let them have some of ours. Gradually more artists had their work there. At first they expected the antiques to carry the art, but Edith found she could sell contemporary art; she did not need the antique business. Later on, with the help of Holger Cahill she collected and built up a market for Harnett and early-American art—folk art. She went in for Americana on the side, promoted it from the art angle, and became quite an authority. When the Rockefellers were re-creating Williamsburg, she was a great help to them and found all manner of fine and interesting folk art for them.

What to name the gallery?

Edith and Bea thought of "Our Gallery," but I said, "After all, the other galleries are all uptown. Why not call it the Downtown Gallery?"

And that is what it became. Edith was full of ideas. In order to get people into the gallery and used to coming there, she had evening talks and gatherings of artists and people interested in art and she served coffee. The critics came and the reputation of the gallery grew. A gallery thrives by the quality of its shows and the enthusiasm and personality of the dealer.

As Edith and Bea became more and more involved in gallery affairs and the business of selling, this created difficulties for their husbands. Both were older men—lethargic, and used to being taken care of. They regarded the gallery as a pleasant club and sat around there afternoons and evenings playing cards and checkers and smoking big cigars. Not only did this embarrass the girls, but they were always in the way of the customers. Finally Sam got a job teaching painting in Detroit. That solved that problem, and shortly after Edith sued for a divorce. The day the divorce came through, Edith got a telegram that Sam had died of spinal meningitis. Later Edith and Bea separated and Edith carried on alone.

One evening a man came in, looked around, and asked where they served the drinks. This was in the days of prohibition and many village speakeasies were hidden behind a pretense of business. Edith persuaded him this was a legitimate art gallery. It seems he was very much interested in art and he became very much interested in Edith. He asked Edith if she had any Arthur B. Davies lithographs. She told him she would have some in a few days. She rushed up to the Weyhe Gallery on Lexington and Weyhe let her have a number of Davies. This man was Duncan Chandler. He became a regular visitor and customer for small things at the gallery. One day Edith told him that if she could only get hold of a Winslow Homer somewhere she would put on a show of American watercolors and show collectors that there were men today that would hold up with Winslow Homer. Homer was selling for $10,000 and contemporary watercolors were selling for a few hundred. Chandler said he would borrow a Homer for her and he did.

One day a tall, aristocratic lady came in to see the watercolor show. Edith told her she did not know who owned the Winslow Homer, but she was sure if the person who owned it could see the contemporary watercolors of Marin, Demuth, and Zorach hanging alongside the Homer, he would want to own them too.

The lady said, "I think you are perfectly right. I own the Homer and I would like to buy the other watercolors."

This was Mrs. John D. Rockefeller, Jr. and it turned out that Duncan Chandler was the Rockefeller architect. I believe Mrs. John D. was fascinated by Edith. Edith was attractive, lively, with real intelligence, and full of enthusiasm for modern art. She also sensed that Edith was not out to take advantage of her. There was a period when Mrs. John D. would come down to the gallery before Edith was up, ring the bell, and wait for her on the doorstep.

Edith built a beautiful little one-story exhibition gallery in the back yard at Thirteenth Street with a small patio between it and the front gallery. We all participated. I did the grilles and doors and Marguerite designed the floor in colored concrete in a handsome abstract pattern. The light was beautiful for sculpture as well as for paintings.

I had finished my "Mother and Child" and had my first sculpture show in this gallery in 1930. The show made quite a sensation in the art world. I exhibited all my carvings. I had about ten pieces besides my design for the frieze for the Los Angeles City Hall and the wood carving of the Schwarzenbach doors. In art and in other things I guess every dog has his day. This was my day. The publicity and appreciation was tremendous. Fame and recognition had come to me. I was under the illusion that there was a permanence in this; I did not realize that a new order would take its place and there would be new gods. I think I sold a few things. I only remember the sales that did not go through. Edith asked thirty thousand dollars for the "Mother and Child." A Mr. Bixby wanted to buy it for his garden. He had no qualms about the price but he wanted his landscape architect to see it first—most rich people are controlled by decorators and landscape architects. He wired for his architect to come back from Cuba. He came and he didn't approve. He told someone afterwards that he liked the sculpture all right but he wasn't going to have Edith Halpert horning in on his customers. He persuaded Mr. Bixby to buy a classical garden piece from an English collection—the conventional garden sculpture for a rich man. So the sale didn't go through. Now I am glad it didn't. I am much happier to have it in the Metropolitan Museum, which is where it belongs—for all people to see and enjoy; but they didn't buy it until 1955.

At the time I first showed "Mother and Child," the Metropolitan was also interested and Mr. Blumenthal, the president, came down to see it. But by the time he got around to it the show was over. The "Mother and Child" had been magnificent in the center of the gallery. He saw it crowded into the little patio, six feet by six, between the buildings. It was not an interesting display. They did not buy it—it may have been that they had to get used to it because it was different.

The "Mother and Child" was invited to the Chicago Art Institute, where it won the Logan medal and a fifteen hundred dollar award in 1931. It was exhibited in the Cleveland Museum for several years in the entrance to the Rotunda. They said they had no money to buy it—only money for ancient gothic textiles and jewelry. It was exhibited in the garden of the Museum of Modern Art for six years. They wanted me to find someone to buy it and give it to them. I said, "What about Mrs. Guggenheim?" "Oh," they said, "she's our patron; you have to find your own patron." I dropped it, that wasn't in my line. It was on display in the Metropolitan Museum as a loan during the war years—several of the curators told me it was the one piece of sculpture that held up over the years after the newness of seeing it wore off. But they did not buy it. I now realize that few things are ever bought, they are only sold. It came back to my studio. Twenty-five years after it was first shown, the Metropolitan Museum purchased my "Mother and Child" on the recommendation of Robert Hale and Francis Taylor, who was then the Director. I feel that that is where it belongs and I am very happy about it.

In 1930 plans for Radio City Music Hall were in progress. Edith Halpert interested the Rockefellers in having a young modern designer, Donald Deskey, plan and execute the interior. There were no appropriations for art—either murals or sculpture. What Deskey did was to set aside a small sum for art by cutting a bit here and there on items he could simplify or eliminate. We were all so impressed with the opportunity to work for a modern theater and the idea of modern art in a modern theater that we were willing to work for almost nothing. Or maybe we just wanted to work and the idea was exciting. As always we were told how valuable it would be for us to have our work in this most important project and of the future commissions that it would mean for us. And as always we worked wholeheartedly on these projects and not a future commission ever came from it for any one of us. But we received lots of publicity and that is supposed to count. Edith asked me to make some designs for sculpture to go in the downstairs lounge and in the foyer upstairs. Ed Stone and a couple of other architects looked over my drawings and selected a figure called "The Spirit of the Dance." It was the figure of a dancer kneeling just at the finale of the dance. My understanding was that it was to be only thirty-six inches high and that they had only eight hundred and fifty dollars to spend on it. I agreed to do it. When Deskey showed me where it was to go, we both realized that a figure three feet high would be ridiculous in that space. It had to be at least six and a half feet, which, since she was kneeling, meant proportionally a nine-foot figure. Nothing was said about the discrepancy between the cost of the two figures. I went ahead and created this figure in my studio. I always get so interested in an idea and so eager to see it develop that I never wait for a contract or even a go-ahead signal. I went right ahead and modeled "The Spirit of the Dance" full size. I worked on it all spring and into the summer, and when the figure was finished and cast in plaster, I told Deskey the sculpture was ready. He said he would get the committee down to O.K. it. It was a very hot summer. I was tired and exhausted and I waited and waited and no one showed up. Finally I left the key with the janitor, wrote Deskey to take the committee up when he could get them together, and went to Maine. When I came back the janitor told me there had been quite a session, a riot of loud, noisy arguments. That one man—it must have been Deskey—put up an awful fight and it went through.

The Radio City figure was cast in aluminum. I had another cast in bronze hoping to make up a bit on the sale of the second one. It traveled to various museums all over the country. At one time I offered it to Los Angeles for five thousand. They said they had no money. Museums are like charitable institutions—almost all their money goes to upkeep and salaries. People have to donate art to make up their collections. Finally I had "The Spirit of the Dance" shipped to Maine, where I anchored her on a natural ledge among the pines and oaks overlooking Robinhood Cove in front of our house. We enjoy her, our friends enjoy her, strangers come to see her. Marguerite discovered that a sightseeing boat comes by and the captain stops and runs a bit in shore and gives the passengers a lecture about the statue and the famous artist that lives in the house above. I have never checked what the captain says; it's probably like all the baloney handed out to tourists—maybe it's better not to know.

I didn't get much money for "The Spirit of the Dance" but I got a tremendous amount of acclaim and notoriety. I never know whether or not this has any importance. It is appalling that publicity, bad even more than good, is responsible for a consciousness of art accomplishment among people. But there are so many unsavory angles that are involved in the buying, promoting, and even appreciation of art that it is better to shut off your awareness and not think of these things. But when they hit you and knock you down, then you have to meet them.

I was out in Greenwich, Connecticut, at the time I got a telephone call from Edith that my figure had been thrown out of Rockefeller Center and had disappeared. I was stunned. After all a sculptor's work is his life. Destroy it and you destroy him. I was desperate. They weren't going to have it because it was nude . . . it was immoral . . . it was unfit to exhibit in a public place . . . Roxy wouldn't have it. This caused a terrific sensation in the art world. Artists protested, art organizations protested, public-spirited people protested. It was most interesting and revealing to see which organizations protested and which artists and people remained silent lest they stick their neck out or get in wrong with the Rockefellers or harm themselves by being on the wrong side of the fence. Even the Society of Independent Artists refused to say a word in my behalf or in the behalf of art.

The plaster model was exhibited at the Architectural League in a beautiful display by Joseph Urban. Edith exhibited it at the Downtown Gallery. It was invited to the Pennsylvania Museum, the Newark Museum, and the Cleveland Museum. Everywhere it was received with enthusiasm and appreciation.

After a while the "Spirit of the Dance" was replaced in the original setting. I never knew just what happened or why. I sometimes wonder if it was all a publicity stunt on the part of someone. I'll never know. Roxy was the man that sold the Rockefellers the idea of building the music hall. Broadway was in a terrific slump. The country was now really in the depths of a depression. The Music Hall was to save the theater. I never felt too happy about the setting of this figure. The room was a beautiful room but the ceiling was too low and the lighting, though well planned, was rather on the dark side. But what I really minded was the row of telephone booths in the background and the ladies' powder room on one side and the men's room on the other. I just didn't like it as a setting for my sculpture. I complained about this to old Henry Watrous, President of the National Academy of Design. "It's an excellent place," he said. "At my age I have weak kidneys and I have a chance to enjoy your sculpture very often."

"The Spirit of the Dance" is still there—in spite of the crank letters I got. One man wrote that he couldn't stand the idea of some young squirt standing in front of that naked statue with his daughter and ruining her morals—one thing could lead to another until it was too late. However no real disaster has been reported as yet.

The world is full of people without an idea in their heads. Painters who can't paint until they realize what another has seen in the world surrounding us, who can't be conscious of relationships, compositions, and forms until they can see them through another's eyes; writers who cannot write until they hear a story from another man's lips; inventors who have no approach until another man has seen a vision. And there are those within whose fertile brains ideas develop faster than they can handle them.

Edith Halpert was always full of ideas and projects. She didn't have to depend on anyone. She did not follow in the footsteps of others; she did not take the easy way of promoting and selling European art where the path was clear and well trodden. She set out to promote American art because she believed in it and realized that if this country was ever to have an American art it had to come out of American artists and not out of American collections of European art. This she made her goal and she has stuck to it with a single-minded devotion. American art owes her a great debt.

The Armory Show had been such a sensation Edith wanted to see if she couldn't repeat this success and put modern American art on the map with an all-American Armory show sponsored by the municipal government. When La Guardia was elected Mayor he was persuaded to take an effective interest in the idea. He was willing to let Edith have an Armory but Nelson Rockefeller said, "Who is going to pay for all the expenses of installation and advertising. Why don't you let us have the exhibition in Rockefeller Center and we will take care of expenses?"

A lot of politics and maneuvering came into this but the Municipal Exhibition went through. It was understood that all schools of American art were to be shown side by side with no labels to differentiate them. The architects, through Nelson Rockefeller, designed and equipped some very handsome galleries especially for this show and made them available to the city. This was the first time that the Mayor of the City of New York had given official support to a contemporary art exhibit. There was still a bitter conflict between the academic organizations and the moderns, and many artists were unhappy at the company they were forced to keep. Still it was an exciting and successful show.

I was interested in the sculpture situation. When the traditional sculptors exhibited at a large show like this, they seemed to have nothing of importance to send—a general's head, the head of a horse, a little model for enlarging—no creative work, only jobs. They were always complaining about the younger sculptors taking the limelight and getting all the attention in the papers and from the museums, but when it came to showing anything creative or unusual they seemed to have nothing. To me it looked as if they were always too busy doing commissions and had no time for anything else.

Holger Cahill was to be director of the exhibition, but he fell sick and was in the hospital the whole time. That left no one in charge except the hanging committee, of which I was one. We took over and arranged the show. One of the critics asked me to pick out something for him to reproduce in *The Times*—something that was different from anything else in the show. I showed him a picture by Florine Stettheimer—a large picture, very effete and elegant—of her friends and family painted on a heavy white ground, freely and delicately drawn, and lovingly painted in very bright and lovely colors. He reproduced it in the rotogravure section of *The New York Times*. Florine said to me, "Isn't it strange? After all these years the newspapers are beginning to pay attention to me."

Before my "Mother and Child" went out to Chicago, because shipping the stone was a very expensive and risky thing, I had a piece mold made of it and then a copy in plaster. I painted and colored this copy to look like the stone, and when I was invited to exhibit the "Mother and Child," it was very simple and inexpensive to send this copy. I showed this in the Municipal Show and it received favorable reviews.

There were few sales made at this show but there was great interest.

One day Edith had me bring the Jonas tapestry that Marguerite was working on down to the gallery. It was practically finished but unframed. Edith said she wanted it to show to a customer who might be interested in having one made. It turned out to be Mrs. John D. Rockefeller, Jr. That summer Mrs. Rockefeller invited us to her home in Seal Harbor and we spent a week with her. We discussed the subject matter and size of the tapestry. It was to be of the family, their home, their life and their surroundings on Mount Desert, Maine.

One morning when we were there, I got up at daybreak to paint a watercolor. I couldn't find the light switches and bumped into things around the house, and after that, I had great trouble getting out the front door onto the porch. The night watchman came along and I asked him to get me a pail of water, which he did. When Mrs. John D. came down, she was horrified for fear that I might have been shot for a burglar. It had never occurred to me. When I am visiting I always get up at dawn and paint a watercolor. The dawn is always full of magic.

Mrs. Rockefeller drove us all around the place in a horse and buggy, showed us all over the island, and took us sailing. It was fun being with them. Marguerite loved the gardens and was intrigued at the men going over the rocks and woodland carefully removing the less attractive weeds and plants. I remember a dinner one night when they had butter-pecan ice cream especially for Dahlov and the embarrassment when it was so salty no one could eat it except Dahlov—she ate it. The cook had used salted pecans. And I remember another dinner when a prominent English woman was present. John D. asked her about the "dole" in England. He did not approve.

"But," she said, "if we didn't have the dole we'd have a revolution."

Said John D. Jr., "A revolution is much more healthy than the dole. People can recover from a revolution. They are undermined spiritually and morally by the dole."

Everyone was surprised and disturbed—it was considered too controversial a subject for the dinner table. But I had a greater respect for John D.'s thinking after that.

One day Mrs. John D. took me aside and asked me what commission Edith Halpert got. I told her Edith got 33⅓ per cent on sales, the standard gallery commission, but she had agreed to take only 25 per cent on the embroidery because of the great amount of labor and time involved. Then she took Marguerite aside and asked her the same question. Marguerite of course told her the same thing I did. Mrs. John D. said she considered it a very large commission for work of this kind. After I got home I wrote her I didn't consider the commission exorbitant and reminded her that when she bought an old master the dealer often made one hundred per cent and that sometimes the dealers' profits were even more fantastic because they bought and sold and took whatever the market would stand. This is what I said—I couldn't tell her that I, too, considered the commission unjustified on a work which required so much time and labor as well as creative effort. It should have been rated as a mural at ten or fifteen per cent. When Edith found out I had discussed the commission with Mrs. Rockefeller, she raised cain—telling me an artist had no business under any circumstances to discuss commissions with a client. But Mrs. Rockefeller was a very direct person. She had asked me and I had answered her question. If we had not been frank and honest with her there would have been no embroidery.

Some clients feel the poor artist should be getting the full price of a work of art—that the dealer is cheating the artist by taking a third. I don't see how they figure a gallery can operate on that basis. Others want to buy direct from the artist and expect the artist to deduct the commission. Some people always want to get something at a wholesale price. They never seem to think the situation through. Even Mrs. John D. liked a bargain. Certainly she did not like to feel she was being charged more than the next because of her great wealth. I always say the rich want to enjoy the pleasures of being poor as well as the pleasures of wealth. They love a bargain, forgetting that with wealth a bargain is meaningless.

Mrs. Rockefeller wanted to pay for the tapestry by the month; Marguerite always preferred to wait until the work was done and then be paid in full but it was not too important. Each month the check would come, Edith would deduct the commission and send Marguerite her share. Marguerite did no obvious work on the design. She was thinking and planning. I was horrified and desperate. She spent a year planning this tapestry in her head, figuring out the design, fitting ideas together, mulling over the family, and finally drawing a cartoon, just line no color. When she was satisfied with it, she began the embroidery. She was three years executing it. Like all artists she gets so fascinated by the work that time means nothing to her. Sometimes she would get so exhausted she would put it away for a week. She had sense enough to know when she should put work aside and replenish her soul, even if it was hard to separate herself from it.

I have always loved this tapestry. The creative vision, the interweaving and juxtaposition of colors and forms; in the sea, the clouds, in the details of woods and rocks and plants; in the way the ugly mansion is kept true in detail and yet becomes a part of the whole; the incorporation of the members of the family in the landscape; the exquisite detail in the minute scenes. John D. Sr. playing golf on the church lawn, the Socony filling station, the cows in the meadow.

The tapestry was to be a surprise gift for John D. Jr. Mrs. Rockefeller never told him she was having it made, and I'm sure it was a real surprise and that he did not like it–it was too modern for his taste. It was intended to be hung in Pocantico, but after Mrs. John D. died it went to Nelson, who has it in his home in Seal Harbor.

At the time Duncan Chandler was building the Play House at Pocantico for the Rockefellers, he asked me to design some figures of athletes to be placed on the wall around the large front terrace. I made a tennis player, a basketball player, a baseball player, and a football player. Mr. Rockefeller was not one bit enthusiastic, but after all architects have to create enthusiasm in their clients–not wait for it. Chandler persuaded him to have me enlarge one of the figures and put it in place so that he could really get the idea. I enlarged the football player and patined it to look like granite. The Rockefellers sent the truck to pick it up and put it in place and Chandler made an appointment with John D. to see it and talk over the project. We went out to Pocantico and waited and waited for John D. to show up but he never did. I had seen him hurry across the lawn in his riding clothes and disappear into the woods as we drove in. He had made the appointment, this man was his architect, had built his house at Pocantico and the one in Seal Harbor, and yet he ran away from a meeting–he could not face him–which is hard to believe. Afterwards Donald Deskey wanted to use some of these figures in the Music Hall but John D. said, "No! Do I have to see those awful things again? They are haunting me."

Later when the "Football Player" was in red Swedish granite to my own satisfaction, I exhibited it. I had no place in my studio for large pieces of sculpture and during the depression I loaned it to the Newark Museum.

They put it in the garden and sent me a receipt: "Will you kindly hold this and when the loan is returned to you, please sign the sheet as indicated and return it to us in order that your name may be cancelled."

That was on August 8, 1935. Some time later I met Miss Winsor, the curator at Newark, and asked her if she would try to get the Museum to buy my piece.

In April, 1941, I received a letter from her: ". . . The Museum is in no financial position to purchase your football player. It has been in the Museum garden since 1935 and I remember when you first brought it over, you relinquished it to the Museum since you had no place to take care of it. . . ."

That gave me a jolt. I wasn't in any position to give a granite carving on that scale to a museum at that time. I needed a sale, not a giveaway.

Miss Winsor then wrote: "My dear Mr. Zorach, I am sorry you feel as you do because you really did say to me in your letter of July, 1935, 'I hope you will like the "Football Player." If you don't, well, dig a hole in the garden and bury him.' "

I explained to her that I was appalled—"What if all the museums to which I have loaned my sculpture for exhibition purposes, and where it, I am sure, has been regarded by the public as part of the museum collection, feel that in some mysterious way I have relinquished my rights to my work—that it is no longer mine but theirs? . . . I don't doubt for a minute that I facetiously suggested digging a hole and dropping in the 'Football Player'—I've felt like that many times as my studio got more and more cluttered—but that is not exactly presenting the work to the museum as a gift. Now we have a studio in Brooklyn and, if no one will buy my large pieces, at least I have a place to keep them even if it becomes the Zorach Museum. You make me feel guilty at asking for this piece back—almost as if it doesn't belong to me. I had better ask for this one back before I get the feeling too strongly."

We live in Maine half the year and have always been interested in Bowdoin College. They have a fine little museum with a beautiful collection of American portraits—Fekes, Stuarts and others—and also some magnificent Assyrian reliefs. They also hold exhibitions of contemporary art. I had a grandson in college there and in 1958 Bowdoin gave me an honorary degree, Master of Arts. I was now sufficiently well off financially to feel free to give works of mine, no matter how important and valuable, to places where I am happy to have them. It occurred to me that here was the place for my "Football Player."

I visualized it on the green campus but they said, perhaps wisely, "No, we can't risk it there." So it sits in the Rotunda of the Walker Museum near one of their magnificent Assyrian reliefs and the two works of art are on good terms with each other.

The year before, I had a bronze made of the round mother and child, called "Devotion" which the Laurance Rockefellers have, carved in light gray granite, on their terrace in New York. I gave this to Colby College, where there is so much real interest in and appreciation of American art and especially Maine art—and where another grandson went to college.

CHAPTER NINE

THE ROCKEFELLER TAPESTRY had been finished and paid for. The depression had deepened. The Gallery sold little. The artists in the gallery were discouraged and distracted. If you are with a gallery you are not free to sell outside the gallery. What could one do? I said to myself, "I'm certainly not going to sit here and starve or go jump in the river. If the gallery can't sell my work I've got to do something about it myself. The world isn't coming to an end. The sun is still shining, there are still people of wealth, there are still museums with funds with which to buy art."

I tried discussing the situation with Edith Halpert but it was very difficult. Of course things were not easy with her, but then I felt as if I could never get anywhere talking with Edith—there seemed to be little give and take between us. It was probably my fault. I went home and wrote her a letter saying I could not sit home waiting for her to sell my work, nor could I make her unhappy by pressuring her to sell it when she couldn't. I'd have to go out and shift for myself. I had to make an effort. But at least in that case I was under no obligations as to price and I could not continue to give the gallery a commission on sales I made myself. Edith couldn't see that. She said she was through with me forever. She was through with Marguerite too. To Edith the wife is always to blame; she would never have believed that Marguerite did not want me to take this step, but I was so disturbed and miserable I couldn't go on. I felt that I had been instrumental in building up the gallery and it was not easy to move out, but I saw no other way. Every gallery thinks it owns its artists body and soul. The separation was not easy and getting on without a gallery was not easy. But I was now free—on my own. I am no salesman. I can sell a work of art to someone who wants to buy a work of art, but a salesman can sell a work of art to someone who doesn't want to buy it. That I could never do, nor would I want to.

I went to see Mr. Winlock, director of the Metropolitan Museum; I pointed out that they owned nothing of mine and that they had the Hearn Fund for sculpture, which they had not used, and then showed him pictures of my available pieces. He said, "You're perfectly right, but I don't know that I can make the board of directors see it." Nothing happened. But later when I met him in an exhibition where I had a granite cat, he looked at it and asked Jonas Lie, the president of The National Academy of Design, if it was really good. Jonas Lie was enthusiastic and the Metropolitan bought the "Cat in Red Granite."

I made an appointment with Nelson Rockefeller. I said, "After all, you are building Rockefeller Center. Why don't you have the architects use some of my work?"

He said, "I'll talk to them."

Nothing came of it. Architects are used to working with professional architectural sculptors like Lee Laurie, Paul Manship, and Leo Friedlander. They can rely on them to meet a deadline and they know what the finished work will be like. They were right. I could have met a deadline but they did not know it. I was an artist doing my own creative work to please myself and exhibiting in galleries. I had no background of collaborating with anyone. And in a way I think they had a point. Architectural sculpture is essentially design—not expression—and essentially I am not a designer; it is in the conception and power of expression that the value of my work lies.

I could interest architects but I could not sell myself to them. One day a Mrs. Dougherty came to see me. She was a person who made it her business to promote artists, introduce them, and get them commissions. She knew I was on my own and thought it would be a real opportunity.

She said, "Colonel Woods is the man who has the final word on all work being done at Rockefeller Center. I'll make an appointment and introduce you to him. Take down a portfolio of your work."

This came about. With Colonel Woods were all the architects of Rockefeller Center. They said they would give me fifteen minutes—they spent two hours going over my work and discussing it with me. They seemed interested. But again nothing came of it.

I heard afterwards that someone said, "What's the matter with that fellow Zorach that he comes down here with a woman to introduce him; can't he stand on his own feet?" I thought it a joke and a rather nasty one—that the work meant nothing.

In the years between 1935 and 1939 almost all the young artists and many of the older ones were on the W.P.A. It was the most wonderful time in the world for the art of America—a period that infused art with life and gave artists a place in the world. It took art out of the field of dealers and New York cliques and spread it over the whole country. There was much criticism over boondoggling. Much bad art was produced on the W.P.A., but a lot of fine art was also produced and the stimulus to art was of incalculable value for all time.

I was teaching out at Rosemary Hall, Connecticut, one day a week. A woman came to me and said, "The government is very much concerned that so much poor work is being done on the W.P.A. and there is so much criticism. The standard of art is being lowered to the point where everyone is worried. We are afraid there will be so much pressure that it will stop the project. Mrs. Force [the director of the Whitney Museum], who is in charge of this area, is very much concerned. The government wants her to get a few of the best artists to do a few worthwhile things to raise the standard of the project and give it stature. Would you do a monument for Greenwich, here where you teach and are known?"

I said I'd like to do this but I was not on W.P.A. nor was I in need. I couldn't do it if it were considered relief. But if it could be arranged I'd do the work for nothing—as a gesture of good will.

Mrs. Force had John Sloan, myself, and a few others, come down and discuss the matter with her. But we had to sign a paper to do this under the W.P.A. in order to put the work through—and the form said we were in need. We were told it meant nothing—that governments functioned that way and it had to be done that way—and this is certainly true of governments. It sounds ridiculous but that is what happened.

I was working on a sketch for this monument in my studio when a couple of reporters knocked on my door and said, "We are from the *Herald-Tribune* and we understand you are going to do a monument for the government on the W.P.A."

"Yes," I said. "Mrs. Force asked me to do this. They wanted to get some well-known artists to do some work to counteract the poor stuff being turned in."

"Oh," they said. "You're going to be right across the front page of the *Herald-Tribune* tomorrow."

"What for?" I asked.

"You wait and see!" they replied. "Boy, are you really in trouble."

The *Herald-Tribune*, a Republican newspaper, was eager to get something on the Roosevelt Administration. Next morning a screaming headline all across the front page said, "Zorach and John Sloan, famous artists, are on the W.P.A. on relief."

I was shocked. I called the newspaper and said, "What do you mean by such headlines? We are not going to be paid anything for this work. We are just doing it out of the goodness of our hearts to help art in America, by producing something worthwhile through the W.P.A."

Well, they printed a retraction—you know—three lines on the back page in the shipping news. But we got write-ups and crank letters and telephone calls over our scandalous behavior, saying what an awful, unscrupulous thing it was for us to do—to horn in on government money meant for desperate and needy artists. Of course that ended it—no work was done by us.

One day in the Milch Gallery I met Ned Bruce, the head of the Section of Fine Arts, which was under the Treasury Department. He said, "We're developing some sculpture projects. They have nothing to do with the W.P.A. or with relief. We are going to have competitions and want to have the finest artists do these jobs. This time instead of the usual eagles and cornices that are used for ornamentation, we are going to have sculpture and murals."

He asked me to come to Washington and talk it over with Mrs. Henry Morgenthau and Ed Rowan, the head of the P.W.A. Art Project. I suggested they ask competent artists to send in photographs of their work and from these we would select a number of artists to take part in the competition for a particular project. Of course the old guard was still in power in Washington and had a strangle hold on all government art. The only people getting commissions were members of the National Sculpture Society, professional architectural sculptors, and traditional muralists. I gave Mrs. Morgenthau a talk on the younger generation of sculptors growing up and needing encouragement—how they would, if given a chance, bring new life and creative vision into a jaded and decadent art. And I brought up the point that these men were eager to work and for far less money than the professionals.

The first competition was for a series of postmen for the niches in the Postmaster General's reception hall, the next competition was for a six-and-a-half-foot figure of Benjamin Franklin, the first Postmaster General, to be placed in the same hall. There was also one of Osgood, the first Postmaster General of the State of New York to be placed in the hall opposite the reception hall. Ned Bruce sent out a questionnaire to the museum directors and critics of the country asking them whom they would choose to do these two figures. Paul Manship and I got most of the votes and were chosen. Manship, Bruce, and I discussed the project over lunch at the Harvard Club. Bruce asked what a six-and-a-half-foot figure in marble would cost.

Manship said, "That's a twenty-five-thousand-dollar job."

Bruce said, "We are working to get the government interested in these projects but we can't pay these prices. All we have allotted is eight thousand each. Would you be willing to do it for eight thousand?"

We thought it over and, because it seemed an important step, we agreed.

Bruce said, "Of course you both want to do Franklin."

Manship said, "Of course. How are we going to decide?"

Bruce suggested flipping a coin. We did and I got Franklin.

I had never done a conventional statue before. You just can't do a figure of Franklin and not have it exemplify Franklin to the people of the United States. And yet it had to be a work of art as well as a likeness. It is simple enough to make a likeness but to make it a work of art as well was a real challenge. Certain of the Academicians were venomous over my getting this commission and did everything to thwart me. The Fine Arts Commission refused to O.K. my sketch. They wouldn't approve my quarter-size model, they found fault with every detail as well as with the whole.

Finally I said to Ed Rowan, "I don't want to do this job if that's the way they feel about it and if they are going to hamstring me all along the line."

Ed Rowan said, "Look, we want you to do this figure, Ned Bruce wants you to do it, Mrs. Morgenthau wants you to do it. We will stand in back of you; you can't let us down."

Ed Rowan and I went to see Lee Laurie, who was chairman of the Fine Arts Commission. I showed him my sketches; he looked at them and criticized them and we discussed my ideas. It was a good meeting. I found Lee Laurie was a serious person, an artist who understood artists. And when he met me as I was, not as an abstract entity, an ogre horning in on the world of monumental sculpture, he felt interested and sympathetic. I listened to his ideas and criticisms and agreed to give them thought and consideration. I went ahead with my enlargement.

I had no place equipped to execute the full-sized figure. Manship told me of a shop in Long Island City where a man had an enlarging machine and a stone-carving machine. This was where he had his monuments done. The figure had to be made full size by me for my own satisfaction—not just thrown up and carved from the quarter-size model as is usually done. I would like to say here that, while I carve directly in stone and find it my most satisfying expression, this method can't be used when it comes to commissions and architectural sculpture. First, the small model must be made and approved. After that a full-sized model is required. I usually do this myself, although most sculptors when executing commissions, give the small model out to be enlarged. Full-size models can be cast in bronze or carved in stone. The sculptor cannot copy it in stone—there is something destructive and uncreative in a sculptor copying a model, even his own, especially when the model has to be identical. It is only possible to supervise and see that the copy is perfect. Secondly, there is the question of time. No time is ever allowed by architects and builders for the artist to dream and think—everything has to be finished yesterday. There are contracts and deadlines that only a machine can meet.

The shop enlarged my quarter-size model to full size, and I developed and finished the clay model in the shop. This was one of the most miserable experiences of my life. Here I was trying to create a work of art in a big shop full of workmen and noise, and the man whose shop it was and who considered himself a sculptor talked constantly, telling me what to do, criticizing, and talking, and talking. He was one of those fellows you can't shut up—the next minute he's back again.

It was in the summer of 1937. I had to take a long trip every day from Manhattan to Long Island City at rush hour, and then walk a mile to the shop. The building with its corrugated roof was like a furnace. I worked all day, every day, until my sacroiliac gave way and I was in agony. I lost a tremendous amount of weight. I couldn't eat or sleep properly. Marguerite and the children were in

Maine. It was hell. I lived through it, but it took some vital energy out of me that was never fully replaced. A lot of it was my own fault. I cannot take things lightly—I give every bit of myself, mentally, physically and emotionally to my work, even in a noisy, hot bedlam with a mosquito-like academician continually buzzing in my ear.

I hired models and costumes to see what could be used to make the Franklin authentic in his period, but it was vital not to let the costumes weaken it as a work of art. I finally got the full-sized clay finished, cast, and approved. Then, I had to have the men execute it in stone. I stayed there and watched the carving, and this time it was I who was so particular and exacting, making this man who had been torturing me pretty miserable in turn. I insisted on perfection, regardless of the time involved. I had a great admiration for the skill and craftsmanship of his Italian stone-carvers. He would rave at my speaking to them or discussing the work with them.

"You'll give them ideas," he said. "First thing you know they'll be asking for more pay."

I finally finished, after all the misery and heartaches. The figure was delivered to Washington and set up. No one ever asked the Fine Arts Commission to look at it or to approve it. Bruce just took the matter to Roosevelt and he O.K.'d it.

Afterwards at a reception at the White House I met President Roosevelt and he said how much he liked what I had done. He especially liked the gesture of the hands in the waistcoat. Usually, Franklin is shown with a manuscript in his hand and books at his feet. I had wanted to do something a little different. To me, the gesture I used showed the independence and sureness of the man. A marble figure has to be supported. I used a cloak of the period. I borrowed an authentic one and extended it to the floor. The back fell in marvelous folds and supported the figure. I studied the bust of Franklin made in his lifetime by Houdin, as well as all the contemporary portraits I could find. But the Houdin bust gave me the best idea of the appearance of the man. The great stature and extraordinary personality of Franklin had to be realized through my own understanding of him as a great human being.

I felt I was doing something for the American people. People have a definite image of Franklin, Washington, Lincoln—you can't just ignore this image if your sculpture is to have meaning to the people. I tried to augment that image and give it greater power, dignity and authenticity. The only thing I regretted was that it had to stand in the Postmaster General's room on the third floor and therefore would not be available to the people of America. Imagine my pleasure when I went back to Washington a few years ago and there stood my Franklin in the lobby of the Post Office building on the ground floor where all who had eyes and interest could enjoy it.

Late in 1939, six sculptors were asked to compete in creating a monumental figure of Thomas Jefferson to be placed in the center of the Jefferson Memorial in Washington. Considering how unfortunate my experiences with competitions and committees had been, I was not in the least eager to win this competition. I could not forget how I had been driven to distraction when making the Franklin. I knew exactly what was wanted, but I decided to do Jefferson as I thought he should be done—a figure that would satisfy me as an artist and not a committee. I did a thorough research job on Jefferson. I read books, studied the various pictures, and made a careful study of Houdin's bust which was modeled from life. I built myself a picture of the man. Jefferson was a cultured man, an idealist, and of superior mentality. Physically, he was tall and thin, with a small, narrow head. He was a wonderful dancer and moved with grace. I based my conception on Jefferson's statement, "I have sworn on the altar of God, eternal hostility to every form of tyranny over the mind." This, I inscribed on the pedestal.

My Jefferson was tall and thin and lacked all the qualities of conventional and costumed historical figures. The jury had no trouble at all with it. Mine was the first eliminated. Lee Laurie won the competition but they did not give the commission to him but to another academician, Rudulph Evans. His figure is based on a picture I saw in the library where Jefferson wears a long fur-lined coat with a fur collar. The figure is a huge mass on top of which sits the conventional small head of Jefferson.

When I first visited the Lincoln Memorial—although I don't think the Lincoln Memorial or the figure of Lincoln is a great work of art—when I walked up the steps and entered the interior of the monument I was tremendously impressed and almost moved to tears at the sight of this figure of Lincoln in this setting. And if I, a modern artist, can be moved to tears by a conventional piece of work that is not a great work of art, there must be something else than art that is necessary in a monument. I visited the Jefferson Memorial and, although I am not greatly impressed by the figure of Jefferson, the whole idea of the memorial is impressive. A modern work can also thrill people. But in the final analysis a monument must be something that impresses people and moves people. It must be awe-inspiring. A monument is not just for the sophisticated people of the art world, it is to commemorate and to give substance to a national figure or a great man in some field of endeavor. It must have meaning to all people and to children. We either put up a monument of him or a monument to him. It does not necessarily have to be a great work of art. If it is a great work of art, then it is wonderful.

The Sculptors Guild came into existence during a period when there was very little opportunity to exhibit sculpture and still less sculpture. It was like working in a vacuum. These new sculptors had to find a way to live and produce sculpture. The school of welders and wire workers developed later. Many of these men and women carved directly in stone and wood. They were full of creative ideas and enthusiasm and eager to do great things. The Academy and the National Sculpture Society ignored them completely, they wanted no new ideas.

Some of these men came to me and wanted me to help them organize a sculptors' guild. I told them I knew nothing about organizing but I was with them heart and soul and would help in any way I could.

The Sculptors Guild was organized in 1938. The first catalogue lists fifty-seven members. One of the most active members was Dorothea Greenbaum. She was most experienced and helpful. Her husband, Eddie Greenbaum, the lawyer, was a man with professional and executive background which made her even more helpful. We needed honorary sponsors and after that, patrons, and finally we got together a very imposing list of sponsors—Mrs. Eleanor Roosevelt, Mrs. Henry Morgenthau, Jr., Fiorello La Guardia, Robert Moses, Stanley Isaacs, and other important people. We also had about one hundred and fifty patrons, all of whom gave money—Winslow Ames, director of the Lyman Allen Museum; Joseph Hudnut of Columbia; Holger Cahill, National Director of the Federal Arts Project; A. Conger Goodyear, President of the Museum of Modern Art; Mrs. John D. Rockefeller, Jr.; Mr. and Mrs. Laurance Rockefeller; Mr. and Mrs. Edward Bruce; Mr. and Mrs. Edward R. Rowan; and Herbert Winlock, Director of the Metropolitan Museum. The committee had composed a very good letter. Then they had brought it around for me to sign.

I asked, "Why me?" and they said, "We have to have someone with an important name."

I hesitated but I signed the letters and they went out. The response was wonderful.

We went ahead with the plans for our exhibition. There was no gallery with sufficient space. Someone suggested we have an outdoor sculpture show in a vacant lot. Some of the sculptors felt that wouldn't be the right thing. I felt that it would be a marvelous opportunity to show sculpture in its natural setting, out of doors. It was finally agreed. Dorothea and her husband, Eddie Greenbaum, got the Mayor to give us the empty lot on Park Avenue and Thirty-eighth Street. We paid a token fee of one dollar. The lot was just weeds and rubble. We got a landscape architect to help us with the planting. Du Bois Fences furnished the fence, woven out of natural wood. Bobbink and Atkins furnished the plants. There were some ten tall birch trees growing around the lot which we dug up and moved about. They were glad to be moved and responded beautifully. Everything was going along fine. We were ready to print the catalogues and the show was to open in a couple of weeks. We had to move fast.

I got a telephone call to come down to the lot. They were having trouble getting any of the sculptors to come down and work and it was snowing. I put on my Maine boots and rough clothes—overalls and a wool shirt—and I took a shovel and a pick and went down to the lot. Only one sculptor was there and working, John Hovannes. He was a good man with a hammer and a saw and he was putting up a ticket booth. I don't know what the sculptors were dreaming about, or how they expected the show to go on, or who they thought was doing the work. The thing that shocked me most was that I had signed all the letters to all those important people and I would be responsible if the show didn't go on. I got on the telephone. I told the boys that if they didn't show up on the lot with shovels and boots ready to work, they could just stay home and there would be no work of theirs shown in the show. I had to get tough. One by one they showed up and began to clean the lot. It was an interesting experience; I found that certain men will work and others will just stand around and watch other men work. I had to be a tough foreman and so I told the ones who wouldn't work to get out. Under pressure I suddenly acquired a certain kind of ability I didn't know I had at all. Some of the sculptors didn't like it. They said they didn't like having a boss.

I had another difficulty with the group because they wanted publicity and they were all desperately jealous of each other's publicity. I had been around long enough to know you can't tell reporters what to write or whom to write about. But you can talk to them if they will listen and every one did his best. I told one of the boys to call up *The New York Times* and the *Tribune* to have reporters sent down. Reporters came and took pictures of all of us—sculptors working. This was news.

The sculptor John Flannagan came around at the day's end when we were all worn out and tempers were short. He leaned on his cane and said, "How's the Zorach Guild?"

I didn't realize he drank as much as he did and was not exactly accountable.

He said, "Where are you going to place my piece? I see you've got yours in a prominent spot."

It was absurd but annoying. Nothing had been placed, things had just been brought in and put down anywhere. In this show no one artist placed things. The sculptors fought it out among themselves. All day they were moving their pieces around—except for the few big things that couldn't be shifted from one spot to another.

The publicity had been sent out, the catalogue printed, the critics had seen the show and had gone home to write their reviews. The opening was to be the next morning when one girl decided to change her exhibit. She had sent in an enormous piece, the largest in the show. We all said, "No." The next morning she came around before eight o'clock with a big truck, took her piece of sculpture out, and put an even bigger one in its place. She also sent out a special release to the press complete with pictures.

I began to wonder what kind of people these were. I had known and loved artists all my life but had never had to work with them in organizations before. It was quite an experience. Naturally everyone wanted to be in the center, but whenever a piece was placed, when you looked around it was somewhere else. They didn't want to be next to this man—he's imitating me—or this one—his piece is too big or too small or too bad.

I said to Dorothea, "What is the matter with these people? What can we do with them?"

She spoke to her husband, the lawyer.

He said, "Dorothea, it isn't just artists. You're dealing with people and people are all that way."

I said, "This is a crazy world. How does it function as well as it does?"

Finally we got the show beautifully landscaped and arranged. Sculpture never looked more beautiful. It created a sensation. I think we had twenty-five thousand people visit the show. They paid an admission of ten cents. The show received world-wide publicity and it put sculpture on the map. Everybody was very happy; quarrels and misunderstandings were forgotten.

The next show held on the same lot the following year was a still more fantastic affair. We started from scratch again—landscaping, everything. But this time we had experience and success behind us. The Board insisted upon me being head of the grounds committee again. After my experience of the year before I was very wary. I am not a committee man. I would leave the meetings feeling ill. I didn't know where to start or what to do and yet I'd let myself be roped in. All I wanted was to be left alone. I was fed up with organized activity and with all these temperamental people craving for recognition. Yet I was involved because I am an artist and art is my life.

The committee that year gave the contract to build the stands for the sculpture and the little shed to house our working paraphernalia to the husband of one of the sculptors, because he could get lumber wholesale and his was the lowest bid. They advanced him two hundred and fifty dollars.

I said, "Gene, I'm not in favor of your undertaking this work but I have been overruled. I know you mean well but this job has got to be done, done right, and done on time. If you let us down you won't live."

Again I felt responsible. I knew Gene and I knew what we were up against. He was a nice fellow, a dreamer, an idea man. He had a new idea every fifteen minutes. There was nothing practical about him.

I said to him, "Gene, where are you building the stands?" We had to have about a hundred sculpture stands. He said he was building them out in New Jersey on a railroad siding sixty miles from New York. Then I told his wife, "We'd better take my car and go out there and see what is going on." Two hundred dollars worth of cardboard was piled up in a shelter at the siding. He was going to have the stands out of cardboard.

"But Gene," his wife cried, "these stands have to hold up in the rain and they have to support hundreds of pounds of stone and bronze!" Not a soul was in sight.

"But Gene, where are the workmen?"

"Let me take the car and we'll get some men," Gene said.

"You'll not take my car," I said. "I'll take you to get the men." We went down the road and he saw a group of W.P.A. men working on the road. He asked the foreman to let him have some men to help with the stands.

The man said, "These men are working for the government. I can't let them off to help you."

He stopped at a couple of farms but found nobody home. We went back to the siding.

I said, "Look, Gene, just forget about it." And we drove back to the city.

His wife was just frantic and kept saying she was through with him forever. We got a little carpenter shop to do a rush job and they made us very good stands out of wood. We painted them and had them up just in time. The money paid Gene was a complete loss but we made enough at the gate to pay for everything.

We hired a man to take care of publicity.

He came to me and said, "What can I do? Every time I come up with a wonderful idea all the women sit on me. After all I'm here to get them publicity. For instance, I think I could get Ringling Brothers to bring a couple of elephants down to the lot to haul some of the sculpture around and we could put some monkeys to work—think what a sensation it would cause. But these women say it would be undignified."

I said to the women, "Look, when a man comes up with an idea, don't sit on him, leave him alone. That one idea may not be any good but he's trying and he will come up with another one and that may be a good one. Never discourage a man. There are not going to be any elephants or monkeys—he can't get them. But he'll come up with another idea."

A few days later he came over to me. "Mr. Zorach, I know the man in charge of the subway ads and I can get a free ad in the subways. When I told my friend about this show he said, 'I'm not interested in giving you any advertising in the subways. If you have an idea that will put nickles in the slots, all right. But people on Park Avenue are going to come to your exhibition and come in limousines not in subways.' Then I told him that there were all those sculptors working up there and he seemed amazed. He said, 'If you can get those sculptors working I'll get you a free ad in the subways!' "

The publicity man meant that they were digging and planting trees. The subway man thought he meant the sculptors were modeling and carving. Again the ladies on the committee said it would be undignified, "Nobody wants to model or carve in public."

I said, "Go ahead with the idea and I'll get you a number of sculptors who will be happy to model outdoors on the lot."

I announced to the sculptors that we were going to have a model pose on the lot—we would get an important person—and to bring clay and a modeling stand. They were delighted. We had Major Bowes, and on Mother's Day we had a nice motherly mother. Some days we'd pick someone from the audience. We'd set them up and model them. They liked it; the audience liked it. The photographers came—it was the first public demonstration ever given in the making of sculpture. It started a whole chain of activity. It was done at the San Francisco World's Fair, museums have public demonstrations, and it is used in colleges and lectures all over the country now. I think the Sculptors Guild shows may have inspired the Museum of Modern Art to build their open-air garden court for sculpture.

The second outdoor sculpture show was an even greater success than the first. We had two more outdoor shows but not another on Park Avenue—our lot was used for a building. Our last outdoor show was in the lot adjoining the Guggenheim Museum. I exhibited there with my little bronze of a child, "Innocence," but I didn't take an active part in any of the exhibitions after the Park Avenue shows. The Sculptors Guild still exists and puts on very good shows every year. But indoors, not outdoors—there are no more vacant lots available. Vincent Glinsky and his wife, Cleo Hartwig, have held the Sculptors Guild together these recent years. Someone has to be unselfishly devoted to a cause or it dies and they accepted the responsibility. Vincent told me lately that they have decided to elect a president and asked me if I would accept the job. I told him I was sorry but I wouldn't be president of any group, dead or alive, no matter how deeply I was in sympathy with them. That I was tired and no longer had the energy and drive that such a job deserved. I felt I had done my share and had had enough. It was now up to the younger generation and they would have my backing.

Before the days of the Sculptors Guild I had belonged to a very fine organization, The Society of Painters, Sculptors and Graveurs. This group was formed from the more progressive elements of the older art societies, and they also invited some of the younger and more progressive men on the outside to join them. They held annual exhibitions and were a very fine group. Leon Kroll was president; he had all the qualifications. He was active, broadminded, and had the good of the society at heart. He was a wonderful administrator and his name carried prestige. After a few years the more modern and progressive artists began to feel Kroll was not modern enough to represent them and that he was getting all the publicity. They voted him out. I tried to make them see what a wonderful job he had been doing and that he was a man who would not be easily replaced. I was unsuccessful. A very fine artist, who had no organizational or administrative sense, was elected president. Everything fell apart and the society died. This was a valuable lesson to me when I was working with the Sculptors Guild.

CHAPTER TEN

SCULPTURE IS A MONUMENTAL ART. It depends primarily on a magnificent design. If these essentials are visualized and incorporated in a small work, they become stupendous and awe-inspiring when the scale is enlarged to monumental proportions, and the larger the scale the finer the sculpture becomes. There is a point however where enlargement becomes so far removed from contact with the sculptor that the work becomes straight decoration. Even then it doesn't lose its power and majesty; it does lose the human and expressive quality.

Small works are beautiful with life, but even they expand in sculptural quality when made life size, and when twice life size they reveal beauty and power on a scale never suspected. Maybe every sculptor wants to do monumental work—to see his powers and talent used in all its potential. There was a time when I wanted desperately to do monumental sculpture, but monumental sculpture cannot be done without a commission, and the agony and frustration of working through and with a committee is heartbreaking. And in the end I realized that monumental sculpture was not my true expression. A deep and profound contact with life and the universe was my contribution.

I entered a number of competitions. The ideas were a challenge and I enjoyed solving the problems, and I suppose there was always the hope that I might be chosen to execute them. I had a small machine shaft and some gears lying around my studio. I played with these and it seemed to me they might be used as a suggestion for an interesting monument. Then one day I met an artist on the street who told me that, as a gesture of good will, Russia was holding an international competition for a Lenin Memorial to be built in Leningrad as a lighthouse or as the Palace of the Soviets in Moscow. When I got home I studied my pieces of machinery and an idea took hold of me. I used the gears as a base and the shaft as a tower in the center and on top a simplified figure of Lenin himself. The proportions were beautiful and it had great simplicity. I designed the cogs supporting the column as workers. The interior was to house Soviet history and the inside of the column was to be decorated with murals depicting Russian activities. I wrote an appropriate thesis, had it translated into Russian, had everything carefully boxed, and shipped the model to Moscow at my own expense through the Amtorg Corporation. I received no acknowledgment from Russia that my model had been received.

My friends said, "In Russia an artist as an individual doesn't count—and as to letters, they just throw them in a big basket and that's it."

Then someone came back from Russia and said, "I saw your model on exhibition in Moscow. It looked great. I think you won the competition."

Nothing happened and I forgot the whole thing. Then one day I happened to open *The New York Times* and there was a picture of the proposed new Palace of the Soviets. It was to be the highest building in the world. And behold! There was my design for the Lenin Memorial incorporated on top of the proposed Soviet Palace. It was not a coincidence of ideas. It was clearly my model, sitting on a sort of wedding cake effect. I was perturbed and mentioned it to a reporter on *The Times*. The next day *The Times* reproduced a picture of my model and a headline, "Sculptor Charges Soviets Stole His Idea." This was picked up by the other papers but we never heard a word from Russia. This was at a time when the United States had just given recognition to Russia, and I thought it would be best to drop the whole matter. Of course, I never got my model back.

In 1934 I met Burnham Hoyt, an architect from Denver, Colorado. He wrote me that there was a fund of a hundred thousand dollars to build a memorial to Mayor Speer of Denver. It was decided to hold a competition and invite fifteen nationally known artists to compete for this monument. Burnham Hoyt asked me if I would design a sculpture in collaboration with a landscape design and setting which he would create. I made a number of small sketches. Burnham Hoyt was very enthusiastic over my design of two figures, each to be thirty feet high on an esplanade with a pool and fountains and running water. It was to be in the very heart of Denver on the plateau, with the Rocky Mountains in the distance. It would have been magnificent. He asked me to submit two three-foot models of the figures with his rendering. This I did; the models were very complete. Maurice Sterne, painter and sculptor, was chairman of the jury of seven.

It was announced in the Denver papers that Arnold Ronnenbeck, the Director of the Denver Museum, had been awarded the commission. When Maurice Sterne, who was already back in New York, heard this he was scandalized. It seems I had been first choice and Ronnenbeck had been fifth. He at once wired and protested and all hell broke loose. There were screaming headlines all across the front pages of the Denver papers and a terrific scandal seemed to be in the making. Ronnenbeck's friends, it was suspected, had maneuvered things so that he would get the commission regardless of the jury. It was war. I was out of it, on the sidelines. It was fought over for a number of years and in the end there was no monument. The money was given to the hospital.

At the time of the Texas Centennial I won a commission for a monument to the pioneer woman of Texas. I had made a family group and thought it suitable. I did not take it very seriously. It was an open competition and I didn't think I stood a chance in the world. When reporters arrived at my door and said I had won, I couldn't believe it. When I sent in my model I wrote a short thesis stating that, while as an artist I preferred unclothed figures and was presenting my model unclothed, if there were any objections I would be glad to clothe their nakedness in simple garments that would not interfere with the sculptured forms. The uproar in the Texas papers was over the question of nudity. The newspapers said that if a Texas pioneer had gone around in such a state of nudity he would have been strung up on the nearest tree—and here was a woman with two children and no wedding ring on her finger as a symbol of a Texas pioneer. Gutzon Borglum was down there at the time and I was told that he said my figures looked like a bunch of apes. He was a traditionalist and a politician; he could never have liked my work. The art committee and the jury put up a fight, but the Board of Control maneuvered and juggled the funds and in the end gave it to another sculptor, Leo Friedlander.

On the Denver thing I worked very hard in collaboration with Burnham Hoyt and felt we really had something fine. Not being allowed to carry it out was a great disappointment. The Texas competition I had never taken seriously. But this all happened at a low moment—the depression, no sales, my "Spirit of the Dance" thrown out of Radio City, this Denver affair, all the trouble I had with the Fine Arts Commission in Washington over my "Franklin." On top of all this I got a letter that my son Tessim, who was just about to graduate from Johns Hopkins University, had to be operated on for appendicitis; and Marguerite had to be taken to the hospital to be operated on for a tumor and was brought home on a stretcher. It was a nerve-racking period. Just too much at once.

After this I had two commissions that were a pleasure. The Mayo Clinic in Rochester, Minnesota, was building a new diagnostic building and planned to use both murals and sculpture to add interest and beauty. Ellerbee and Company were the architects, and they had an art coordinator, Warren Mossman, who had worked out an impressive program to use art in this building. They asked me if I would be willing to do the sculpture.

I wrote as I always do now, "After you have eliminated all other possibilities, I would be glad to consider a commission, but I will not enter any competition."

Mr. Mossman wrote back that this was not a competition; he wanted to consider the best art possibilities for the building. He would like me to collaborate and see what we could work out. He sent me blueprints and the schematic material. The subject was "Man's achievement through labor." I made several sets of drawings and sent them out. After some very amiable discussion, we arrived at a satisfactory idea and composition. I made four small models, which they approved, and I enlarged them to full size. They were cast in bronze and shipped out to

Rochester and hung on the building. Later when I went to Des Moines, Iowa, as visiting instructor on the Cowles Grant, I flew over to Rochester and saw my sculpture in place. It was about eleven in the morning—the light was superb and the figures were most impressive. I was thrilled by the impact I got from them. They are in high relief and project from a sheer slab of white Georgia marble sixteen stories high and a block wide. They are hung on stainless-steel rods, projecting and casting shadows on the building. It was a most satisfying commission for everyone concerned.

James E. Shepard was one of our great Negro educators. He started with a log cabin and a few pupils and became founder of the North Carolina College at Durham. I was asked if I would consider making an over-life-sized statue of Dr. Shepard as a memorial. I do not like to work from photographs, a contact with the living man is worth more than any amount of photographs. But when a man is dead there is no choice. Of course they wanted a likeness as well as a work of art. I tried to give them both, and while the statue is more realistic than most of my work it is still impressive. Ordinarily I would not make a portrait statue, but Dr. Shepard was such a wonderful man and accomplished so much in his lifetime that I was happy to do this. It stands on a plot with green grass and flowers in front of the entrance of the college. I attended the unveiling. It was a charming ceremony. I donated my fee to the college scholarship fund.

During the depression there were many attempts to do something about it. The architects got together and promoted the idea of a World's Fair. I went to a number of meetings. Each artist was asked to do a monument; we were to be paid five per cent of the cost of enlarging, casting, and so forth—there is never any money for anything in a project like a World's Fair, at least not for the artists—they just do it for self-satisfaction and fame! I submitted a sketch of two figures, male and female, in a posture of a dance. The figures were seated back to back—quite angular postures using space between forms—but the man's arm was around the woman's figure, evidently too close to her breast. It seems you can have almost unlimited sex in ads and publications but never a breath of its existence in public art. The architects had been enthusiastic over my sketch but when it came down for the final decision of the commission everyone was very strange.

"Oh, oh," I thought. "Something's going on."

They told me the sketch I had submitted was not the kind of thing they wanted for the World's Fair. It was a bit suggestive. Mr. Winthrop Aldrich, the president of the Fair, didn't believe in sex, at least for the masses. He was afraid the crowds might find too much of it in my figures.

They asked me to submit another sketch.

I said, "Gentlemen, this Fair has to be built and it has to open. We have spent six months on this already. It takes lots of time to create and enlarge and cast a plaster model full size. If you want my work represented in the Fair you had better send someone around to my studio and see if you can use a model I have already made. There is no time for me to make a new one."

William Delano came to my studio. I had a number of models I had made at the time I had had the Denver Monument in mind. Delano liked one of a group of figures flanked by two horses. He thought it was very appropriate because it was of working men, builders and pioneers. We called it "Builders of the Future." The committee was happy. The small model was enlarged by professional enlargers to eighteen feet and was to stand on a ten-foot pedestal. When I saw the plaster model enlarged I was horrified. I just couldn't accept it. Those professional Italian enlargers! They were so happy to be working on sculpture! My model was just a starting point for them to let go and create their own sculpture. They put all their rococo and baroque techniques into it. The horses looked like Coney Island merry-go-round horses and the figures were worse. The committee asked me to work on it and see what I could do to rescue it. They said I'd get the union wages of thirty dollars a day. I never was so well paid before in my life. I worked a month on the enlargement, climbing on rickety scaffolds under the roof. But I got it back into shape so that it was presentable. My "union wages" were the only compensation I got for the work. But the monument looked very handsome in the Rose Court at the Fair. It photographed beautifully and I got much appreciative publicity on it.

Holger Cahill, the head of the W.P.A. Art Project, organized a sculpture exhibition for the Fair of original sculpture from all over the country, a tremendous show in volume. I wrote the foreword to the catalogue. Everything was going so fast and furiously; the deadline of the opening was so close! They had just laid the asphalt floor of the tremendous sculpture hall when they brought all this sculpture in. A lot of it squashed into the floor, which hadn't had time to harden. The grand opening was the next day. I spent the whole night until five in the morning helping Holger Cahill arrange the show. Of course we had helpers to move and set up the work on stands. We were utterly exhausted.

Juliana Force, Mrs. Whitney's secretary, was the hostess at the opening of the show and she had sent me an invitation to the opening. I showed my invitation to the man at the gate and he refused to let me in. I was furious—after working all night on the show for nothing, I was not going to pay to get in and see what I had done nor was I going to walk away. He refused to call anyone higher up and I stuck to my point. There was quite a scene and do I know how to make one! Finally someone took care of him. It was all foolish but to me it was just the last straw.

There was quite a fanfare with a lot of speeches. Mayor La Guardia made a speech and all I remember of it is his condemnation of everything modern and calling it distortion. I looked at him, this little man with his big head and his great long torso and his stubby legs—like a piece of African sculpture—up there talking about the distortion of the human figure in modern art. It was fantastic.

There was some wonderful sculpture at the World's Fair, none of it in permanent material—all in plaster. It was a question: what to do with all this sculpture? It made me ill to think of certain pieces being destroyed. I wrote to Robert Moses and asked him if it wouldn't be possible to put some of these monuments—where the artist had put in so much creativity, artistry, and expense—into some permanent form, if not in bronze at least in cement. Moses wrote me that they had no funds for this purpose—not even cement; that the Metropolitan Museum had funds to put sculpture into bronze but not this sculpture. So all this work was junked and buried in Flushing Meadows. I still have my quarter-size model. It may yet make a fine monument somewhere.

There is something which moves humanity in a sanctuary—a church, a synagogue, or a monument—regardless of whether it is modern or classical. In our cities of block architecture a religious edifice is a welcome relief and I always regret seeing one torn down "for progress." Nor am I happy at seeing the modern churches taking on the form of a school or a factory. I like the spire pointing to heaven and the dedication of a building to the spiritual needs of men. I was deeply impressed when I visited Dallas, Texas, and saw their beautiful new synagogue with its superb modern design and simplicity, and its most beautiful use of colored glass—not as stained glass windows but as walls designed in broad, subtle colors that diffuse an exquisite glow and mystery over the interior. I think in the final analysis it is a matter of taste and scale that gives a monument its expressive quality and makes an impact on the beholder.

I would like to record here the story of the Monument to Six Million Jews destroyed in Europe by the Germans. A Mr. A. R. Lerner had organized a vast committee with hundreds of sponsors, of which the Mayor of New York and Robert Moses were ex-officio members. The idea was to build a monument on Riverside Drive as a memorial to the Jews who were killed—"Lest we forget." It was decided to have a competition of seven artists. Lerner and Mr. Rogosin came to see me and asked me if I would compete. A small round plot of definite dimensions had been given by the city for this purpose. I was willing to do this because I felt so deeply about the horror and destruction visited upon the Jewish people.

In planning his monument, I asked myself how one could best express the terrible thing that happened. All people are deeply moved by such senseless, deliberate, and inhuman slaughter, but they should not keep this horror constantly in their minds nor have it constantly before their eyes. If so they would cease to be moved by it or even see it. We can only take so much horror. But the heroism and the grandeur of the Jewish people under persecution is something that can never cease to awe and inspire mankind. A monument that expresses this will always be an inspiration.

I tried to express the ascending power of a people in a mighty shaft, simple and expressive, above the Drive, which would be visible to the ships in the river. In this shaft I incorporated the eternal symbol of the Menorah—not as a thing apart but as an integral part of the monument, the culmination of light over the world. The sides were to be engraved with the story of the extermination of six million by the Nazis. One side was engraved in English, the other in Hebrew. On one face of the shaft I had the figure of a man, to be about twenty feet high. This man expressed the dignity and suffering of a people and their faith in their God. "In my distress I called upon the Lord and he heard me. Out of trouble and distress a new Israel was born." On the opposite face of the shaft was the figure of a woman protecting a child, expressing the strength and pity, the human warmth and generous help given unstintingly to the innocent little victims of these terrible times.

I thought it most appropriate that in these United States, where human life and individual freedom have always been protected by the Constitution, that this monument be built as a symbol of human rights and the dignity of man. I worked on this with the committee for over a year very seriously. The models of the seven sculptors were exhibited; everyone had his friends and followers and most of them wore blinders—they only saw what they had come to see. It was a very interesting experience, full of complications and controversy. And in the end the whole project was buried in committees, as so many projects are, although it gets a new lease on life every now and then.

46. *Black Cat.* 1941. Black porphyry. 16″ long.

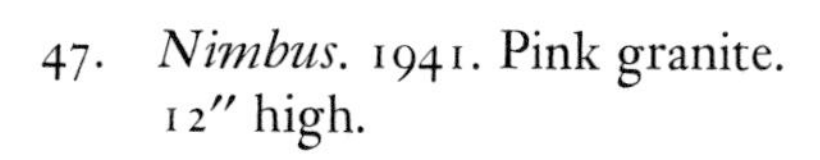

47. *Nimbus.* 1941. Pink granite. 12″ high.

48. *The Future Generation.* 1942–47. Botticini marble. 40″ high. Whitney Museum of American Art, New York City.

49. *Seated Nude*. 1942. Pencil. 18½″ x 22″. The Downtown Gallery, New York City.

50. *Awakening*. 1942. Colorado alabaster. 34″ long. Virginia Museum of Fine Arts, Richmond.

51. *Quest*. 1942–43. Pentelic marble. 23″ high. The Roland P. Murdock Collection, Wichita Art Museum.

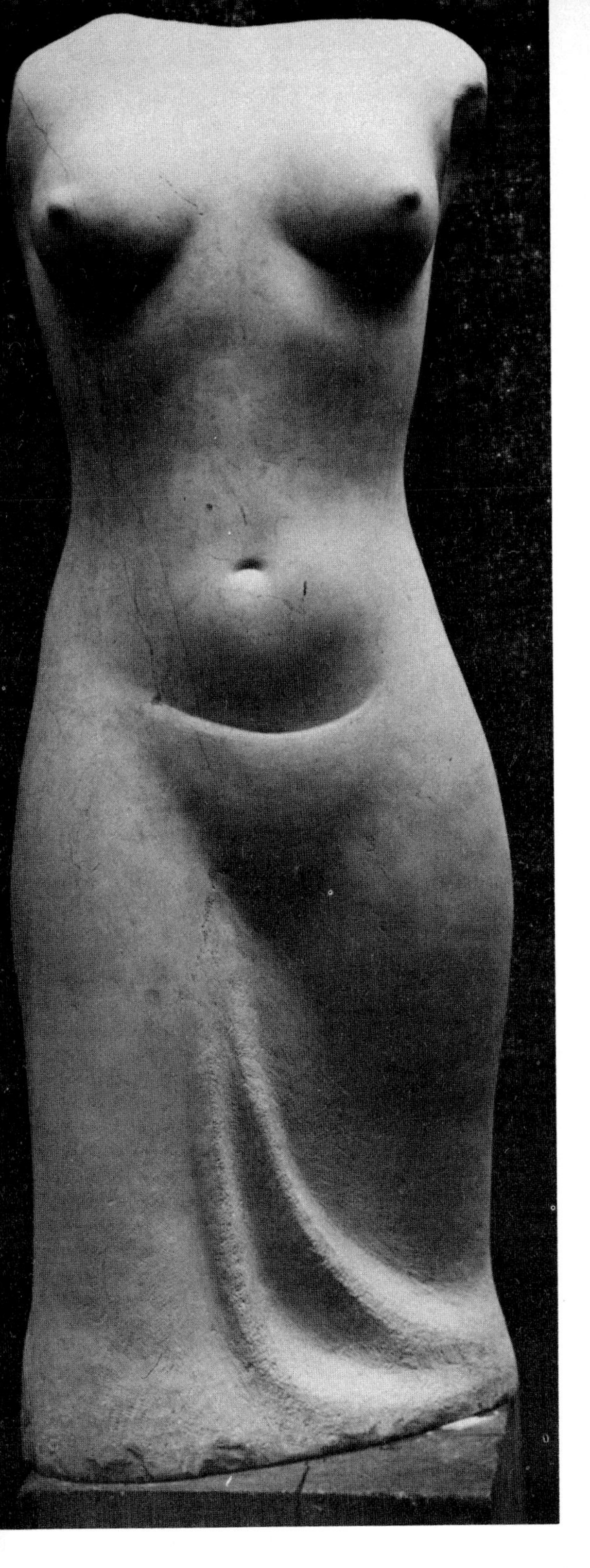

52. *Victory*. 1945. French marble. 43″ high. Collection of the Zorach children.

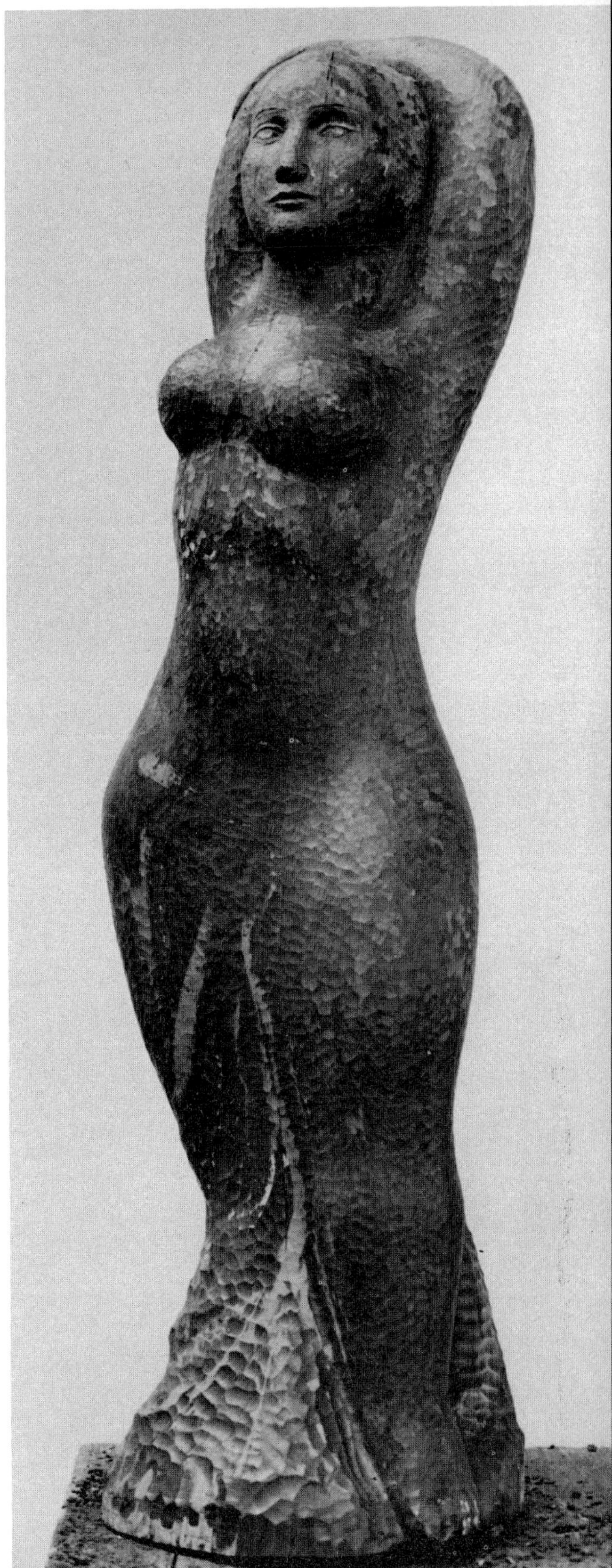

53. *Tree into Woman*. 1945. Rosewood. 55″ high. The Downtown Gallery, New York City.

54. *Head of Young Woman.* 1947. Pentelic marble. 21″ high. The Downtown Gallery, New York City. Head in background is *Tessim.* 1925. Granite.

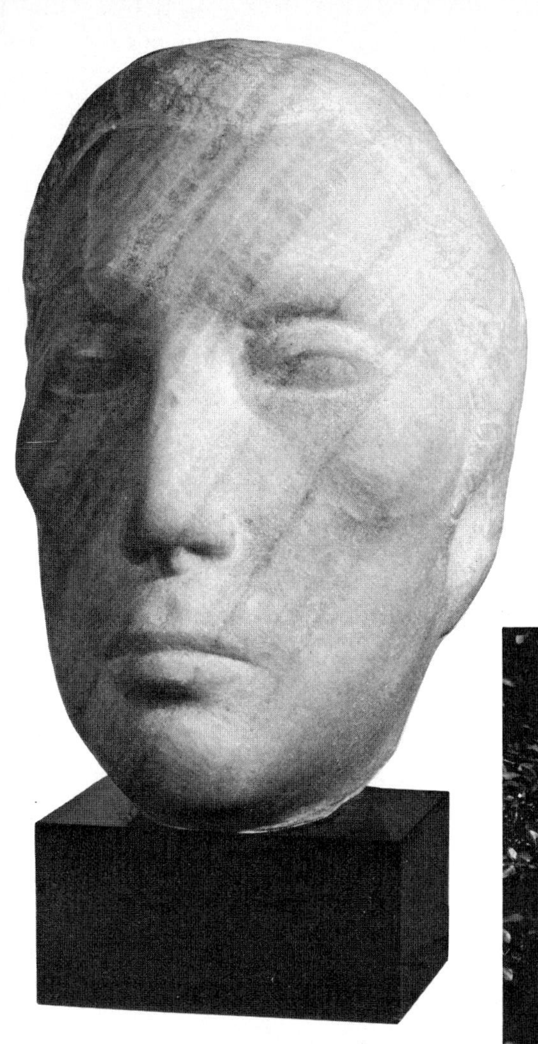

55. *Mask*. 1946. Onyx. 10″ high. Collection of Mr. and Mrs. John J. Carney.

56. *Devotion*. 1946. Granite. 34″ high. Collection of Mr. and Mrs. Laurance S. Rockefeller.

57. *Memorial to Six Million Jews.* 1949. Plaster model. 36″ high. Collection of the Zorach children.

CHAPTER ELEVEN

WHEN WE MOVED DOWN to West Tenth Street, we had the top floor of the old Cushman Bakery. Later on we took over the second floor for the children and William Holly. In 1930 we took over the street floor for a studio because I was bringing my two-ton marble, "Mother and Child," down from Maine and had to have a ground floor. The light was not good and the ceiling was low, but I managed to work there for a year or two despite the disruptive nature of life on Tenth Street. There were constant telephone calls, models who rang the doorbell looking for work, and all sorts of people who dropped in.

I looked around for a studio away from home and found a large skylight studio on the top floor of an old building, a former mansion, at 2 West Fifteenth Street. With a big empty room and fine light, I could spread out in all directions. Everything was peaceful, no telephone—I refused to have a phone. But every time I got an important call at home Marguerite would have to run over and give me the message, which made life very difficult for her. I finally put in a phone. I had been delighted with the idea that the building was a honeycomb of artists—all busy creating art, all minding their own business, and all absorbed in their work. I soon found the building was as full of problems as it was of artists. I was constantly bombarded with their problems: art problems, financial problems, personal problems, every problem involved in work and art and life.

Nat Kaz was a very young, talented boy just out of the Art Students League. He asked me to take him on as an apprentice. I thought it might be a help to him and also a help to me to have someone to keep the place in order and give me a hand. I gave him a corner to work in and told him to go ahead and do anything he wanted to do. He hung around and kept telling me he didn't know what to do. I told him to take his sketch pad and walk down Fourteenth Street towards First Avenue and he'd see enough material in one day to last him the rest of his life. One day I asked him to straighten things up and mop the floor when I left. In the morning things were just as when I left the night before. That afternoon I mentioned it again. In the morning the floor was not mopped and Nat's things were all over. I said, "Did you leave the little gremlins to do it for you in the night? I can't be a boss and I won't be a policeman. We'd better call it quits." Later he married our friend Kaye and took a small studio across the hall and we were all very good friends.

A young woman came in one day and said she was very interested in a talented young fellow from Canada and asked if I would take him on as an apprentice and let him work in my studio. The young man was Jean Lacaze. Jean had talent but he was much more interested in dancing and girls than he was in art. He stayed up all night folk-dancing and carrying on, and when I came to my studio to work in the morning I would find him sound asleep on the cot. I'd wake him and tell him I found it very demoralizing to have someone asleep in my studio when I came to work. I felt the morning was when an artist was fresh in mind and spirit, full of energy and ready to work. It made no impression; every morning he was there asleep. Finally I got so annoyed I poured a bucket of water over him and said good-bye to him. I was still fond of him and wanted to help him. That summer I had him come up to Maine and help out around the place and study sculpture with me. The first morning, he came down in white pants and a sporty shirt, and after breakfast he and a couple of girls lay out on the lawn relaxing. I said, "What do you think this is, a country club? Go up and put on a pair of bluejeans and get to work." He was pleasant to have around but not much help and he couldn't keep his mind off the girls; not that they minded but they were there to work—at least during the day. He always wanted to go out in the woods "sketching" with the girls—that's what we called it in those days. I soon gave up the idea of apprentices.

At the far end of the hall on the Fifth Avenue side lived Milton and Estelle Horn in a little studio eight by ten. There was hardly room to turn around in. There was a tiny closet with a little gas stove and sink. The toilet was a community affair down the hall. Milton Horn had a nose for antiques and picked up fabulous things at auctions for practically nothing—gold and silver ancient Persian armor black with grime, one of the most beautiful early American pictures of a child which I have ever seen. One day he came home with an ancient canvas covered with dirt and grime. He cleaned it and found it was a watermelon picture by Rembrandt Peale! I rushed down to the gallery and told Mrs. Halpert about it. She specialized in Americana but she said, "The world is full of watermelon pictures." She wasn't even interested enough to look at it. That fall she told me she had seen the most beautiful watermelon picture in the world in the Springfield Museum—marvelous! I asked Milton about it. He said it was his picture. Milton had paid five dollars for it and had sold it for several thousand. He would have sold it to Edith for a couple of hundred.

The Milton Horns went out to Chicago, where he became very successful doing architectural sculpture.

An old sculptor named Dykar had a studio across the hall. I used to look in on him once in a while; he seemed so much alone. He was carving a bust of General Pershing in Carrara marble. He did many prominent senators and even Presidents, which are displayed in the Rotunda of the Capitol in Washington. Although seemingly successful, he was very unhappy. He would come into my studio, look around and say, "I wish I could be doing creative work. I studied in Paris; I showed great promise but now all I do is portrait busts." He seemed very disturbed.

I said, "Why don't you go out in Washington Square, sit in the sunshine and relax. Then get yourself a nice model, do a figure composition, and get away from doing busts."

He came into my studio the next day and asked me to lend him a hundred dollars. He said he was broke. I went over to the gallery on Thirteenth Street and got a hundred dollars and brought it to him. He refused to take it, wept, and said it was very kind and no one had ever offered to loan him money before. He walked out and a few days later I learned that he had thrown himself under an elevated train. His wife came. She was a fine appearing woman. She said, "He didn't have to do that. He was not in need. He was getting along fine financially."

There was another instance where a young sculptor called me on the phone. He was desperate, he was broke, and he had to have a hundred dollars. Again I went to the gallery, got a hundred-dollar advance, and took it over to his studio. But when I went to give it to him he laughed and said, "Thanks, I don't need it anymore. I just sold something for a thousand dollars."

A young girl working at the Art Students League rented a tiny studio in the building. Now doctors and dentists love art and often prefer to get art instead of money, but I have yet to hear of a landlord that loves art. The son of our landlord, who ran the elevator at times, was quite taken with Lillian. We all said, "Why don't you offer to do his portrait and maybe he'll take it for rent." She did but he wanted his rent and wouldn't take the portrait. Next summer when I came back I looked at him in the elevator.

"What happened to your teeth," I asked.

"Look again," he said.

"Why, you've had your nose lifted too," I said.

"Right," he said. "When I saw that goddamn portrait I couldn't bear to look at myself; I had to do something about it!"

There were a number of young women working in a large studio next to mine—talented, serious young women. One of them was a quiet, unassuming girl by the name of Ann Weaver. I used to drop in now and then for a chat and sometimes I'd give them criticism—more advice and discussion than criticism. Some years later I received a letter from Ann Weaver asking if I would recommend her for a teaching job at the Norton Museum down in West Palm Beach, Florida. I was glad to and she got the job. Ralph Norton had bought my life-sized marble group of "Youth" for his museum and I had had some contact with him. Some years later our friend, Cramner Greenman, invited us to visit her in Palm Beach. I had always been anxious to see my sculpture in place. I gave a lecture at the Museum and Ann Weaver was there. I noticed in a conversation on art that Ann stood up to Mr. Norton and told him where to get off as far as art was concerned, and he liked it. A few years later his wife died. One night he took Ann out to dinner and asked her if she would marry him. She said she'd have to think it over, but she didn't think too long and she married him. Ann had been penniless when she married him, and while he did not leave her his entire fortune when he died, he left her a rich woman. Now Ann is spending her life creating a memorial to him—a group of huge figures, completely modern, which she had enlarged from her sketches and is having carved in granite. The group is to be placed on the grounds of the Norton Museum in West Palm Beach. It should make an unusual and striking monument when finished.

We have lived at 276 Hicks Street, in Brooklyn, for twenty years but I still feel as if we just moved there and that my life was lived on Tenth Street in the Village and this is just something that came after. There must be an excitement and a vitality in our first living that we never repeat. Everything was wrong with Tenth Street as a place to live. The rooms were numerous and small and the heat would never go from one room to another. We had to furnish our own heat. We had coal stoves, gas heaters, electric heaters, and even bought wood for the fireplace. It was all very expensive and we were never warm in winter. In a cold spell we couldn't work but had to go visiting or Museum stalking. The children's rooms downstairs had a little heat from Cushman's Bakery but it was turned off weekends and evenings. But we loved the place—so much of our life was there. We had put so much work and loving care into it.

When old man Cushman died, the bakery vanished. Instead there was only an agent who took care of nothing and was interested only in collecting the rent. Without the bakery heat underneath, the water pipes froze. Once we had to carry water for a whole week from the firehouse on Greenwich Avenue. In each emergency we would have to get the Board of Health on the job and they were slow moving. The wooden stoop fell apart, and someone dropped a cigarette in the debris and started a fire. Fortunately it was seen and put out. But we were disturbed.

It was hopeless. We gave up and found a top floor on Ninth Street. There was a magnificent studio but it was a five-flight climb. Here the plumbing barely worked at all and the heat came up with a blast at five o'clock when people came home from work and for the rest of the day it was mighty chilly. I couldn't do sculpture on a fifth floor with no elevator but I still had my Fifteenth Street studio. Marguerite worked in the top-floor studio. When we moved in we agreed that we would be really sensible and plan things so we would only climb those stairs once or twice a day. But we were not sensible, and in no time we were running up and down all day long. People climbed our stairs. I remember one day Edith Wetmore, a wealthy old dowager who collected art, came up to buy a picture of Marguerite's.

She said, "I have just come from Raphael Soyer's, where I bought a picture. Nasty little man, isn't he! A communist."

I said, "Raphael Soyer is the nicest little man in the world. Whatever made you think he was a communist?"

"Maybe you are one too," she said.

"Oh no," I said, "I'm an anarchist."

"Goodness," she said. "That's worse still. At least a communist believes in something."

But she bought the picture.

We were very sentimental about our old home on Tenth Street. It had our beautiful red floors, our murals on the kitchen walls and in the hall, our color schemes in the rooms, and our hopes and dreams and life imprisoned in its walls. At first we couldn't bear to go back and look at it. Finally we did after two years. It was empty and unlocked. All trace of us was gone. The walls were a gloomy gray with paint just slopped on; the floors were a soupy brown—no murals, no vermilion buttons on the hot water tank. There was nothing of us there, no tiny reminder that we had ever been there. The imitation marble blocks of the old Cushman Bakery were gone and so was the white wooden canopy that rounded the corner over the whole sidewalk. It was like walking on a grave; we never looked at it again.

My wonderful empty studio began to have more and more things in it until finally there was just a little empty space in the middle where I could work. Here I had done my seven-foot figure of "The Spirit of the Dance" and here I kept a full-sized model. I had a beautiful and enormous armature for the two figures I didn't do for the World's Fair. I had had a "mother mold" made from the large "Mother and Child." That was there. I also had just finished my "Embrace," a seven-foot group of two over-life-sized kneeling figures. And innumerable smaller works cluttered up the room. Besides the lack of working space, I began to be unhappy about a lot of things. The building next door had been torn down and the excavation caused great cracks in our building, and when I saw strips of daylight widening down the joint in the wall through the bricks, I decided it was time to move before the whole place fell into the excavation. Then there were fires—three in a week with sheets of flame shooting up and down the elevator shaft.

Everyone started to look for a new home. Milton Horn told me about a place he had found in Brooklyn—a deserted carriage house in the Brooklyn Heights section.

"Go look at it," he said. "I can't buy it, but maybe you could do something with it."

Now a carriage house is every sculptor's dream, a huge ground floor, high ceilings, and living quarters upstairs. I rushed over. The place was a complete wreck–just four walls, a tree growing out of the roof, as well as a crop of grass two feet high. In the back was a wooden building with stalls for twelve horses. There was a bin of oats and two express delivery wagons. The beams were rotting, the walls were bulging and peeling, the doors broken and boarded up. It was about as hopeless a sight as you could find anywhere in the city. But the lot was twenty-five by one hundred. South of it were a group of decrepit carriage houses but none were as bad as this. To the north things looked better. This wreck was next to a firehouse and from there to the corner of Joralemon Street were nice-looking, cared-for houses. This house was at the exact spot where an attractive neighborhood became a slum. Marguerite, who can see possibilities in the most hopeless things, was appalled when she saw this. She had to come back twice and do a lot of thinking. We finally bought it. We paid eighteen hundred dollars for it. And then we wondered what we could possibly do with it and however could we get enough money to fix it up so we could use it.

Marguerite had inherited Aunt Addie's house in San Diego. Real estate was worth nothing in California as well as in New York at that time. But we had no choice and it was difficult to find a buyer at any price. Today it would be worth ten times what we sold it for, but it was our only possibility of cash and we sold it. We also got a little money by borrowing on a few "worthless" stocks Marguerite had inherited–Standard Oil of New Jersey and American Tel and Tel. The Bank said, "Don't sell them, borrow on them. They are so low there's no place they can go but up."

We knew absolutely nothing about building a house. We liked our Ninth Street studio, so we based our plan on that. Marguerite made an exact plan for the whole place designed to scale, and we had a nice Swedish architect draw up the plans for filing. We figured one thousand for roofing, one thousand for floors, one thousand for plastering, one thousand for painting, one thousand for heat, one thousand for bathrooms, one thousand for plumbing, one thousand for carpentry, and one thousand for the kitchen and equipment. And believe it or not, that's as good a way to figure as any. The architect went down to City Hall and filed our plans, and then dropped dead on the steps. This left us with no one to supervise the building and no one to consult.

A friend who had the best intentions in the world got us a contractor. He was highly recommended and very pleasant and plausible and turned out to be a complete crook. We drew up a contract, everything was to be finished by fall. A friend was to keep an eye on the progress while we went to the country. We had no conception of how naive we were.

The wooden building in the rear had to be torn down and was to be replaced with a studio building of cement block with a huge skylight. The first alarming news was that the city required us to build a tremendous foundation to support this one-story studio. I now think this was a scheme on the part of the contractor to get more money out of us, but I was stuck with it. With each stage of the work completed, these crooks were to be paid and we paid them.

One day our friend wrote us, "I think you had better come down and see what is going on. It doesn't look good to me."

We were in Maine and had a house full of students. Our cook's mother had had a stroke and he had returned to New York. Marguerite had found a local girl, very young and very blond and pretty, who was supposed to be equal to the occasion. Afterwards someone reported to Marguerite that she lay on the couch in state with all the boys in attendance and everyone threw meals together and cleaned up. No one seemed to be unhappy. It was decided that I would stay with the students. After all, they were there to study with me. And Marguerite would go down to Brooklyn and look things over. We never saw her again that summer.

Practically nothing was being done on the house except what was being done wrong. There was a burst of activity when Marguerite arrived, but Mr. Brunton, the contractor, only did the things for which he could collect money; and ignored the related steps and materials. There was a suspicious atmosphere. Marguerite would ask the workmen if they were being paid and they would say, "Yes." (Apparently Brunton had told them not to let him down and he would see that they got their money in the end.) Finally she found out nobody had been paid anything—the men who cleaned out the trash, the men who delivered the steel beams, the men who built the rear studio—nothing was paid for, neither labor nor material. The two bandits, Brunton and his buddy, took our checks and divided the money between them.

Afterwards in court they were asked, "What did you do with the money?"

"I don't know," said Brunton. "It's all gone."

We had to stop the whole job, handle the liens in courts, arrest Brunton. Everyone was on our necks. For a month everything was tied up and of course no other contractor would touch the mess. And we were left with all of Brunton's crew—they had been paid nothing for their work. We couldn't fire them, we had to keep them all on and work with them. And in their way, they were really wonderful. They all felt so sorry for Marguerite they did everything they could to help. They bribed the building inspectors, a thing we could never have done, and with a five-dollar bill took care of the nice, honest-looking young workman's compensation man who was making Marguerite's life miserable. She never saw him again. When a big burly Lieutenant of Police was going to arrest Marguerite and all the workmen for laying a sidewalk without a proper permit, the foreman took her aside and said, "How much money have you got on you?"

She said, "Only four dollars."

He wilted, but he said, "Let me have it."

He took the Lieutenant of Police into the back—they were gone some time and presently the Lieutenant returned all smiles and walked away without another word.

Marguerite just hired workmen. She never thought about unions. One day she hired a painter. The workmen came in and laid down their tools.

"Do you know what you've done?" they said. "You've hired a union man. We don't work with no union man."

She had to get another painter. When the Italian stonemason I hired came to me and said he couldn't work for me and I asked him why, he said that the men I had working for me were crooks and wanted him to kick back half his salary. I went to Murphy, our head foreman, and asked him to please let the man alone. I had to get the place finished and if he had to have more money I'd get it for him.

Murphy said, "Mr. Zorach, I can't take anything from you. You've been stuck enough already."

I had come down for a few days only and when I saw the state of affairs I said, "I'm going to have a nervous breakdown."

Marguerite said, "You can't do this to me at this time."

And I didn't. I was so furious with Brunton I wanted to revenge myself on him by giving him compound fractures of the shin bones. I found the workmen covering up a rotten and dangerous section of wall with lathe and plaster. They said Brunton told them to do it, it was artistic. Then I knew he was taking me for a ride. Since we no longer had a contractor, Marguerite had to run around town and buy nails, sheet copper, angle iron, and brick to match the small neat English brick on the face of the building. The beautiful antique, random-width oak floor boards we got for the price of cheap pine through a friend. These fellows took a rake-off on everybody and everything, but they also hired a truck and went out to Jersey in the middle of the night at personal risk and brought back the radiators for the house when there was a long, drawn-out strike on and everything was tied up, and no one could work in the cold.

There was very little of the original building we could use except the walls. The front we didn't change, just repaired. We put in new beams where necessary, we laid a new floor upstairs, built a stairway, lowered the center portion so we could have an upstairs terrace and light and air in the two bedrooms. We put a big skylight in upstairs and another in the back studio, both resting on steel beams. We did everything very simply. And because we had to be there and tend to everything ourselves, we were able to see problems as they came up, make changes, and have things the way we wanted them.

And how did we get the money? I had to get the money and I simply went out and sold things to people—something I would never have thought of doing. Now I was under pressure, and necessity can make one do the impossible. I had never developed any ability to sell. I found it difficult even when someone wanted to buy, but by now there was quite a back-log of people who had said they were eager to buy some of my work sometime but never had. This was the time. I had to go after them and some of them came cross.

Marguerite stayed with our friends, Dr. Tom Shanahan and his wife Katherine most of the summer. They wouldn't hear of anything else. We have always appreciated their kindness and support in those difficult times. Marguerite couldn't sleep nights and was torn apart with worry over the decisions she had to make in the dark, without knowledge, and the unbelievable crises that were always coming up. When I came down in the fall we moved into a hotel in the neighborhood until we could get into the house.

About Christmas time the place was finished and we moved in. It was all we hoped for; a huge room upstairs where we lived and Marguerite painted, and downstairs a space twenty-five by one hundred feet for sculpture. The front forty-four feet were for housing and displaying sculpture, with counters and cabinets for small sculpture and paintings. In the center was a casting room, which also housed on one side a bathroom, a furnace room, and a storage room. Marguerite envisioned me doing all plaster work here, then showering, changing my work clothes, and coming upstairs. I'm afraid I never got the habit, I just track plaster through the house but she doesn't complain. In the back was my working studio, a large space with high ceilings and a tremendous skylight. Beyond this was a sort of glorified window box—the space the city made us leave, a long cement walk and a plot twenty-five feet by twenty-five inches. The yards in back are ten feet below, and there is a retaining wall. There was no soil, only coal ashes with the thinnest layer of earth. Here Marguerite planted a crab apple tree, a rose bush, a fig tree, a forsythia, and a wisteria. She didn't expect anything from them. The crab apple tree is now thirty feet high and the glory of the neighborhood in the spring with its deep rose blossoms and even furnishes a certain amount of crab apple jelly to neighbors in the fall. It has overcome all the shrubs in between and is now crowding the wisteria.

It is an enchanting place and we are very happy with it. We had a housewarming and I think a thousand people came—at least it seemed that way. I swear the floor upstairs settled an inch all around from the weight. Again I had all the space in the world in which to work. It was wonderful. But gradually work began closing in on me and the clutter began to accumulate. I am a hoarder, I just can't throw things away.

I can't get rid of old casts, old molds, work I don't like or want, and well-made packing crates—I might want to ship something. I even thought of buying the house next door, another empty wreck of a place, just to house my clutter. But when I saw myself gradually extending down the block from house to house, the picture was too appalling. I restrained myself. I am glad I did. The house next door was bought by a lawyer, Meyer Parodneck, who made an impressive place of it and who is a wonderful neighbor.

CHAPTER TWELVE

I TAUGHT ONCE A WEEK for thirty years at the Art Students League—from 1929 to 1960. At the League there are no requirements; it is absolutely free for all, like the Paris art schools, and this is its great value. This is what produces artists. Anyone can get in according to his needs; anyone can absorb as much or as little as he is capable of and at his own pace. He can come in today and be gone tomorrrow. There are no restrictions; he can be very young or very old; he can have great talent or none at all. All these people are thrown together, they see what everybody is doing. They learn from one another as well as from their instructors. No matter how bad you are, there is always someone worse; no matter how good you are, there is always someone better. The instructor takes it hard at first when the genius disappears after a week and the inept old lady killing time stays year after year. But the old ladies and the professional students support the school while the young and talented get a shot in the arm and move on to greener pastures. Some few talented ones stay for several years and one becomes proud to watch their development.

One time I was interviewed on radio. I was asked about my method of teaching.

I said, "I don't teach; I watch talent unfold."

"Well," said the interviewer, "what does this method produce?"

"It produces geniuses," I said.

Then he asked, "What are the names of these geniuses?"

"I never remember names," I answered.

I found the basement studio at the League very inadequate in every way. It was full of pipes of all sizes going everywhere and the ceiling was very low. It was crowded with the stands of the morning classes, an afternoon class, and an evening class. It had no facilities for sculpture. However, it was wonderful training in how to work under the most adverse conditions. The first winter I was there I wrote a report on the practical needs of a sculpture studio and handed it to the Board of Control. I was told the League had no funds to make any improvements. I gave up and did the best I could. I could at least give them explanatory talks on method and procedure and the philosophy of sculpture. I would tell them what they should do to produce a good piece of sculpture, and then it was up to them. As to my instruction, they could take it or leave it; they were free.

Really talented young people I left very much alone; I just gave them encouragement and guidance. But the elderly who wanted entertainment and a sense of self-expression and accomplishment, I was inclined to help along. They needed it. But even among these some could never get enough help and others wanted to do it all themselves. I had a dignified old lady from Boston in my class one winter. She dribbled clay on an armature tentatively and put a little ball of a head on top. She had never heard of Giacometti, she was just helplessly inept. I asked her why she wanted to do sculpture. It seemed a friend of hers thought it would be a good thing for her to busy herself with. She worked for months on this armature putting little pellets of clay here and there. I tried to help her, but she said, "Please, Mr. Zorach, don't touch. I want it to be all my own." When she had gone as far as she could, she asked me to get one of the students to cast it for her. I called in Raoul Hague, who was my monitor at that time and was eager to earn a little money casting. When Raoul looked at the figure he said, "But Mr. Zorach, there's nothing to cast."

I said, "I know it's an impossible job. Look here, you usually get fifteen dollars to cast a figure. This is a special job and I told her it would be twenty-five dollars. Now fix it up and cast it for her."

I asked her what she was going to do with it. She was planning to put it in her garden in Boston, and she invited me to come down and see it in place.

There was another very cute old lady named Fanny Benjamin. She was absolutely helpless with clay. I would help her and put her work together here and there and she was very happy.

But one day she said to me, "Mr. Zorach, I wish you wouldn't work on my piece. You know I sent a head to an exhibition in Rochester recently and I got first prize and my friends said I couldn't have done it myself—that you must have helped me a lot."

So I left her alone but she was completely hopeless. One day I took a tool and began cutting a little form into it.

"Please don't," she cried.

I said, "After all, Fanny, I can't treat you like an eighteen-year-old girl, you haven't that much time. I have to treat each student according to his needs."

Fanny began to weep and left the class.

Some years later she came in to see me. "You'll be surprised," she said. "Guess what I'm doing now? Non-objective art. And the Baroness von Rebay at the Guggenheim Museum likes it very much."

Every Christmas after that we got a non-objective card from her.

During and after the Second World War, the classes in the Art Students League were packed with soldiers and sailors studying under the G.I. Bill. The government paid their tuition, so the League benefited from it. Most of these men were hopeless and uninterested. It was very disturbing and demoralizing to the class and even to the instructor. The government not only paid the League to teach these men but paid the men to go there and be taught. Some merely collected the money and never showed up. Finally a roll call was instituted in each class but that, too, was easily taken care of. When the names were called there was always someone there to answer present. The minute the roll was through the G.I.'s threw their tools down and vanished. Those who stayed were almost more of a headache than the ones who beat it. One elderly seaman worked all winter on a tiny wooden panel of a bar, with whisky bottles, a mirror, and a stool with a lone figure sitting on it drinking. At the same time he was carving a winter landscape with a deer in the snow, pine trees, and a church steeple behind. If a student happened to move in between him and the nude model, he'd shove her aside and yell, "Get out of my way, I can't see the model." Apparently he had to see the model to carve a saloon and a snow scene.

There was an elderly army officer carving in marble; whenever I said anything about his work he would argue with me. He couldn't take a word of criticism so I left him alone. Then one of the students asked me to do something about him as he was demoralizing the whole class. He was going around criticizing everybody else's work, telling them what to do, and saying that I didn't know what I was talking about. One day, I asked him what he thought he was doing.

I said, "After all you're an army officer. You should have some sense of obedience and rank. I am the instructor here and you are in my class."

He said, "I don't consider myself a student, I don't want your criticism."

I told him then that he had no business in my class. The next teaching day he was still there pounding away at his stone. I asked him to stop pounding while I was criticizing the class so the students could hear what I was saying.

"After all," I said, "you have all week to pound. If you have no consideration for me, you at least should have some for your fellow students."

He said, "I have to pound. The government is paying me to work."

He kept on pounding.

I went upstairs to the office and told Stewart Klonis, the director, "Look here, I've stood enough from this character. We are not renting space here for people to work. We're running a school and conducting classes. You will either have to dismiss him or I leave."

It was difficult for the League to dismiss him because of their arrangement with the government, but somehow eventually he was eliminated.

There are two avenues always open to young artists as a way of making a living—teaching and doing portraits. To me both of these are legitimate if you don't get too involved in them. The danger with teaching is that after a certain point you find yourself trapped by your own teaching, and with portraits you find yourself seeing the sitter through other eyes than your own. I always tell students that it is impossible to be a fine artist and be a successful portrait painter. To do a successful portrait, you have to have the God-given gift for getting a likeness and a great desire to please people. I tell them this story. A pupil of mine tried to get a job at Macy's Department Store to sell pictures. They asked her if she knew anything about art and she said, "Oh yes, I studied at the Art Students League and have a very good understanding of art."

They said, "We can't give you a position with the art department here. We don't want anyone selling in the art department who knows anything about art."

She said, "I got a job in the corset department, and do you know, that's the most difficult place in the store to hold a position."

I asked, "Why?"

She said, "Because you insult so many people."

So I tell the would-be portraitists, "That is why it is so very difficult to be a good artist and a portrait painter. Because if you are honest and sincere, you insult so many people."

When Benito Buffano did a portrait of his mother, she said, "Benny, you should only do animals. They can never complain of their likeness." Only Epstein did his sitters in the raw and they liked it. Some of them were wise enough to forget personal vanity and realize that this was one way to achieve immortality.

I have done a few portraits of friends in bronze either because of friendship or because the abstract forms of the head interested me. And I have done certain heads as commissions. I did one of Etta Cone in Baltimore. I did a marvelous factual likeness. She was a Martha Washington type. But Matisse had made drawings of her years before and she was convinced she looked like these drawings. They too were a likeness but I couldn't see her through the eyes of Matisse. The head I did is in the Baltimore Museum with the Cone collection. I don't think Etta ever liked it; it was a new way of seeing herself. I had a miserable time making this portrait. It was during the war and Etta had arranged for me to stay at a hotel in the neighborhood. It was the worst hotel in the world. I was really shocked. The bed sagged horribly, the towels were rags, and everything was filthy. I got the room cleaned up and spread newspapers to walk on but I was miserable there. I remember Etta saying, "I hope you like the hotel. I really don't know what it's like now but forty years ago it was a very nice place to stay." I didn't like to disillusion the old lady, but if there had been another place to stay in the vicinity I would never have stayed there.

I did a portrait of Lisa Marin, the two-year-old daughter of young John Marin, Jr., and Norma Marin. I just put her on a table and gave her a lump of clay and we both finished at the same time; she looked at mine and said, "Oh–Lisa!"

I did a head of Dr. W. E. B. Du Bois which was presented to the Schomburg Collection on his ninety-second birthday. I felt there should be some real record in the way of a portrait of this fine gentleman and scholar who had devoted his life to the Negro people and their problems, who had edited and published *The Crisis* ever since our early days in the Village, and who at the time I did his head was living in our neighborhood on Brooklyn Heights. I occasionally like to make a portrait of someone who interests me.

I cannot see portraits made from photographs. The form is dead. A person talks, his eyes move, his mouth changes, his head moves, there's life, animation. The clay catches this life but it is lost in plaster; a plaster cast is dead. In bronze it comes to life again; you can see the form, it changes in every light—it lives. A true artist gets this living quality in a portrait. When students and amateurs do a head, too often it is like a corpse. When a great artist does it there's a living rhythm, there is pulsating life. That is why Epstein's portraits are so alive.

Marguerite painted a life-sized portrait of me before we left Tenth Street. She has seldom done anything of this kind. She had done a great many portrait drawings in pencil, an oil of Madeleine Islin, and one of Marianne Moore and her mother, members of our family, and this one of me painted on a six-foot canvas in dark, rich colors. She did it because there were no portraits of me and because she thought photographs ironed me out and made me too good looking, too much like a movie actor. She wanted to paint the side of me nobody else knew, the side that suffered and struggled and was torn apart by life and inner conflicts—not the gay and friendly side I showed to the world. I think she succeeded.

I have never carved a self portrait. In my youth I painted a few self portraits in water color and I made a few line drawings of myself from time to time. Sometimes in a weak moment I have posed for some female who was desperate to paint me, but I was always horribly bored and when I saw what she was doing I walked out. I couldn't take it. George Biddle painted a picture of Marguerite which is in the Metropolitan Museum. They call it "The Letter." When I look at this portrait I get a very unpleasant sensation—there is something in it that bothers me because it is not in the character of Marguerite. The one he did of his wife, Helene Sardeau, bothers me in the same way. And when George did a portrait of me I was horrified. Yet I think George has done some fine portraits—Frieda Lawrence, Man Ray, William Gropper, and the one of the old butler in the Museum of Colorado Springs.

There is a disconcerting thing about portraits. Someone does your portrait and you don't like it, your friends don't like it; everyone says it doesn't look like you. A few years go by and you look like that portrait and all your family and all your friends say, "What a good likeness." People, they say, begin to look like their dogs. Maybe this is somewhat the same thing.

I had had two life masks done. It is a horrible thing, like dying and going to hell—certainly not heaven—and then being resurrected, a terrifying torture.

When I showed the first one to Marguerite she said, "It's an interesting head. Who is it?"

So you can't even win with a life mask. A portrait pins us down. It gives us a definite image of ourselves. We can never wholly escape from it into fantasy. If a portrait is alive the layman says it reveals the very soul and perhaps it does, but it is not only the soul of the person; it is also the soul of the artist.

Albert Sterner, the portrait painter, said to me, "You know, most people don't like their own faces. I did a portrait of a celebrated actor one time and it was reproduced in the rotogravure section of *The New York Times*. The next Monday I got a telephone call from a man who said, 'Mr. Sterner, I saw the portrait you did in the *Times*. You are very kind to your sitters, aren't you?' "

Sterner replied that he always tried to do his best.

The man said, "I would like to have my portrait painted by you."

When the man came over to see Sterner, he told him his work was very expensive. That didn't bother the man and Sterner painted the portrait. The man studied it and was satisfied.

He asked, "Can you tell me where I can get this photographed? I would like about two hundred and fifty prints."

Sterner said, "Peter Juley does all my photography. He'll be glad to do it and you will be well satisfied."

He said, "Will you arrange to have two hundred and fifty prints made and have them sent to my office?"

Sterner said, "Certainly. And where shall I send the painting?"

"Oh," he said, "you keep the painting. I don't want the painting. I just want the photographs."

So Sterner said, "What's the idea?"

The man said, "You know, I'm a broker and I want to send these photographs around to my clients so they can see I'm a very good looking and upright gentleman and they'll be glad to have me handle their business."

I have always been interested in the dance. From the beginning I felt that, in order to handle sculptural form and have it function rhythmically, one had to sense the correlation of form in one's own body. I remember Martha Graham telling me that she used to study my sculpture for the expressive gestures she found in it. And I used to study her dance for the same reason. One of my students took me to a recital of East Indian dances by Hadassah. I was fascinated by the beauty of her movements and postures which, although derived from traditional East Indian dances, were authentic and lovely in their own right. Some time later I heard that she was conducting a class on Fifty-ninth Street. I wanted to talk with her and see how she conducted her classes. She gave a most beautiful demonstration of simple movements of the body. But when the group of students began prancing and clodhopping around trying to follow her directions, I had to look away and cover my eyes. It looked like the insane carrying-on in a snake pit. I asked her why she taught.

She said frankly, "I haven't the energy to travel around and give concerts and this is the only way I can make a little money."

I went back to my classes at the League. I looked at my students, the young, the old, the middle aged, a sprinkling of all kinds of people, and I realized that while I had asked Hadassah how she could endure the feeble attempts of her untalented beginners, I was actually doing the same thing. However, one builds up a tolerance for the feeble and the inept and is grateful for the few with real talent. After all, they are all human beings trying to find a place in the world to the best of their ability. They must have consideration and help in so far as they can absorb it.

I wrote to Hadassah a few times. I hoped to see more of her as a dancer and a creative artist. But each time her husband answered my letters. I took Max Weber to see her dance and he was delighted and wanted to meet her. So I wrote her, inviting her to come over to my studio to meet him.

She phoned, thanked me for asking her but added that, after all, she was married and her husband wouldn't approve.

She said, "He works hard in a book shop at Columbia and is very good to me."

I never saw Hadassah again. I realized she lived in another world—not an art world. Evidently she and her husband considered me just another admirer on the make.

CHAPTER THIRTEEN

MAX WEBER:

I KNEW Max Weber for fifty years and there developed a rare friendship between us. There is no one I have enjoyed more than Max Weber. We have wept together and laughed together and complained over the lack of recognition and the hardships of artists with each other. There are people in this world with whom you develop a casual friendship, and there are a few who leave a permanent impact on you, a permanent friendship. This kind of friendship, I think, is related to your own world, the world of art. Way back in 1914 I heard a great deal about Max Weber from various artists and especially around Stieglitz at his "291" gallery, where there was always much talk of art and artists, and there was always an undercurrent against Weber in their talk.

Weber was holding an exhibition at the Erich Gallery on Fifth Avenue; it was in 1915. So I went around to see the show. I saw this very little man vibrating around the gallery, wrestling with the pictures and talking with people;—a very intense man and very serious. I introduced myself to him. He was delighted to talk about his pictures and explain them to me. He had a picture there that I remember, "Women in Tents," a beautiful harmony of blues. There was also a picture called "Interior of the Fourth Dimension," which was a subject I didn't understand. I was much impressed by his seriousness. He approached art with the attitude of the scholar. Art was a serious matter of exploration of what he felt was the most profound reality of form, color, and space. It was not merely a two-dimensional presentation but a searching for a greater depth of communication. At that time he had a deep religious and racial conviction which permeated his paintings. From my early youth I was fortunate enough to have a true instinctive sense of who were the real artists and who were the phonies. Weber was a real artist, a person with natural-born talent and not an artificial or synthetic product.

I went around to Stieglitz after seeing Weber's show and was surprised at the unfavorable criticism I heard there. I later learned that Stieglitz had been most enthusiastic about Weber's work at first and exhibited it when Weber had first come back from Paris. But there was considerable jealousy in the little clique at "291." Stieglitz had considered Weber his protégé. Stieglitz and Weber were both too egocentric and Weber couldn't be a protégé. Stieglitz was an impresario who took artists up as much for his own glory as he did to promote art or an individual artist. Weber sensed this and resented it. He could not become a worshipper, even when it was to his advantage, and again he found it hard to share. Stieglitz's promotion with others. There is a certain psychology in some young people that makes them feel they want to make their own way in the world. They do not like to be promoted, and they are not willing to pay the price of promotion. I went back again to see Weber's show after listening to all the talk around "291," and I decided that Weber was a serious and extremely intelligent kind of artist and not a bit as I had heard him described.

Weber was accused of having adopted all the various techniques of Picasso, Matisse, and others of the time, but the fact that he was a contemporary of these people was ignored. If he had stayed in Europe he would have developed a reputation just as Picasso and Braque and the others did at the time. They were all just as much influenced by each other as he was, and yet remained individuals as he did. He was a precocious young man. He deserves great credit for the fact that when he came to Paris in 1905 as an art student, he sensed what was going on and his whole art instinct took him directly into the Fauve camp and into friendship with Henri Rousseau. No one else among thousands of art students going to Paris every year was that sensitive to the forces of art around him. I, too, sensed the same thing when I arrived in Paris; I knew I was entering a new world and could no longer live in the past.

Painting, to Weber and a few others in the small group around him, was not mere decoration or a mysterious private language into which esoteric meanings could be read, nor was it a picking up and using of new trick forms of art. It meant a searching for a greater depth of communication. I sensed this in talking with Weber and I felt that Weber's art was not decoration but communication with deep religious and racial convictions. He had a fine sense of harmonious relationships of color and specific patterns—making color and pattern a vehicle of communication and not the end—not degenerating into mere visual vernacular or momentary fashion. He broadened the range of my vision; he made me conscious of a more three-dimensional vision. To him it meant the third dimension that Cézanne saw in the world about him. To me it opened a new vista that led me away from painting and into my true medium of sculpture.

Recently Weber showed me a number of canvasses in various stages of completion.

"Max," I said, "to create a picture in a vacuum without benefit or hindrance of models, without the thing seen except with the inner eye, must be like tearing out your very guts!"

"Yes," he said, "how I suffer—yet what a joy it is to paint. You know how I love art, what it means to me. It is my life. See," he said pointing to his palette, "I use no tricks, just paint and brushes, and sometimes a little varnish."

Weber's life was not any more difficult than any other poor artist's; even less so, for in those early days he acquired a patron, Mrs. Nathan Miller, who loved and bought his work and did endless kind things for him as long as she lived. But he could never cease weeping over the hard lot of the artist and the terrible struggle life had been for him. He never could feel that he had the recognition or the position in art that was really his. He was consumed with misery and resentment especially over the success of Picasso. There is some jealousy in all of us, but I learned very early that all sorts of things go on in the world—people get prizes, recognition, commissions, they make sales. If you do not know the person it is not too important to you. You cannot allow yourself to be jealous of another's success just because you know him. It is absurd. But Weber was always terribly personal. He was jealous of anybody's success, especially that of friends. If I was lucky enough to have good things happen to me, he put me indignantly out of his life. But if I was ill or had something terrible happen to me, he was all sympathy and kindness, eager to do anything to help, calling me every day. But when something happened to him he couldn't stand sympathy, he just wanted to be left alone. The sympathy he wanted was for his lack of honors, his lack of appreciation by the public and the art world. I believe suffering is part of life and is necessary to the development of strength and quality in a person. That is, up to a certain point, not to the point where it destroys a person. Weber believed recognition and adulation too early in life is not healthy.

There is a power of expression, of awareness that runs like a thread of permanence through Weber's art, a rare and personal flavor—a translucency and bloom in his color, a beautiful tonal quality that is peculiarly his own. Spirit and form and color are welded into life, a complement of intellectual power and emotion. He could descend into the depths of gloom, overwhelmed with the suffering and injustice of the world, and he could sparkle with fun and dance with joy before a beautiful work of art or a beautiful song. Here was a biting wit, a twinkle in the eye at the absurd tricks of life, and the naive excitement of a child at a new revelation of art or a new manifestation of the human spirit.

ORONZIO MALDORELLI:

Back in 1936 I accidentally bumped into Oronzio and Tillie Maldorelli at the Grand Army Plaza subway entrance in Brooklyn. Oronzio and I had been students together in the Academy and, while I had seen his work around at exhibitions, I very seldom saw him. I was on the jury for sculpture to be used in the new Post Office in Washington. I suggested that he send in photographs of his work for the competition. He was awarded one of the twelve postmen to do. After that we saw quite a bit of each other. We became very fond of both of them and spent much pleasant time together. He was teaching sculpture at Columbia University, and for several years I gave lectures at the summer sessions. I would visit Oronzio and talk with his students and, when he was ill, take over his class for him. One winter he had to go South, and I substituted for him as instructor of sculpture at Columbia. His students went in for direct carving and produced some fine work. Now that he is dead, I hear they are all doing welding.

Oronzio was an Italian, a classicist at heart. He loved the particular grace and sensuousness of the human figure. He felt no need to go into the world of abstraction or delve into the morbid and unhealthy crevices of life. There was too much joy and magnificence in the world for him to express. His work is beauty in the finest sense and conveys a lovely and sensitive human quality. Like so many of us when he was young he experimented with the more abstract forms of art, but they were not for him and he realized it quickly. He was depressed at the trend of sculptors towards the ingenious devices and contraptions of a conglomeration of junk. He was not interested in clever, intriguing, and fashionable direction in sculpture. He had something else to say and give to the world.

To Oronzio the female figure was the most wondrous thing in the world. His work is a paean to the warm, luscious, sensitive, and tender half of humanity that is woman.

HUGO ROBUS:

There are artists who follow the trodden paths but rise above the others in stature. And there are odd souls—hardly of the art world—who draw from within themselves some ingrown form that is wholly theirs and amost unrelated to life or humanity or art. Hugo Robus is such an artist. For years in his loft on Fourteenth Street, where he and his wife, Irene, lived, he produced large sculptural creations in smooth white plaster—strange, rotund, boneless forms. It was sculpture of a sort of strange elegance and born of weird fantasies. The man himself was handsome, quiet, restrained, and strictly conventional. He was an ingrown type, a kind of tortoise who rarely emerged from the folds under his shell. But his work became more and more strange, expressive, and superb, making one question; what was going on inside the man? What fires were burning, and what reactions to life were being expressed and evolved in these fires?

JACOB EPSTEIN:

To me Jacob Epstein is the greatest sculptor of this age, just as Rodin was the greatest sculptor of his time. Although born in America and holding an unquestioned position in England, the country of his adoption, he has never been well known or appreciated in this country except by the few. He has never been promoted by any dealer or clique, something that plays an important role in creating an artist's reputation in Europe just as it does in America. In 1927 Epstein had an exhibition here at the Ferargil Galleries. When I went to the show I was shocked at the way the sculpture was displayed; the pieces were standing around as if in a storage warehouse–on the floor and against the walls in a downstairs room without proper lighting and with odds and ends scattered around indifferently. When I met Epstein he told me he was equally shocked at the way his sculpture was shown and at the way the publicity was being handled. The Gallery had hired a young woman to do the publicity. She wanted to excite the public by sending out a release to the papers that Epstein's work was degenerate. This gave Epstein a jolt; he told the gallery he had never hired a publicity agent and would not have anything to do with it. The critics more or less ignored him and were unappreciative.

I met Epstein through Tom Benton. Tom had invited Epstein to dinner and I was surprised and happy to meet him. Later I visited Epstein at his apartment and met his wife and daughter. I remember Mrs. Epstein couldn't get over the way the old women in this country dressed and made up to look young–"as if it fooled anybody." She said the old women in England never pretended to be young and were content to take their place in the world as old women. Epstein was doing a bust of John Dewey while he was over here, to be presented to Columbia University. We became good friends. They had dinner with us at Tenth Street and I gave him a couple of my watercolors. He wrote me later from London that he too was doing watercolors and having a show of them. Jacob was most unhappy about the sculpture show and his visit to America. He told Felix Wildenstein what a fiasco it had been and Wildenstein was shocked. He said he would give him a real show at the Wildenstein Galleries any time he wanted it, but Jacob was through; he was never coming back to this country.

I've had many interesting letters from Epstein. We corresponded for years. Then, a few years before he died, he came over to America once again to see his daughter who was living in South Carolina and his brother, Dr. Irving Epstein on Long Island. I suggested that Dr. Epstein ask Mr. and Mrs. Max Weber to his home to meet Jacob. Dr. Epstein thought he'd have a nice dinner of lobsters. Jacob loved them and so did Marguerite and I. But it turned out that the Webers wouldn't touch them because they were not kosher. It was a rather difficult moment for everybody, but we all saw it through and had a very pleasant evening in the end. I took Jacob to the Museum of Modern Art.

He was pleased to see that his "Mother and Child" in bronze was exhibited in the museum garden, but when he saw the huge Jackson Pollock he said, "I notice he wrote his name perfectly legibly. Why didn't he make his name as illegible as his painting?"

I always felt as if Jacob was an older brother of mine. People said we looked alike. It is a curious thing that many sculptors have something similar about them, a sort of family resemblance. People used to stop me on the street thinking I was

Lachaise, and certainly I think there may be a sort of family resemblance between Chaim Gross and Lipchitz and myself.

Jacob Epstein was a man whose medium was essentially bronze. He worked in clay as if it were molten metal, alive and fluid. There is a tremendous vitality in his bronzes, a great power of expression, a dynamic and at times brutal power. Brutal is not quite the word. I should say an expanding and overpowering force. There is nothing pretty or sweet in his work but there is beauty, a savage beauty. His art had made an impact on our age. Sculpture, like any other art, to make an impact on people has to amplify its expressive power. Epstein did this in his work. He was a great intellect and had a tremendous appreciation and understanding of all the great art of the past. He was direct and honest; he hated hokum and pretense and did not hesitate to say so. In one of his letters, he wrote:

> . . . I am harassed by calls for work which I have foolishly agreed to do. I went for years here without any commissions of any sort, then when the commissions came I took them on. Now I am absolutely single handed & only have the plaster modeller to help me with the casting. . . . I want to write of other things. . . . We have now in London at our Modern Museum an exhibition of the latest "Living American Painters" large canvasses daubes I would say, empty of all meaning which have been shown all over Europe and hailed as examples for us to follow. I can say you know who these fakers are, fellows who haven't given one day to any kind of study drawings or paintings. These characters are taken quite seriously now & oust any one who is really capable. I am myself in a rather special position apart from all cliques, not at all fashionable, but sought after for all kinds of sculpture, for buildings and also portraits. . . . I enclose an example of the kind of silly (I cannot find it) abstractions turned out now. We have rubbish by Paolozzi, Moore and Hepworth and a dozen more as well as European. . . . The flood of "modernism" threatens to overwhelm us and destroy all values. . . . I am sure you ignore our silly modern rubbish and keep on as you always did."

Marguerite and I went to Philadelphia to see his bronze group "Social Consciousness," commissioned by the Fairmont Park Association. It completely overpowered Rodin's "Burghers of Calais" displayed on the opposite side of the entrance to the museum. This surprised me because I had always felt Rodin had great power and strength. But Rodin was theatrical and realistic while Epstein was mystical and remote, transcending the flesh. He took us beyond ourselves into a cosmic realization of life and art. "Social Consciousness" had been a commission and yet the artist did not compromise. In it is all the power and freedom and a great conception of the soul of man. To me there has been nothing done in our time to equal it.

CHAPTER FOURTEEN

DURING THE WAR YEARS—the Second World War—we had from five to seven art students living and working with us each summer in Maine. We had our cook, William Holly, so Marguerite was free to paint—and one of the boys usually helped around in return for his tuition. It was refreshing to have a group of young would-be artists around. There was plenty of room for them to spread out on our hundred acres with woods, rock hills, a lake in the woods, and a mile of shore. They worked outdoors and in my studio, in the attic and in the boathouse-studio Tessim had built down through the woods on the shore where the old shingle mill had stood. Sometimes romance got so hectic around our place that we were very disturbed and saw visions of headlines in the *Mirror*, "Zorach Love Nest Uncovered in Maine!" I certainly didn't want to be a policeman, but some of those girls were so young I felt responsible—unnecessarily so, it turned out. I guess I'm just old fashioned.

I remember one summer I gave Tessim and the friend who was staying with him a talk on the facts of life. I thought I had done a good job until John Kelley, Tessim's friend, said, "Mr. Zorach, wouldn't it be better if we were just fixed like cats?"

Aggie Straus and my nephew, Jason Schoener, spent several summers with us. It was quite a romance. We were very fond of them both and sort of hoped something would come of it. But they were both very young and the war separated them. We still feel Aggie is one of our daughters. Jason went on to become a fine artist, married a lovely girl from California, and has a charming old farm house on the island about three miles from us. He and Ginny and their two cats commute from California to Maine every summer.

Then there was Winslow Eaves, who developed into a real sculptor and is now living on a farm in New Hampshire and teaching at Dartmouth. One Sunday in Maine, Winslow and our cook went down to the village and rented a little sailboat from Mr. Peterson who kept the store. I can't understand why he rented it to them: neither one of them had ever been in a sailboat before—they couldn't even row. They started off up river with the tide, through Hellgate whirlpools and then Little Hellgate rapids, where even good seamen have drowned. The tide turned when they had almost reached Bath, and they turned with it and sailed down the Sasanoa to Wiscasset. The tide turned again and they started back for home. But by now it was getting too dark to see and the wind was against them; so they tied up to the shore, took down the sail, wrapped up in it and went to sleep—as well as they could, that is, considering our Maine mosquitoes. At dawn they started back and arrived in Robinhood that night in time for supper. We had no idea of what had become of them but we pinned a medal on them for "recklessness beyond the call of reason."

One evening Marguerite and I rowed across the cove to have dinner with some friends on Low's Point. It was the most lovely evening; we sat on the rocks enjoying the afterglow. Suddenly the water turned the color of molten lead and began to curl and spit dragon teeth. Black clouds rushed in from nowhere. I said we'd better go. We were a third of the way across the cove when the storm hit. In a minute it was wholly black, the wind and waves picked us up and drove us back against the shore. We managed to pull the boat up onto the rocks on an incoming wave and tied it to a tree. We never expected to see it again. We were cast up in a wilderness of woods, underbrush, brambles, and huge rocks—every size and kind. There were no houses, no roads, no paths in this wilderness for miles in any direction. And it was utterly black. If it hadn't been for the lightning we couldn't have seen anything. The thunder and the wind roared and the rain beat down on us. All we could do was hope we could work our way along the shore to our friend's house on the point, a good two miles away, feeling our way around every rock and cliff and boulder at the water's edge. We finally made it around midnight. They had been worrying about us and put us to bed with hot drinks. In the morning the sky was as fresh as a new-washed glass, the cove was like polished silver and our boat was standing on end where we had tied it. We found the students comfortably having breakfast. No one had missed us.

This is an age obsessed with security. To the young today, there is no such thing as facing life without money, without a job, with only courage and a belief in oneself and a belief in one's innate talent as an artist. It is not faith in a religious sense, because you do not count on God to see you through; you count on yourself to see you into life and into the future. Of all my students—and their number is legion—Winslow Eaves had the courage and this faith. My example may have been an inspiration, for Marguerite and I had this courage and lived by this concept. But the others wanted to be secure first and after that would come their art. Winslow worked with us in Maine. He was in the war, came back and taught in Utica for a year, married Faye, gave up his job and went to Paris, and when they came back they faced the unmapped future. With a wife and two small boys and the wolf sitting on their doorstep, Winslow took a job teaching art at Syracuse University for two or three years. But he was not satisfied to teach and do art on the side. He had the guts to give up his job and get a place in the country and make sculpture his life. This was no easy way but it was the real way. Now he does sculpture and teaches on the side. They are a great family and have my deepest respect and admiration.

It was in the winter of 1918–1919 that a socially prominent woman, Eleanora Theodora Laroque, came to take private lessons in watercolors from me. I gave her one lesson a week in the dry method I was using at that time. When I came back from California she wanted to continue. When I suggested she wet the paper and work the color into the wet paper she said, "Why that's the way I used to work, and you told me to work only on dry paper."

I said, "So I did and that was the way I was working, but I'm working on wet paper now and I think I get better results."

Like most students she followed my instructions implicitly. I told her it was valuable to try different methods and see which was most suited to one's temperament but this only confused her. She wanted to be told just what to do.

The Laroques had a beautiful estate near Bernardsville, N. J. We enjoyed visiting them, and the gracious way they lived. Their woods, their flowers, and their animals were all delightful. Mr. Laroque had the most handsome and immaculate pigs we had ever seen. The Laroques had a delightful daughter with black hair and a charming way about her. She grew up into a lovely but restless and unhappy woman. In turn she had a beautiful child, Diana. Diana was thirteen when I first saw her and I fell in love with her at once. She was a very talented child with a passionate love of animals—a spirited thoroughbred little creature.

The following summer Diana's mother asked us if we would take Diana to Maine for the summer and let her study with us. We loved having her around and she developed in her work and her personality. There were a number of students at that time and we had a special summer. Diana's mother was a woman with conflicts, married twice and divorced twice and considering a third marriage. Her own life was so unsettled and involved that she had no time for Diana. But I do not think it left any scar on Diana. We practically became her second parents, giving her the love and attention every child needs. She was with us many summers and in the end she married one of our students, Bob Folley. Bob was the son of an Irish family in New Jersey; his father was in the trucking business. They had no money and lots of children but they were as warm and outgoing as Diana's people were ingrown and tight in their world, and Diana loved it. Bob was a talented fellow, full of life; he took no nonsense from anybody, even Diana; he was rough, bold and tender. They got married and went to Europe on practically no money, had a baby there, bought a motorcycle and rode all over Europe, even going into Greece. Bob made a tray with straps to hold the baby in front of Diana and she sat behind him on the motorcycle. They slept beside the road when necessary and bought what food they could along the way. Busses ran them into ditches and cars almost ran over them; their life resembled "The Perils of Pauline," but it was great adventure. Now they live in the country and have three small, handsome boys. Both Bob and Diana have the gift of making any place they live charming. One way or another Bob makes a living, not at art but in projects mostly related to architecture. Neither of them has much time for art at the moment, but Diana makes most imaginative and creative little animals in ceramics. They have a kiln in the cellar and fire them. Bob is one of those men who can do anything and do it well. Nothing is too much for him.

Bob and Diana lived two summers in our boathouse—the first year they were married and the year after they came back from Europe. There were no conveniences of any kind in the boathouse; no water, no electricity, nothing that meant convenience or comfort, but they managed and they loved it. It is an exquisite spot. The path to the boathouse is a rare pleasure, through the woods of tall pines and old oaks, along a cliff with fresh green moss underfoot hiding the carved stone steps of earlier generations. It drops sharply over the cliffs and down to the shore; only the young and surefooted can manuever it easily, and if you are the kind that can make it you can do without conveniences in the pleasure of living in such a spot.

Sometimes Bob and Diana stop for a few days with their children and would not think of staying any place else, and when they talk about it together we can see how much the years of living with us meant to them and it makes us glad.

I got up one morning and discovered a sixteen-foot dory on our lawn in front of the house. I wondered how the devil it ever got there. The next morning I saw an elderly man tinkering with it and I asked him what was going on.

He told me, "I just bought it from Mrs. Westall down the road. I intend to use it to go fishing." He said he was a building contractor from Marblehead and had lost his money during the depression; that someone he met had told him about a deserted farm back in the woods along the Robinhood Cove shore and suggested he go there and that he could make a living off the wild blueberries and the fishing.

I said, "You can never make a living here fishing. Even the fishermen can't and they've worked here all their lives."

Then he told me he used to live in Maine on a farm. I thought for a moment and asked, "Can you milk a cow?"

So Mr. Farrow came to work for us. He had no natural enthusiasm for work and he was a genius at avoiding it. He smoked a pipe and that pipe had to be emptied and cleaned fifty times a day. It was a magnificent ceremony. Both he and his wife insisted on living the role of superior people who had come down in the world.

"I've seen their kind before," said our neighbor, Ed Clary. "They arrive in

Robinhood with a suitcase, take to the woods and a year later leave with two loaded trucks and never do a stitch of work."

I let him live in the house on the hill which is now Dahlov's place, for the winter. It was furnished and I paid him a small salary for looking after our place. He had milk, eggs, chickens, and ducks, as well as the bacon he was smoking for us. In the spring he and his family would move back onto the farm in the woods. One spring we came up too early or he became too relaxed. The Farrows had moved out and left the place filthy. Marguerite was so mad she set off through the woods to their place to tell them to get right over and clean their mess up. There was no one home at the farm where they lived. The doors were open, the windows were stuffed with rags where the panes were broken, the yard was piled with trash. It was a fine old house with a huge kitchen with a counter running all around it, now piled high with all kinds of debris. In the center of the floor there was a pile of empty tin cans five feet high, left from the food they had lived on the previous summer. The sink was full of dirty dishes, and on the table were the cleanest of the lot scraped off—unwashed—ready for the next meal. After seeing that, what could we expect? Never hire people without seeing how they live!

When we arrived back home the barn door was off its hinges. I was fixing it myself when Farrow showed up. "Nice job you're doing there, Mr. Zorach," he said.

"Yes," I said, "but you are out of a job."

I made him come back and clean and scrub our place end to end, and I worked right along with him till I knew it was done. Despite his faults, he was a wonderful father to his three children. He always had time for them and made all the little things of life fascinating to them. He took them into the fields and made all the wildlife real and exciting to them, telling them all about the plants and insects and sea things. He was a true educator in his home. I never knew of his taking another job and I don't know how they lived. It must have been pretty tough. They never gave up the farm in the woods, and now their son, who became an artist and writer, lives there. One of the girls lives in Iowa, has a nice husband and children, and we enjoy them very much when our paths cross.

We first came to Maine during Prohibition. Ed Clary was town constable, a real, genuine New Englander. He would sit in our kitchen and tell us tales of rum-running and of how the rum-runners would bring the liquor into the cove and the local boys would meet them with a truck and deliver it to the right man. But "You wait"—he was going to catch up with them and the rewards were going to be great, both financially and politically. And who was the liaison man for the bootleggers? "Why, Walter is, of course!"

"But, Eddy," we said, "you sit right alongside Walter all day on the road truck working on the road together."

"Yes," he said, "but after dark I follow him and chase him in my Ford, and sooner or later he'll lead me to them."

I said to Katie, our local washerwoman, "What's this about Eddy working with Walter all day and chasing him all night?"

"Sure," said Katie, "he chases him all night, but he wouldn't be mean enough to catch him."

One night by accident Eddy—who had just been appointed deputy sheriff—stumbled into a bootlegging operation on the other side of the island. It was a great day—until it turned out that the county sheriff was in on the bootlegging. Eddy got demoted instead of promoted!

Eddy kept a skiff down at our shore. Early in the morning before we were up Eddy would pass by and pick a bunch of flowers from Marguerite's garden without asking. We found out that they were for some woman on MacMahan Island, where he worked days.

On his way to MacMahan he had to hug the opposite shore to get through the terrific current in Goose Rock passage. One day I was going to bail out my motorboat after a storm and stepped into Eddy's skiff. My foot went right through the bottom. The next morning I got up early to tell Ed about this but he never came by. Later I noticed his boat was gone from the shore. I was certain he'd gone out in the skiff and drowned; everyone knew he couldn't swim. I blamed myself and felt terrible. Every day I waited to hear the sad news. Six days later I saw Eddy going by the house. What a relief! I mentioned the hole in the boat.

"Oh, that," said Eddy. "The hole is in the bow and I sit in the stern and row and that keeps the bow up out of the water. I'll get around to fixing it one of these days."

Ed was always a little devious and he was especially so about work. But we enjoyed him and his indirect ways and his stories. When he began opening our beehives in the winter, taking the honey out and leaving the bees to starve and digging under our potato plants and sneaking out the potatoes and leaving the wilting vines untouched to deceive us—that was too much.

Nevertheless, I like these old state of Mainers. They used to stop in for a word when I was working in my studio. One thing about a Maine man, he never stops in for too many words—just enough. Walter Reid was a native islander and had been a clam-digger, but he had a flare for high finance. I remember one spring Ed Clary stopped by and said to me, "That old clam-digger, Walter Reid, went down to Wall Street and made a hundred thousand dollars in the dead of winter."

In his later years Walter Reid gave miles of beautiful beaches and sea cliffs to the state. The first public beach in the entire state was Reid State Park.

Another time Lon Twombley asked me what I had done with the cat I was carving out of a boulder that I had picked out from a load of gravel he sold me. I said, "I took it down to New York and sold it to Mrs. Rockefeller for a thousand dollars."

Twombley's eyes popped out. "Highway robbery," he said.

A few years before, Lon's housekeeper committed suicide by jumping in the well. His neighbors always said he threw her in, but when they found she had left a note and since Lon could neither read nor write, we all knew he didn't go that far even if he may have made life not worth living for her. He was a violent man when drunk and he was almost always drunk. At eighty he was strong as an ox and moved huge rocks all by himself when rebuilding our road.

Cal Powers was a lobster fisherman in the village. He was one of the local boys who had married the schoolmistress—a common fate of country school teachers. Agnes was a nice, intelligent person and our local postmistress. One day Cal was standing out on Blacksmith Shop Ledge with Bill Bunyon talking things over. "Now take this fellow Zorach. He's a curious one. He don't go around and do things other folks do. He goes around picking up stones and then sits around chipping away at them. Now that's a mighty funny thing for a man to do—just chipping stones."

Bill said, "You know he sells those stones he chips and sometimes he gets thousands of dollars for them."

Cal didn't say a word. He looked down at the granite under his feet. Then it came out, "Jees-us, we're standing on a gold mine."

One of our most enthusiastic patrons is the woman who helps out in the summer. Since Marion has been working for us she has developed a real love of art, especially Zorach art. We give her things and she has bought one of my best watercolors out of her wages. We took her to New York for a visit one winter and she had the time of her life. She exhausted New York and herself. She didn't miss a thing.

Joe Totman lived across the cove from us, with his ancient mother in a dilapidated little house. He slept in rags on an old couch and lived on parsnip stews and clam chowders. Joe was a powerfully good looking old fellow with a white mane of hair and old-fashioned, courteous manners. To us, he was a delight with his stories and his Elizabethan English. As he put it, he was a good axe carpenter and ready for any odd job that came up. But to the islanders Joe was a menace. He would never owe anyone a dime, but he would have no scruples about taking away anything of yours that you weren't using that he thought he could use.

Joe was insulted when anyone accused him of stealing. He would say, "If Charlie Campbell wanted that lumber I took home with me, all he had to do was say so."

It was said that the pictures on his wall were labeled "Stolen by Joe Totman" with the date and from whom. When Joe was eighteen he was sent to prison for rape.

According to Joe, "That wasn't rape! I just made the mistake of getting caught, and what could she do but yell 'Rape!' "

When we first met Joe he was seventy, but the village women still shuddered when he went by, and even put a chair under their doorknobs nights. To them he carried an aura of excitement and danger all his life.

One winter he got hungry and he started thinking about all the jars of food

Marguerite had put up that summer going to waste in our cellar. He had no trouble picking the lock on our front door, but the old lock broke and when he wanted to leave he couldn't get out. He could have gone out any window or any other door, but he lost his head and started to chop his way out.

One summer a very young and pretty girl from a Theological Seminary came to hold services at our Robinhood meeting house. We were amazed one Sunday to see cars driving onto our front lawn and across the meadow into the woods. No one stopped or said anything to us. We finally found out there was to be a baptism—a real dunking—on our shore. And who was it to be? Why, Joe Totman himself! It was quite a feat for a five-foot girl to dunk a six-foot, two-hundred-pound man—and in the ice-cold water of our cove, stirring up the black mud of the clam flats. But it was done and Joe was saved. Not that it changed him a bit, and when the summer was over and the lady minister left, Joe's church-going days were over.

Joe had a good sized sloop. It was old and I suspected pretty well rotted—I knew the sails were so delicate you didn't dare lay a hand on them, but Joe could handle a boat and he treated this one tenderly. He took Tessim and me on a two-week trip up to Bar Harbor. We stopped at all the little harbors along the way and I sketched and we tied up and waited out the fog. We even survived a hurricane that was taking us right up onto the shore and into the hills. The wind died in the nick of time. I paid Joe by the day—it took us eight days to get to Bar Harbor—we just seemed to inch our way along the coast. When I told Joe the money was running out—like an old horse Joe turned and headed home. We were back in three days!

Then one day Joe dropped dead down on the Five Islands wharf.

Ed Clary, who had despised Joe with an unholy hate, for which he may have had reason, stepped up and pulled off Joe's boots. "Just a shame to waste that good pair of boots," Ed said, as he walked off with them.

CHAPTER FIFTEEN

KENNETH FRANZHEIM, a modern architect in Houston, Texas, had at various times asked me to submit estimates for architectural projects he was working on. Some years before, he had bought my large figure, "Vita Nova," and placed it in the entrance to his garden. He was most enthusiastic about my sculpture and always hoped we might collaborate on one of his building projects. In April of 1953 I got a letter from Franzheim. He was preparing designs for a new bank building in Houston and asked if I would be willing to make a few preliminary designs for reliefs to be placed over the three building entrances. He said the sketches would be purely speculative on my part. I did not really want to become involved in an architectural project; I knew from experience that I was not temperamentally equipped to cope with committees, workingmen, foundries, and all the contractual problems involved. But Franzheim was very persuasive. For six months, I worked up various drawings and ideas and sent Franzheim some simple pencil drawings to fit his blueprints. He mailed these back to me with suggestions. I, then, proceeded to develop the sketches in color; since at that time they were thinking of using enameled aluminum. My idea at the time was to express, in somewhat abstract design, ideas relating to banking and its relationship to people and industry.

Franzheim kept these designs for months without saying a word. I'd forgotten all about them and was happily working on my own projects in Maine, when I got a telegram asking me to come to Texas to discuss the question of sculpture with the president of the bank and the board. They wanted me to bring with me a portfolio of photographs of my work, my books, my newspaper clippings, etc.

To my surprise, when I showed my photographs and newspaper clippings to the board, they were very pleased and I had a pleasant and satisfying meeting with them.

The question of how abstract or non-objective, the question of costs, the question of a competition and what that would involve, all came up and were discussed. I explained to the board what a competition involved and told them of my experiences as a judge in various governmental and private competitions. I explained that no sculptor of standing would enter a competition without being paid a substantial fee for his sketches, and that most sculptors of standing would not enter a competition, fee or no fee. I warned them if a jury decided on a certain design they might not like it—and there would be no end of trouble.

I said to them, "Gentlemen, you have seen the kind of work I do and this is the kind of sculpture I would do for you. If you do not want this kind of sculpture, we will go no further."

They didn't know what to say. I asked them who would pass final judgment and approval of the models I submitted and they said, "Of course we don't know anything about art. Mr. Franzheim is the architect of the building and our advisor, and whatever he approves of we will agree to."

I spent the evening with Franzheim and Mr. and Mrs. Bryan. Mr. Bryan was president of the bank at that time. We discussed the subject matter of sculpture and art and life in Texas. Mr. Bryan gave me a copy of his letter to Tamayo, who had been commissioned to do a mural for the interior of the bank. In it, he explained that in the abstract treatment of the mural he hoped Tamayo would incorporate something of the background and history of Texas so that people coming into the bank would see something with literary meaning, something about Texas which they could understand and take pride in. If I would try and incorporate these ideas in my sculpture he was sure the trustees would be pleased.

Tamayo did a painting of a sprawling nude fifty feet long that stretched all across the interior of the bank, while I tried to incorporate some of the uniqueness of Texas in a sculptural work of art. I was very foolish. Tamayo's mural is beautiful and the bank is very happy with it. My work was rejected, but for other reasons.

Everything was most amiable. Franzheim's assistant took me out to the San Jacinto Museum the next day to acquaint me with the past of Texas. On my return I submitted drawings, contacted foundries and enlarging shops for estimates and mailed them all to Franzheim. The estimates for the bronze casting from the three foundries I consulted were $100,000, $45,000, and $36,000. This gives the impression that the work at one foundry must be vastly superior to the others, but that is not true. They are all equally good and often their estimates are about the same. These estimates varied more widely than any I have ever come across. The foundries' estimates were for the large panel only; there would be two additional smaller panels to be installed over the side doors.

The design they accepted was of a group of figures. On one side there was a primitive figure of an American Indian and on the other, one of a man and a child representing education and growth. At the bottom was a figure of a nude woman, sitting on the ground, representing the Spirit of Texas. Sam Houston's horse was lying down behind her. All this was against a background of the five flags that

58. Zorach Exhibition at The Downtown Gallery, February 20–March 10, 1951.

59. *New Horizons.* 1951. Plaster. 44″ high.

60. *New Horizons.* 1951. Bronze. 44″ high. The Shelburne Museum, Shelburne, Vermont.

61. *Man and Work.* (Mayo Clinic Relief, Rochester, Minnesota.) 1952–53 Plaster model.

62. *Mother and Child.* (Mayo Clinic Relief, Rochester, Minnesota.) 1952–53. Clay model.

63. *Puma.* 1954. Labrador granite. 40″ high. Philadelphia Museum of Art.

64. *Reclining Figure.* 1954. Sienna marble. 17½″ long.

65. *John the Baptist.* 1955. Porphyry. 12″ high. The Downtown Gallery, New York City.

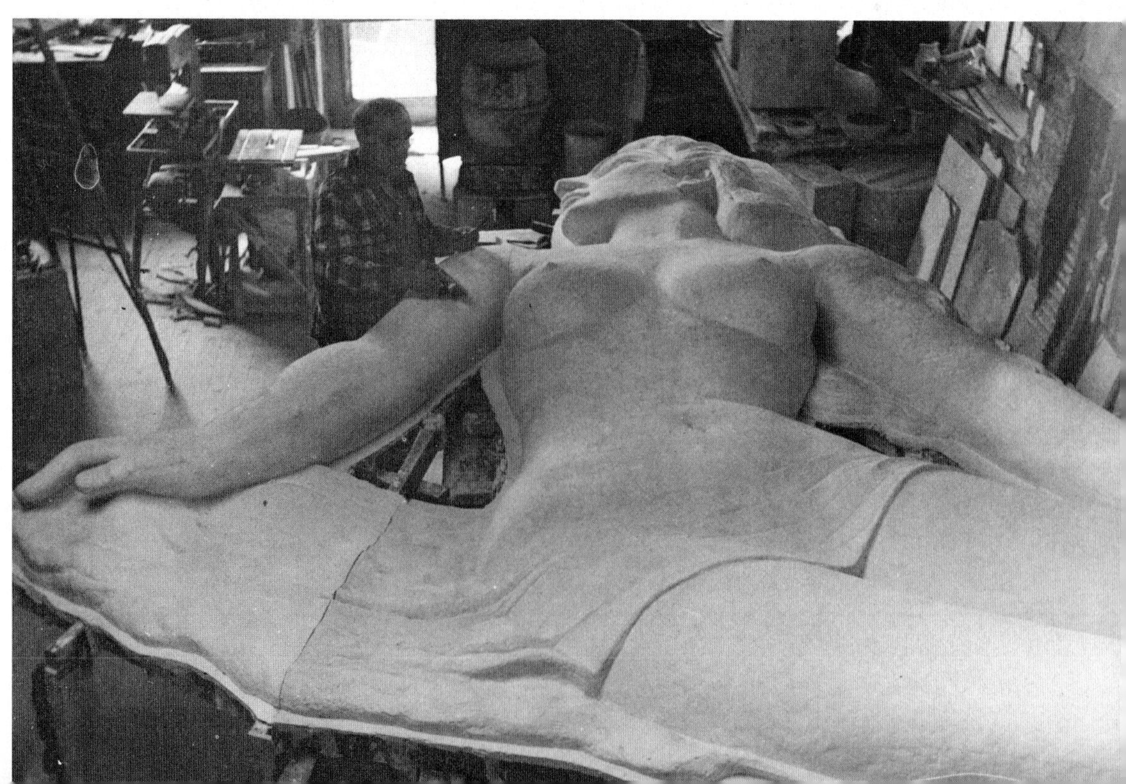

66. The sculptor working on full-sized enlargement of sculptured panel (*The New State of Texas*) that was to be cast in aluminum for the portal of the New Building of the Bank of the Southwest, Houston, Texas. Ultimately work was hung on library wall, Fairleigh Dickinson University, Teaneck, New Jersey. 1955.

68. *Head of Moses*. 1956. Granite. 36″ high. Columbia University.

67. Full-sized plaster model of female figure for *The New State of Texas*. 1955.

69. *The Family*. 1957. Granite. 20″ high. Collection of Arnold Weissberger.

70. *Lovers.* 1958. Italian marble. 10¾″ long. Collection of Miss Marilyn Karnes.

71. *Love.* 1959. Botticini marble. 23″ high. The Downtown Gallery, New York City.

had flown over the State of Texas, and behind them was a delicately engraved star of Texas. Above it all there was a bird.

I had a scale model of the facade of the building made with a small plaster model of the design they had accepted, boxed it, and sent it off to Texas. It was greeted with complete silence. Finally a letter came. The bank did not like the model; they thought it was too complicated. A layman sees only the small thing before him; he cannot visualize what the finished work will be. He must have the same faith that he automatically has in the man who builds his dams and hangs his suspension bridges. The bankers had no faith; they wanted to see it before it existed. This put a damper on my enthusiasm but I decided I must see the thing through. I restudied my model and sent in another model. Again here was a silence that went on all winter. I did not make changes in my original model; I simply made casts of it and incorporated their suggestions so they could see the results. Normally I would have quit when I ran up against this complete indecision but it was a big job and I wanted to see it through.

First they wanted everything based on the star of Texas—then they didn't want a star. Next they wanted Sam Houston's horse, which had been shot out from under him—then they didn't want a horse. Suddenly they wanted a bird—but then they were afraid the bird might be taken for Picasso's "Dove of Peace" and, instead, wanted a sunburst. First they wanted the child facing in—then they wanted the child facing out, of no importance in the design. They wanted the figure on the left changed to an Aztec Indian (a change I enjoyed). They wanted their beloved flags toned down. They wanted the female figure more full blown (delighted). And, in the end, after asking that she be nude, they began to be afraid that she might offend the Baptist women of Texas and asked if I would drape her slightly. A harmless change; I put a slight, almost invisible drape over the offending nudity. I made six different casts incorporating their suggestions, some of which were valid and more of which were ridiculous.

If I had been left alone, undisturbed, to carry out my first version, I would have done a more exciting and finer piece of sculpture. This is always true, but the customer can never leave the artist alone; he must worry and meddle and annoy and in the end defeat himself. However, I felt at this stage of my life I could battle it out and still make a fine work of art, which I did.

Franzheim asked me to make one more model. I agreed but I said, "This is absolutely the last one. This kind of thing can go on forever." The sketch was approved. I signed the contract and went ahead with the quarter-size model. This model would be nine by ten feet and would be enlarged by pentagraph mechanically in sections to the scale of the finished relief, which would be thirty by thirty-two feet. These sections would have to fit perfectly.

By now the bank had a new president and had changed its name to the Bank of the Southwest in Houston. I was working happily on the full-size model with the enlarger, crawling over those stupendous figures, seeing that the form was developed truly and that the measurements were kept correct—all during the hot summer and the cold winter in a large shop in Union City, New Jersey. But this time, unlike in my experience with the Franklin, I had wonderful men to work with. The models were finished and cast in plaster, then in aluminum, which has much less weight and is easier for a wall to carry than bronze. I was ready to ship the sculpture; the bank had been rushing me. I telegraphed them that it should be there within three weeks.

The next day I got a special-delivery letter from Franzheim with the appalling news that Mr. McNeese, the new president, had decided he didn't want any sculpture on the new building. I was stunned. I didn't know what to do. The shock of it made me sick. It was my life. You can't work on something that long, that hard, and under such terrible pressure and then have the rug pulled out from under you without getting a terrific jolt. The shock made me ill. The doctor was worried and was on call all night. I had suffered a slight stroke three years before, and he didn't know what this might do to me. Marguerite had been in the Virgin Islands and got home that night. They called her at the airport so she would be prepared.

In a few days I was better and could face the situation. I had received certain payments that covered materials and enlarging but nothing at all for myself, and I owed the foundry thirty-eight thousand dollars for the casting, a sum I couldn't conceive of ever paying. Edith Halpert got in touch with a lawyer she knew in San Antonio. I got in touch with my friend George Hourwich, a very fine lawyer in New York, and he negotiated with the bank officials. They would give him no explanation; one minute they said it was too modern, the next that it was too conservative. Then they finally said they just didn't want it. Furthermore, they didn't want to pay anything beyond the expense I had been put to. However, George held them to the contract and they paid in full for the work completed and they relinquished all claim to the sculpture.

The bank never offered me any explanation of its apparently senseless action but eventually I discovered the reason for it. At the time, a small watercolor of mine, called, "The Fisherman," happened to be on display in a Sports for Art show in Dallas sponsored by the American Federation of Art. It was a very minor little picture, but if this small thing had not been shown in Dallas my large relief would be over the entrance of the Houston Bank.

A group of Dallas artists started to make trouble because they felt the Dallas Museum exhibited and bought pictures from artists in the East while neglecting their own. The American Legion, along with some patriotic women's clubs, accused the museum of harboring subversive art and left-wing artists. They wanted all "Communist" art removed from the Museum. They accused all modern art of being "Communist Art." (I guess they had never seen the art put out by the Russian communists—the most conservative, academic art in the world.) In this exhibition they singled out Leon Kroll, Ben Shahn, Yasuo

Kuniyoshi, and myself as having at various times sponsored subversive groups, such as Spanish Relief, Relief for the Foreign Born, and British Relief. They didn't mention the Red Cross and the War Orphans. A group of super patriots published a most scurrilous paper in the vilest language accusing us of the most amazing things and protecting themselves from libel by saying, "Of course we don't know this to be a fact, *BUT* . . ."

There was more to this. There is a very reactionary member of the National Sculpture Society in New York who may be jealous of me, may be prejudiced against me, or may just plain hate my guts. (He does not know me personally.) He bombards the Un-American Activities Committee with the most curious misinformation about my so-called subversive activities. Sometimes when it has been called to my attention and is particularly objectionable, I have had it retracted; but he never gives up. It had reached the point where it wasn't being taken seriously, but the Bank of the Southwest in Houston took it seriously. They said it had nothing to do with their action, but the timing was too perfect. And I do not blame them; they were in no way committed to fight my battles and certainly they didn't want to be involved in any such controversy, a case of "Caesar's wife."

I did not know what to do with this magnificent panel now that it was in my hands. I wondered where in the world I would find a place big enough for it and someone who would want it. I have many good friends in Texas, and certain organizations there tried to figure out how they could use it and gave me wonderful support. Franzheim took all this very hard; he wanted to wait until things calmed down; he was sure in the end he could get the bank to use the relief. But before this came about he died. There is still no sculpture to enhance the bank—just a big empty space. Eventually Dr. Peter Sammartino bought the panel for Fairleigh Dickinson University in Rutherford, New Jersey.

Dr. Peter Sammartino is an extraordinary man. When he was young and just married, he and Sally went out walking in Rutherford and saw an old-fashioned castle for sale.

It was magnificent and they said, "What a pity. There is no place in the world for such an estate and nobody wants one. All it could be used for would be a school."

They looked at each other and said, "Let's buy it and start a school."

They bought it, and that was the beginning of Fairleigh Dickinson University. All the great institutions of learning in this country seem to originate in the vision and devotion of one man.

When Dr. Sammartino heard about the Texas fiasco he said, "I'll buy it."

"Wherever will you put it?" I asked.

"We can only pay a nominal sum for it, but we'll build a building for it," he replied.

I was very pleased and in a few years it came to pass. The relief was delivered to the college before the new library was started, while it was only a dream. One whole wall of this modern building was designed and set aside for it. With illumination at night and student activities around it by day, it is very impressive and they are proud of it. How much better to have it there than on a bank.

I would like to describe the panel. It is cast in polished aluminum in high relief. The central motif is based on the flags that flew over this country in the past. Each nation represented enriched our culture and our history. The woman embodies the abundance of the land of this great country. She rises clear-eyed and powerful into fulfillment. On her left the past is represented, going back into the early beginnings of history in America; the Indian cultures are embodied in the Aztec Indian, the sun-worshipper, with his gift of corn, his fierce and dynamic art, his closeness to our natural resources and his secret knowledge of this country's past. On the right the figures represent the modern development of man—his proud belief in himself and his ideals, his confidence in life and in whatever the future may hold. The child embodies the ever continuing cycle of the generations.

When this assault upon me, accusing me of supporting Communism, came out into the open in Texas, my first impulse was to issue a denial and a statement of my position politically. Everyone said, "never do that, just ignore it." I spoke to lawyers and to the best public-relations men in the country, and they all said the same thing. I think they were wrong but I listened to them. I believe that if I had gone to Houston and talked to the board at the bank as I wanted to, my sculpture would have been put up. I had nothing to conceal and nothing to fear. I can never see why everyone combined to keep me from speaking. To me silence is close to admitting the truth of the situation. Perhaps they thought I was not equipped to cope with these people. Anyway, I allowed myself to be overwhelmed.

These vicious attacks went on for years; in Congress before the House Un-American Activities Committee, every time I served on an art jury, every time I gave a talk even at an obscure country high school in Maine, scurrilous letters were sent out. But only once, in Flint, Michigan, was a show of mine cancelled because of this. This went on until 1961 when I was working on a fountain for the city of Bath, Maine. When it happened there, I finally put an end to it.

These same people—at least I am sure it was the same men or the same group—caused me endless trouble and expense some years before by asking the government to investigate my citizenship.

One day an official from the United States Immigration Service rang my bell and asked if I was a citizen. I told him that I had been a citizen for over sixty years—that I was born in Lithuania and brought to this country at the age of four and automatically became a citizen when my father was naturalized, and that I had my father's certificate of citizenship in my safety deposit box at the bank and also a passport of mine that I had used when I went to Paris in 1910 to study. He asked me to come see him at the Immigration Department and to bring my papers along. All sorts of complications followed. In the days when my father was naturalized, things were done very casually. Even my own passport, a beautiful big engraved document, mentioned nothing except the fact that I had been granted a passport. Seventy years ago in the big cities politicians who wanted votes rounded up the foreign born and had them sworn in in batches of fifteen or twenty. My father, to whom this must have been a strange and mysterious ceremony, muffed it the first time or, at least, they produced a record to that effect. It took my family more than a year of intensive research to unearth the records. The Immigration Service refused to accept my father's citizenship papers, my passport, or any family records.

Then there was the question of names, and this resulted in utter confusion. Seventy-five years ago in Russia there were no surnames among the common people; a man was simply the son of someone. Relatives who came to this country took various names. My father's name was Orchick; over here it became Aaron but in the stress of becoming a citizen he was put down as Ezra, and someone added the name of Finkelstein for the occasion and the family was known by that name from then on. I had later taken my grandfather's name Zorach which was also my own name. But I kept the William which had been given me by a teacher in first grade in Port Clinton, Ohio.

I thought the family had landed at Ellis Island, but there was no record. Finally we found that my father and eldest brother had landed in Baltimore. Four years later my mother and six children landed at Castle Garden. The more I found out and the more I explained, the more proof they wanted and none of the proof I produced was sufficient. They seemed to be out to get me. What chance do you stand of proving anything after sixty-five years? The public schools keep records no longer than twenty years. Everyone I knew as a child was by this time dead or had vanished. My father and mother were dead, as well as my older brothers and sisters with one exception.

Finally they found a record of my whole family in the census of 1900 in Cleveland, but I was entered as a girl instead of a boy. I got letters from the Cleveland School of Art and numerous affidavits from endless people. But, unfortunately, no one was available who was present when I was born or when I became an American citizen through my father's naturalization.

Documents flew back and forth and then suddenly one day the United States government decided that I was not a citizen. It was a horrible position to be put in and I seemed helpless to do anything about it. I could be deported and the subversive angle would not help my case. I am not an international person. I speak no language but English; I have my home, my family, my work here in the United States. I don't want to be anywhere else. Here I had a life and a country and they were taking it away from me and leaving me suspended. To think that at the age of seventy I should have to prove my citizenship—and after all I am not a man who was unknown, who had contributed nothing to his country—completely floored me. It was incredible and yet it happened.

They said, "You can appeal the decision," and I contacted my friends, Morris Ernst and General Greenbaum. It's hard to involve a firm of busy lawyers in a nasty research job like this. They had little time but they came to my rescue and found the time. At first, no one could get anywhere; they found only dead ends and more confusion. Part of the problem was that they were in New York and the solution was buried in Cleveland. Then my niece, Rosemary Lewis, got on the job. She knew Cleveland politics and politicians and had worked with them all her life. She went to a judge she knew and got advice and help. She got permission to go into the archives of the Cleveland courts and went through the old records, dug through the accumulation of sixty-five years in the basement of the Cleveland City Hall through all the dust and grime until she came across my father's naturalization papers—and even a second verification of citizenship. It took her all winter and I am eternally indebted to her. Even then it took expensive briefs and Eddy Greenbaum had to go down to Washington and argue the case. In the end I came out with citizenship papers and a passport. But I can't help thinking it was a disgraceful business.

We were much surprised to receive an invitation to President Kennedy's inauguration. The Kennedys believed in culture and in art, and realized its value in the life of a country. I do not think any other President of the United States ever invited artists and writers and musicians to an inauguration. Enclosed with the formal invitation was the information as to where we were to stay and where to pick up our tickets for the various parties and events. Everything was beautifully taken care of except the weather.

It was cold but clear when we left Penn Station. A few minutes later it began to snow. We were glad we had decided not to fly. Those who did, in some cases, didn't get there. It was like old home week on the train; we met so many old friends that we hadn't seen since the Roosevelt days—good Democrats rushing back, hoping to take up where they had left off eight years before. By the time we reached Washington, it was a real blizzard, snow several inches deep and no sign of a letup, intense cold and a high wind. I knew it would be impossible to get a cab legitimately, so I found a porter, gave him a few dollars and he rushed us across the street with our bags.

We dropped off our bags at the home of our host and hostess and hurried over to Walter Lippmann's cocktail party. It wasn't far but it was already late and the going was grim. We skidded around curves and struggled up hills.

We made it. I left Marguerite in the cab and went in to pay my respects to Walter Lippmann. All was bright and gay at the Lippmanns'; everybody was celebrating and drinking cocktails, happily, with never a thought of the storm. I told the Lippmanns that much as we would like to stay we were afraid that we couldn't get back if we did and that he would have to put up most of his guests for the night as it was, which turned out to be true.

The next day was clear and cold. No cabs were available; cars were stalled and abandoned all over. We took a bus into Washington and found our seats for the inauguration, in the stand just in front of the grandstand and President Kennedy himself. But we were on the shady side of the street—maybe it was better on the sunny side. We were given bundles of newspapers to sit on and wrap around our legs but we almost froze to death. I was never so congealed in my life. We were seated with a lot of friends and a number of fellows from the Arts and Letters. It would have been festive if it had not been for the terrible cold and the vicious wind. We sat there slowly turning to stone or rather cakes of ice and looked across at the President without a hat or an overcoat and Jackie lightly clothed and without a fur coat and wondered how they could survive. We waited for them to topple over like the soldiers in the street and a few weak spectators. Not a bit of it! They survived the interminable prayers; Catholic, Protestant, and Jewish. They must have been sustained by the excitement of the occasion. Robert Frost was so cold he couldn't see to read his speech and recited a poem instead, which was much more effective and much more enjoyed. It was very touching. He was so old and venerable—and whenever in history has a President been so honored by a poet or so honored a poet?

On the way back to Georgetown our cabby said, "This town is run by hill-billies. Someone cleared Pennsylvania Avenue but you watch, they won't do a thing to the rest of the streets." We had him take us to the place where the inaugural ball was to be held that night to see what the prospects were of getting there. When we saw the distance we would have to walk and thought of our chances of getting a cab back to Georgetown that night, we decided to give up and went to the ball on television.

CHAPTER SIXTEEN

TWO QUESTIONS always come up when artists are discussed—housing for artists and juries. Young artists usually have to solve the problem of finding a place to live without money, and they have to work and develop their talent. Yet in the early years their work does not warrant a place in the art world. It is just not good enough for people to exhibit it or to buy it even if it could be sold. Fortunately they do not know this—neither did we know this when we were young. But if this country is to have a place in the world of art, it will be through these young artists. An artist can give only a small part of himself to making a living outside of art; otherwise he can never develop his art.

The young artist can pay only the most nominal rent. He must find lofts with no living facilities and live in them illegally, broken-down buildings, sheds, and unused warehouses. Artists are quite ingenious in what they can find and use and adapt. Someone is always trying to interest the city or the government or a philanthropist in adequate housing for artists. It never works. It always costs too much, and the people who live in regular apartments have only to lay eyes on a skylight or a fine big window and they rush to rent the place.

I remember one time someone built a house full of studios on Eighth Street for artists. No artist ever moved into one of them. The bankers and brokers from Wall Street rented them to house their girl friends. Even when an artist finds a nice, cheap, disreputable neighborhood and moves in, in a few years people begin to think it's intriguing and attractive and they move in; the rents go up and the artists move out. I see no solution except for the city to leave the artists alone in their lofts and not bother them—that's the least they can do. It is better to leave it illegal than to have no artists.

As for juries: the jury system for selecting works of art for exhibition has everything to be said against it, and yet no one has ever been able to devise a better system. The word jury implies compromise. No group of men or women in any profession see alike, think alike, or are moved alike. The choice of painting or sculpture by a jury necessarily reflects personal preference based on personal judgment, reduced by disagreement, and with compromise as the inevitable total. Some like them hot, some like them cold, some like them new, some like them old. The prize-winner in one national exhibition may have been rejected by the jury of another national exhibition the same year. Max Weber sent a picture to the Art Institute of Chicago one year and it was thrown out. He sent the same picture the next year and it was given first prize. It was a different jury.

A juror's taste may be conservative or extreme; he may approve only of work related to his own, or he may like only work that is basically different; or he may be responsive to novelty and technical facility. Nevertheless experience proves that a jury composed of professionals in the field—of artists, museum directors, and critics—conscientiously select from the works submitted to them those of true merit within each category of interest, allowing for a minimum of blind spots. Once in a while it is well to have a one-man jury—it usually means a homogeneous and impressive show! It is also good sometimes to have no jury or an independent exhibition. In that case, strange and unusual talent shows up and enriches the world of art. The best jury system is for each juror to select his own preference without outside intervention. This results in a more interesting show and there is much less compromise.

It is equally difficult to set rules for the public. The public is entitled to freedom of taste if not freedom of ignorance—but should it have the freedom to condemn? As in everything else in life, a work of art either gives you pleasure or not. The non-objective art of today is a purely visual thing, a cerebral experience. The importance it has is the importance you, yourself, give it. To read meaning into it, whether psychological, musical, or otherwise, is comparable to reading meaning into tea leaves.

The man in the street appreciates a well designed gadget or refrigerator; you have only to look at the sales slips to know that. Of course, industrial design is not sculpture, but industrial designers derive their ideas and inspiration from the forms modern sculptors invent and use. Men have always used abstract forms for utilitarian purposes, but never before had they elevated them to an art status. They have never considered them art expression in themselves. Abstract form is the basic structure of art expression. It is like the structure of a house but not the finished house. A checkerboard is a pleasing abstract pattern. You can hang it on the wall as a decoration—but it is not a work of art. What is happening in a certain period always seems unique and different to the people of that period because it affects them personally. There seem to be no standards today, but someone looking at our art a hundred years from now will find there were standards in all this mishmash that is going on today.

One should not condemn the experimental mind. The search for new forms is invaluable; it enlarges our field of vision and expands our thinking. But research is not art nor is art research. The repetition of new forms and directions by various artists adds nothing. Continually trying out new ways and directions leads to chaos. Some artists are always talking about progress. There is no progress in art; there is only change. Art is art. There is no gain in keeping up with the Joneses in art. It is more important to find your own way than always to have your eye on someone else's way of seeing and doing. It is natural for the young and unformed to shop around for ideas and techniques. It is the way they grow and find themselves. But innovation is not an end in itself. I am shocked when a mature artist who had developed something out of himself throws it all overboard and changes his style with the fashion and becomes an opportunist. He is not finding new power in himself or even originality; he's changing to someone else's style. A true artist doesn't change, he expands the range of his expression and develops greater power.

We are in the last phase of a period of art. Artists are concerned with technique and accidental effects. They are playing with art. It is no longer what is boiling in the pot but what spills over the edge that fascinates them. There is a natural law in art as in all life, of rise and fall and disintegration. Many today feel beauty lies in decay and capitalize on shock and horror. Some do not go this far out but find beauty in a tentative sketch, in the weatherbeaten, the rusty, and the corroded, in discarded junk, in the imperfections in the execution of iron and bronze. They speak of sculpture as "happy accidents" and "found" sculpture. I cannot accept this. The instability of this world has penetrated into art.

Don't think because the Museum of Modern Art gives a thing museum status that it is accepted in the art world, even in the most advanced circles. I remember one day when Max Weber met John Marin coming out of the Modern Museum.

John said to Max, "Go in there and see what painting is coming to. My god, they're going nuts."

A year later I saw the avant-garde painter, Stamos, standing in front of some enormous smears at the Brooklyn Museum. "Whatever is painting coming to?" he asked.

But the next year he was doing the same thing.

People ask, "What next?" I say I don't know, but I do know I won't like it. And I know that if I lived fifty years more I would get used to it and I would like some of it and some of it I would never like. Most of it would be waste material cluttering attics and cellars—as it has been in every age. In the catalogues of the great Paris Salons of seventy years ago, where the great and accepted art of the age was displayed, is there a name we know today or a picture we can locate or would want to locate? And yet there are magnificent and treasured works of art in our museums that were done in that period.

A fine artist will assimilate ideas unconsciously. He will absorb the art of the past and the art of today, and the good and the bad will simmer through his unconscious. He will sometimes be surprised at the similarity between what he is doing and the work someone else is doing. Ideas are not the creation or the property of any one man. The same idea may develop in more than one human at the same time. The human brain, and the world around a human, is common to all men. A good artist does not copy forms but realizes the art of the past and of the present. People do not read Shakespeare to copy him but because they recognize a universal human value in his writing, a fullness and beauty of expression through language.

The reality of art runs through the ages; it is something that has meaning to us as human beings. It affects us in a constructive and not a destructive way. Art is creative and stems from accumulated energy. Just as a garden does not grow without nourishment, art cannot develop without encouragement and intelligent sponsorship. Art expression does not die in adversity, but under encouragement it flourishes. There is only one way to subsidize art. That is to buy it, to take it into your life, and let it expand and enrich your life. I do not believe in subsidies to artists, nor do I think any artist really wants that. How little art the people of this great nation have in their homes.

The Ford Foundation asked me to sit down with them and tell them what they could do for art and artists in this country. I cannot attend board meetings where ideas and plans are lost in irrelevant argument. So I wrote them it was very simple: "The only way to encourage artists is to buy their work and after having bought it, to give it to colleges, schools, hospitals, institutions. Make small collections and give them to small museums around the country." People should try and buy worthwhile work but they should never buy a work as an investment. By using individual taste and judgment, much fine work could be accumulated and the worthless would find its way to the cellar in the end as it does in a museum. We are a nation of all peoples and all traditions as well as a nation in our own right; we should produce a rich and rewarding art if our artists can find encouragement and an outlet for their work.

I do not like to see art made an investment issue, a new form of stocks and bonds to stimulate speculation. I do not like false values and manipulated prices. I especially don't like to see this in the art world, but I guess human beings can use almost anything as a gambling device. We are not a country that values culture or education and learning except in superficial ways. Perhaps our only approach to a position in the art world is through speculation and the accompanying possession of art treasures. Just as Morgan and Mellon and Rockefeller bought up the old masters for prestige, today people buy up the new artists for gain and speculations and status. In the past this has filled our museums with great art to be enjoyed by all who are responsive. It has enriched our national life. But it is the art created by the people in their own country that becomes the living art of that country—not the beautiful art of other countries that we fill our museums with and educate ourselves to enjoy. That has its place and its great value, but it leaves the country sterile.

My brother-in-law, who is a businessman, was once telling me how successfully a businessman could handle art. Suddenly he stopped and said, "The only trouble is, it would cease to be art." He added, "Beware of practical men. They will destroy your dream—and it is out of men's dreams that the worthwhile things in this world are made."

I consider it my duty to serve on an art jury whenever asked unless it is impossible. I exclude the small amateur groups that always consider my name will lend prestige, when in reality there is an open field for them to choose from, some of whom would be honored and any of whom would do just as well as I. You cannot allow your time to be nibbled away by these things, but still whenever possible I cooperate as a gesture for art. I seem to be a man who can't say no.

I have served on so many juries from coast to coast that it's hard to remember many details about all of them, but the most soul-shattering and devastating one was the Metropolitan Museum Exhibition of Modern Sculpture in 1951. There were five sculptors on the jury as well as Roland McKinney, who served as organizer, and Robert Hale representing the museum. Coming back from Washington on a plane I had met Francis Taylor, then Director of the Metropolitan Museum. He told me the "Met" was planning an all-American sculpture exhibition at the museum and that McKinney was organizing the show. He said he was not familiar with the contemporary sculptors (which shocked me, coming from one whose business it was to know) and he asked whom I thought would make up a representative jury. I gave him a list of sculptors. The museum chose the five sculptors for the jury. Announcements were sent out to every sculptor in the country to submit photographs. Thousands of photographs were sent in, and from these the jury selected 101 works to exhibit. I think we spent a week going over these thousands of photographs. The usual procedure was as follows: a majority of four out of seven votes got a sculpture in; one or two votes held a sculpture over for consideration; no votes in favor eliminated the work. There was very little discussion. Photos were passed around to each juror and a stenographer recorded the votes. It was a stupendous and exhausting undertaking. I was suffering from sciatica, and when the pain and exhaustion became too great, I'd have to stretch out flat on a table until I could go on again.

There was discussion pro and con in the magazines and press. Of course the sculptors who were accepted were happy; those who were eliminated were sad and some were furious. As soon as it was announced that I was to be a juror, I was bombarded by requests from sculptors to look at the work they were going to send in. I was even asked to come over to the studios and advise them what to send. To me this was highly unethical, and of course I refused. It was all very silly—after all, I was familiar with their work. I was only being given the opportunity together with six other people to consider it.

One sculptor complained to his friends and to the critics that I was responsible for his not being in the show. He made such a stink and created so much sympathy for himself that it put him on the map, and he benefited more by not being in the show than if his work had been accepted. In this particular instance this sculptor had met me on the street a week or so before the jury met, and, knowing I was on the jury, had asked me to come out to his place and see his work. He said he would come in with his car and take me out to his place in the country and I could look over his work. We had never been on such friendly terms before and this kind of pressure tends to prejudice a juror. When his name came up I said nothing, but I refrained from voting. The funny thing was that no one else voted for him so he was out. When I am on a jury and the work of one of my friends or one of my students comes up, I never rush in to vote. I hold back and give the others a free choice and then put in my vote. On the other hand I do not feel that because an artist is my friend I should not vote for him. It depends upon how I feel about his work. But no matter how fair and impersonal you try to be, there are always the disgruntled, the jealous, the inept, and the frustrated who make a howl and go about running down the jury and the jury system. Of course it is natural to be tolerant of a friend's work and even prejudiced, because you understand what he is trying to do and what he has accomplished, but I try to let this influence my judgment as little as possible.

They used the big entrance hall of the Metropolitan Museum for the sculpture show. They had to keep the whole center space clear for the incoming and outgoing museum crowds as well as the space around the post card and trinket booths. This meant the sculpture was crowded into the two wings on either side. McKinney said the museum had no money for display purposes; everything had to be used as it was. The sculpture did not show to advantage. It was a hodge-podge, crowded and unrelated, at either end of the huge hall. It was one of the worst jobs of display I have ever seen, and yet it put contemporary American sculpture on the map.

An artist's contact with the business world is through dealers (and critics). Some artists can devote themselves both to their art and to handling the sale of their work. Most artists need and want a person who will take care of the business side for them and leave them supposedly free to work and able to ignore the question of sales and money. There are hundreds of galleries in New York that handle and exhibit art. But beyond giving the artist an opportunity to exhibit—and the lesser galleries even make the unknown pay for this privilege—most galleries do not begin to furnish their artists with a living. They take on large numbers of artists, hoping to find one who is an inborn success, and out of the group they manage to get along; but their artists cannot depend upon them alone. But if an artist doesn't have a dealer he is out of luck. He may be a genius and some day he may be discovered, but I suspect he can also dissolve into oblivion. Art has to be shown and seen to live, whether it is today or tomorrow. Occasionally an artist has talent as a businessman as well as an artist and can keep a balance between the two so that he can survive without a dealer, but this combination is rare.

Business arrangements between artists and dealers are usually very vague. No one is ever very happy—neither the artist nor the dealer—over sales, promotion, commissions, or relations with customers. This is true even with the best. In my estimation Edith Halpert is tops among the dealers in New York. Certainly she is the finest and most dedicated dealer for American art and American artists. Between Edith and the artist there was never any contract. Nothing was put in words—let alone on paper. There was just an understanding—never a perfect understanding because an artist always complains about his dealer and the dealer undoubtedly complains about the artist.

As a sculptor I have two real quarrels with the general run of art dealers. First, they expect a full commission on the sale of a piece of sculpture, including the cost of the casting in the sale. Bronze casting is so expensive that it comes to one-third of the sales price, sometimes even to half. This leaves the sculptor with one-third or less as his part of the sale. He is working for the foundry and the dealer, not himself. He has the pleasure and the pain of creating a work of art, but he has to have money to live and for material and for the other expenses that go into sculpture. This system may be all right for painting, where there is only a nominal expense for materials, but not for sculpture. Second, dealers do not necessarily have a consistent commission rate for all their artists. I feel all commissions should be on an equal basis and different commission rates for different artists is certainly unethical.

There is this to say for my dealer, Edith Halpert. Even though she is a hard-boiled business woman—and I mean hard-boiled—she has a soft spot in her makeup. She loves her "boys." She will extract the last penny of tribute from them. But if they really are in trouble and call for help, she's there. No matter how many fights and misunderstandings she has with artists, she is never through; she always comes back. She will take the black sheep into the fold again no matter how much dirt she feels he's done her. She will never permanently relinquish a relationship. It is in a way the measure of her faith in her artists. In spite of her strict business sense, Edith has an altruistic point of view in relation to American art. Edith Halpert deserves all the credit in the world for putting American art on the map—her "boys" are found in museums and collections all over the country.

At one time Edith decided the older artists were getting older, producing less, and doing all right financially. She felt she should give the younger men a chance. She created a special gallery for them, showed their work, bought it, and sold it. The young artists felt she was taking advantage of them and exploiting them. The older artists thought that she was building up the prices of the young ones out of all proportion and they did not like it. After a lot of headaches Edith gave that idea up. She still complains that the older artists don't produce enough work. The truth is that she likes to be carried away by new ideas. Everyone does. Like any good salesman she gets bored with what she has already shown and has not sold. She wants something new—something that excites her customers with its newness. She wants new men and new art but she is no longer willing to put the effort and money and time into building them up. She doesn't need to. All of her "boys" have made the grade with her help.

Dealers and promoters love to make discoveries, but they want to make their own discoveries and their own mistakes, and they make plenty. It is like the collector who comes to your studio and is not interested in the pictures on the walls or the sculpture on display. He wants to snoop in dark corners and see the work turned to the wall—that he discovers and wants.

I could take a young artist of great talent and extraordinary possibilities of development to every dealer in New York and tell him, "Here you have a potential gold mine if you will take on this young person and promote him."

There wouldn't be a dealer who would be interested in even seeing this young person or his work. But they are always interested in taking on someone who has already been promoted if they can get him. I don't believe they trust anyone's judgment, even their own. They are like the girl who can never quite make up her mind to get married and is always waiting to be swept off her feet.

Galleries resist any contacts you make outside. They do not like to introduce you to their customers for fear you'll take them over. And if you bring someone over who wants to buy your work, they are suspicious that you have already taken them over and sold them things. Yet any time I have sent a potential customer to the gallery, Edith has welcomed him and sold him this and that and the other thing.

You don't discard or terminate relationships in life because there is a conflict of interest or ideas or understanding. These involvements and relationships stand—like marriage—for better or for worse. My relationship with Edith Halpert has existed over forty years—as dealer and artist, and friends and human beings. And even though communication is difficult between us at times and all is not sweetness and light, there is a fundamental understanding and mutual appreciation that has persisted through our lives and will be there at the end. She's quite a girl and I am one of her "boys."

There is an illusion that the success or failure of an exhibition depends upon what the critics write in the newspapers. It is always a surprise to me how many people see and read these criticisms. And I suppose it does bring in a certain number of people to see the show. I think this was more true in the days when critics, even the ones recruited from among the racing and sports reporters, wrote serious criticisms of every exhibition. Today they are more inclined to write essays on art and that, too, is enlightening to the general public.

They say nobody ever goes to a critic's funeral. It is an ungrateful job even if it entails a certain power and a certain prestige. Occasionally there are critics of stature, like Henry McBride, Emily Genauer, and John Canaday. The artist should always be grateful for a favorable review and never be resentful of an unfavorable one. Remember that an unfavorable review is infinitely better than no review. The one thing a critic can't stand is criticism. If you write him and tell him he is all wrong, he goes berserk and never forgets it. If you write and praise him it makes him happy, but he is wary of mentioning you in the future for fear the public will fear he's prejudiced in your favor.

Elizabeth Luther Carey, who was art critic on *The Times* all her life, never had any use for my work until she saw my woodcarving—her father had done woodcarving and she was fascinated. She asked me if I would carve her a breadboard for a hundred dollars. She said she never took gifts from artists, but she liked to own their work and she always paid them one hundred dollars because that was what she could afford. I made the breadboard and she was happy.

There were two incidents that I can never forget. One day Arthur Huber, the critic on the New York *Globe,* stuck his head in the door at the Stieglitz "291" Gallery.

Stieglitz saw him and said, "Come in and see the show."

To which Huber replied, "Do I have to eat the whole egg if I find it's rotten?"

Another time at the Michael Kennedy Galleries I was talking to Stieglitz when he saw Royal Cortissoz, the art critic on the *Tribune* come in. He dropped me like a hot brick, went over to Cortissoz and said, "Come back into this room, Royal; I want to show you something in here."

Cortissoz smiled and said, "Is that where you keep the chloroform?"

It is disconcerting that publicity is responsible for an appreciation of art among people—that it is necessary, to make them conscious of the existence of art and artists. There are so many unsavory things that go into the promoting and buying and appreciation of art that I am appalled. Yet real art is eternal and will always be there in spite of any smoke screen. It is better to shut off an awareness to the world and just work.

I am also appalled that museum directors and museum people keep themselves apart from the art world. They are not interested enough in artists' work to go to an exhibition unless it is a super-social event. Museum directors seem to keep in close touch with their patrons and collectors rather than with the artists themselves. It never occurs to them to look up an artist and see what he is doing or to familiarize themselves with the teeming activity of art around them. And yet, this is their life and their business; how *can* they be so uninterested?

I have written about the commissions in which I have been involved, and the occasions when the world outside moved in upon me. These are a necessary and disturbing part of life and our contact with life. But despite the outside pressures upon me, I was doing the things that came from within my soul. The carving of the "Mother and Child" was an inner work of this kind. I mean that in doing this sculpture there was no conflict or problem with the outside world—only with the world within myself.

I have mentioned several of these individual pieces, I cannot write of many of them. I did two large pieces in York Fossil—a black marble. One was a "Child on Pony," a very solid and beautiful carving which I still have. The other was "Affection." It was a child on a dog, and expressed all the love that exists between animals and children. This belongs to the Munson-Williams-Proctor Institute in Utica.

"Youth," a life sized figure of a man and a woman, in Botticini marble, is in the Norton Gallery in West Palm Beach, Florida. Edith Halpert brought Mr. Norton down to my studio because he wanted a bronze of my "Child and Cat," which the Modern Museum owns. The minute Norton saw the marble "Youth," it belonged to him. I never even had a chance to exhibit it in New York until my retrospective show at the Whitney Museum in 1959.

For two summers I chipped away at a large stone of a father and son, the father reclining with his son, called "The Faith of This Nation." The stone is a white Georgia marble with considerable black and gray in it. It was an interesting stone but very hard to carve; but sometimes difficulties are a challenge and bring out more power in the artist. It was shown at the Downtown Gallery.

A private in the United States Army came in and liked it. When he left he said, "Let me think about it until tomorrow." At the Gallery they thought it was a joke, but the next day he came back and bought it. He was Wright Ludington and he has it in his home in Santa Barbara, California.

I spent several summers on and off, during the war years, working on a group which is now in the collection of the Whitney Museum, called "Future Generations." It was a terrific problem to create what I wanted to do with this particular block of stone. I would go as far as I could, then put it away and come back fresh the next year. Each winter I packed it in straw and tied a canvas around it and left it outdoors in the Maine winter. Every spring it was ready for the attack. The stone was Botticini marble and just as uncooperative as glass. I have carved a number of things in this marble; it is so beautiful when finished and polished that I can't resist it no matter how exasperating it is to carve. This time I evolved two practically life-sized figures out of what had seemed a very small stone.

The Sarah Roby Foundation also has a large torso of mine in Labrador granite which I carved back in the days when I had a studio on Tenth Street. A bronze of it was recently given to the University of Nebraska by Frank Stanton of C.B.S. I made another torso, in marble—it is "Victory," perfectly streamlined, and without adornment—in strict simplicity and clarity. It lives in bronze in several places.

I have carved a few portrait heads—of Dahlov, of Marguerite, and one of our friend, Katherine Shanahan. I have also done a number of imaginative portraits—my "Head of Christ" which is in the Museum of Modern Art; a tremendous oversized "Head of Moses" in black granite, unpolished, which was given to Columbia University by Armand Erpf and placed in Earl Hall. There is a "Head of a Prophet" in the Chicago Art Institute also carved in porphyritic diabase, the same stone as the "Head of Christ." This rare stone turns up on the shores in Maine. I found my stones along the cove near our house, boulders brought down by the glaciers. I understand that it is found in only two other places in the world, one in Massachusetts and one place in Japan.

I love carving Maine boulders. I collect them and have them lying around my place; you'd never guess from their dull surfaces what beautiful colors, textures, and patterns are concealed in them, waiting for the sculptor to give them life and form. Now and then I see possibilities in one of them and start to evolve a sculptural form in it. I have carved large dogs and quite a number of cats in these stones and many small heads, which I like so much I sometimes hide them for fear someone will want to buy them. I don't dare leave them on display in a gallery in the open. It is too easy for someone to walk off with them and just that has happened. I seem to like to carve frogs; they hop around the grass after a rain and I capture one now and then and study him in my studio. I have done a fish or two and also birds, but you can't be intimate with birds. I like to know the creatures I do.

I had a commission to do two pumas for Mrs. Gladwin of Santa Barbara. She wanted them life-sized and in lead, which is most impervious to weather and is also a lovely color like pewter. I had to see live pumas to understand the beauty of their movements and their forms. No picture can give you what you want unless you already know the animal. The New York zoos had such miserable, spiritless creatures that I could get nothing from them. Finally I discovered two magnificent specimens in the Staten Island Zoo. Marguerite and I commuted out there for about a week until I got acquainted with the brutes and had made a lot of drawings of them. The lead pumas sit on a terrace overlooking a beautiful, wild valley in Santa Barbara where their live relatives cry at night. I wasn't satisfied to have my pumas in metal. I wasn't happy until I had them in stone. I got a wonderful Labrador granite called emerald pearl. It polishes black and has crystals of deep blue in it which gives it great life. The first one Margaret Strater gave to her son and his family at York Beach, Maine. They have a large new modern house, and the puma sits on the stairway as you go up to the house. Their six children climb over him and embrace him. It makes me a bit nervous. I hate to trust even granite to children with their uncanny ability to take things apart and destroy them. But the children are growing up and the puma is still intact. Some years after, I finished the second puma. It was shown in Philadelphia and bought by the Pennsylvania Museum of Fine Arts. I was also given the Widener Gold Medal for sculpture by the Pennsylvania Academy that year.

Besides the large woodcarving of the "Mother and Child" that belongs to the Lathrop Browns, quite a different one from the marble one in the Metropolitan Museum, I have done a number of important sculptures in wood. One time I bought two large pieces of Borneo mahogany from a German who had cut the trees in Borneo. This is very hard, heavy wood with great depth of color. Out of one of these I carved "Bathing Girl" about forty-eight inches high. It is now in the collection of the young John Marins, where it is very comfortable and much loved, especially by little Lisa Marin. Out of the other piece I carved the figure of a young man, very compact, very alert and with a fine cut surface. To date it has been completely ignored and I consider it one of my very best.

I seem to have given up wood. I don't know why. In the last years I've gotten so involved in working in stone and get so much pleasure out of the material that I think in stone; something happens with stone that doesn't happen working in other materials. It's a sort of resonance; something comes through. It's a metaphysical sort of thing which you are playing with, almost like a sailor's relationship with the sea in which he becomes a part of the elements, of the sun, the storms, and the waters. You are actually creating and at the same time battling hard material. Then there is a peace and a quietness that you get out of the communication—something that is not related to our materialistic world but that goes back to the ancients and the primitives. It takes you back into timelessness, where there is no time and space is endless. If you pry up a boulder that has been lying in the ground or in a sand pit, it's sort of alive, whereas a rock that's been exposed to weather out on a beach or in a quarry is very brittle and not nearly as responsive to carve. There's a sense of eternity in a glacial boulder that's been rolled around for millions of years. It has a marvelous feeling of permanence. When I began working in stone it was a great revelation to me, watching the form emerge from the rock, living and eternal. It was very satisfying. There is a beautiful, heroic, almost Olympian, feeling in these things. I can't tell you exactly how or why I get that into the stone; it comes from inside. It's from the quality of your personality, of your feeling and love for nature and for life, for people and for animals. It's a sort of inner vision. It is seeing with a spirit that is timeless. It is love that is felt so intensely that the artist has to record it and give it back to humanity; for love is not only getting but giving. I would say that the difference between my stone carvings and many of the more modern works done today is that I make a great many studies and observations from nature, and every form and detail is alive and has a certain basis in reality. It is not just stylized carving. Every bit of the surface is studied and undulates. It is a living surface and is based upon something seen or felt.

I have always been deeply conscious of the fundamental elements in life. There is nothing more emotionally significant than the relationship between mother and child unless it is the element of love between man and woman. Life exists through them and could not exist without them. From the beginning I searched within myself for the forms that would express this love. I felt I must give this subject the dignity due this significant moment and imbue it with passion and exaltation. In 1933 I modeled in clay, life-size or over, the two figures called "Embrace." I cast it in bronze. It is now in the Sculpture Hall of the Brooklyn Museum. It seems to many a very daring thing and many people feel a certain shock that I have done this thing, but it is rare that anyone is shocked at the subject itself or the way it is handled. It was shown at the Modern Museum and at the outdoor Sculpture Show and outdoors all one summer at the Pennsylvania Museum, where it received the popular award for sculpture. To me, it is a very idealistic and a very spiritual portrayal of the love of man and woman. When it was shown at the Modern Museum, one of the critics wrote that, in all the history of art in America, no one had ever before portrayed the love of a man and a woman in sculpture. This most momentous element in life had been ignored as if it had no existence. My first idea had been to model this conception in clay and later carve it in stone, direct. But, I consummated the work in clay. It was complete, and no artist wants to copy, even his own work. Doing a thing of this kind in stone would take four or five years and would become a different work from the bronze. I would have liked to have done it. Another thing is that carving a great stone is like painting a big mural—you have to have a place for it. I had the "Mother and Child" around for twenty-five years before I found a place for it. I haven't got twenty-five years any longer to wait for somebody to find a place for a large sculpture of mine and I can only house just so many. And to move these rocks is a project; it takes a crew of four or five men and costs large sums. I often think of distributing these large pieces around the rocks and woods and fields on my place in Maine. "The Spirit of the Dance" is up there, on a ledge overlooking Robinhood Cove. I should have done this a long time ago, but I am so involved in executing things that my impulse, my drive, is not so much to display these pieces of sculpture as it is to create them and keep creating.

One day I saw my son's wife, Peggy, sitting on a bench in Maine, leaning back braced on her arms with my youngest grandson, Jonny, then a tiny baby, lying across her knees. I quickly made notes both with my mind's eye and with a pencil. It was such an unusual composition and so sculptural. I modeled it life-sized in heavy forms, alert and spirited. I called it "New Horizons" and exhibited it in the big sculpture show at the Metropolitan Museum in 1951. There was so much controversy over the show that people hardly saw the sculpture. It was bought by Mrs. Vanderbilt Webb and sits in the center of the main gallery of the Shelburne Museum. It has all the qualities of stone and I still hope one day to carve it in a dark and lively marble. But I am getting older, I need someone to give me a push, someone who wants it enough to persuade me and who has a place waiting for it. Otherwise I will probably go on to new conceptions.

CHAPTER SEVENTEEN

I WORK BEST in the early morning, on Sundays, and on rainy days. There is something soothing about rain and fog. You are removed from the restlessness of the world, and enclosed in your own world—the forces that surround you can't close in on you. You are separate; you are free. I have always had a real compulsion about work; I can work before breakfast and into the night. I also have a compulsion about answering letters and attending to certain things but not everything. I am highly selective; Marguerite thinks I am unreasonable in this. But I spend all the time I can possibly grasp in this hectic world, day and night, on my work. I never know when to stop and I never have what you could call rest periods. Not that I work with my hands twenty-four hours a day, but that I seldom relax. My one real relaxation is sleep. It alone relieves the tensions that build up in me. I can sleep for long hours at any time and any place, and I awake refreshed and ready to cope with life and art. I regret it, but sports and games mean nothing to me. I am entirely lacking in the competitive spirit. I like to see the other fellow win, he enjoys it so much. My only physical exercise outside of sculpture has been the creative dance. Then I really come to life. And in the summer I swim every day, but not enough to call it exercise. I might also add, I find attractive women a diversion and a happy relaxation.

I usually have several projects going at one time but concentrate most seriously on one until it is finished. In this way I don't keep on working on a piece beyond the point of creativity. Sometimes I leave it for weeks or even months at a time, coming back to it again and again. I have one strict rule: "When you don't know what to do, don't do it." Let it rest in your subconscious and it will resolve itself. I have a great many ideas planned ahead in the form of small sketches, in clay or in pencil. When I see something that moves me deeply or when an idea comes into my head, I make a note of it, a sketch. If it grows on me I work it out on a larger scale and develop it. I make many sketches and many changes until the final form develops in my mind. Sometimes I come back and work on an idea after ten years or more. Things grow by themselves in the unconscious, others die and are never revived. I keep all my sketches in an architect's cabinet and in as good order as it possible for me. I am not at all methodical. Yet my mind is always on one project. If something interferes—like a commission—I put my project aside and take it up when the other is finished. I do not find my work suffers from the break; often it improves. My life is not complicated by too many commissions. I do not seek them. But when one captures my imagination I can't resist it.

I work best when alone. The ideas that have come to me as sudden inspirations never develop. At the time, they always seem to me to be my greatest ideas; but when it comes to executing them, they often don't come off. The ones I do execute are of slow growth, developing from one form to another until a satisfying form is arrived at and made permanent in stone or bronze. There is relaxation and pleasure in doing small sculpture, things that take weeks, not years. My heads carved from local stones, from life-size down to a few inches in height give me great satisfaction. The variety is infinite—each one a new conception, a new experience. I love to carve cats in granite boulders and in porphyritic diabase. Cats are subtle and lovable and have no objection to being studied and sketched; whereas a dog, if you look at him, is immediately all over you for attention. A cat, who is imbued with dignity and has a mysterious and aloof quality, also has a beautiful, flowing form. We have had many wonderful Maine coon cats and I never tire of doing them.

I love to carve directly in the glacial boulders of Maine. They are full of exciting surprises in color and texture. I visualize a head or an animal in the stone and start roughing it out and developing the form that emerges as I chip away the superfluous stone, revealing the form within the rock. This is a measure of the artist's sensitivity to what is being revealed. People often ask me what I do when a chunk breaks off my stone accidentally.

I reply, "That's when you need courage and when you have to believe in God; that there is a purpose in everything and that you can find that purpose."

You gird up your loins, take a deep breath, and pray for a new vision. If you are lucky you find out eventually that the disaster has been a great help. It has removed a lot of superfluous stone that you might not have had the courage to remove. Then you must go on to see new relationships and new directions, and form will reveal itself to you once more.

This is true only when the artist is creating. If a workman is copying a plaster model in stone and a chunk breaks away and there is not enough stone to push the form back, he is out of luck. He has to start all over with a new stone or patch this one, and a patch is always a serious imperfection, except in an antique.

In wood I have carved pine, which is very soft and heavily grained, and I have carved lignum vitae, which is dense and hard as stone and in the beautiful black center, almost like carving glass. Teak is one of the most rewarding woods to carve—not too soft nor too hard, with texture but no grain, and practically indestructible. The fruit woods are beautiful but let you down disastrously; they check and crack and sometimes even go to pieces. Once when Marguerite was in California she found a beautiful log of madrone. She thought it would be different in color and interesting to carve, so she sent it to New York for me. The freight was only five dollars, but the man refused to take it off the truck. I hired a man to put it on the sidewalk. He charged five dollars. I paid a couple of other men another five dollars to bring it upstairs to my studio. It was warm and pleasant in my studio and I began to notice strange bugs like flies with long tails emerging from the log. Then one day I came down and my studio was alive with these insects. I rushed and opened the windows and they sailed off over Manhattan.

Marguerite said, "I hope we are not introducing a new and terrible pest into the East."

To get rid of them we painted the log with turpentine, and I had to visit the galleries for a few days—I couldn't stand the smell. Then the wood began to check and split. I gave up. I went out and bought a crosscut saw and we sawed it up for fireplace wood. It took a month!

When I carved "Affection" directly in stone back in 1933, it occurred to me that I tended to be limited in my work to a four-sided relief. I did not like the idea, so I penetrated the stone all the way through this time to get another dimension, releasing space around the legs and bodies. It was the first time I had done this and it took away the flatness and gave the stone a more three-dimensional feeling. In the carving of the "Child on Pony" I hadn't penetrated under the legs of the horse or through the arms of the child. But after I had carved it, I wanted to see what the effect would be if I opened up these spaces. The carving was solid enough to permit this. I had it cast in plaster and did that, and I found it didn't improve it in any way; added nothing. It was even better as it was originally conceived. You never know.

I like my sculpture solid; I have never been tempted to put holes in the wrong places. There have always been holes in sculpture but they have been in the right places. No one ever put holes through the chest of a figure or cracked the skull of a figure right down the middle until Henry Moore appeared. Nor did they break sculpture into separate and almost unrelated sections. These highly stylized effects can be very interesting, a kind of personal idiom and a trademark. And yet Moore's followers are legion. Any new angle seems to excite a rush of "me too's," but I give him credit as someone with the vision to see a possible new direction. Art is infinite with possible directions, both known and unknown, discovered and undiscovered. But art has to go beyond discovery and fashion and it has to survive these to be evaluated.

Bernard Champigneulle, writing in Paris in 1956, expressed clearly and profoundly the course of development of the great trends of art, such as the one we are in today. I quote:

> There is a relentless and historical phenomenon; no sooner has a form of art become the vogue than its field of action multiplies and is vulgarized. Its external signs repeat themselves and its spiritual substance is exhausted. It shares the lot of all fashions, fickle and ephemeral on principle. Shall we see abstract art before long developing into a sort of mechanized decoration, enriching the objects surrounding us while becoming spent itself?

Paul Wingert, Professor of Art and Archeology at Columbia, wanted to do a book on my sculpture. This pleased me very much. I worked on it with him for a year or so, getting together information for him and having photographs taken of the work—not always a simple matter. Some pieces were hard to locate, and it was often difficult to get a good photograph. Wingert did a fine and sensitive job and I was very happy with the book. I am glad someone with appreciation and understanding has written about my work both collectively and individually, because I never could give such a picture and analysis of it, nor is it my place to do so. It was published by the Pitman Publishing Co. in 1938. They printed seven thousand five hundred copies. After they sold six thousand five hundred copies, they wrote me they were giving it up but had a thousand unbound copies on hand which they would bind and sell to me for thirty-five cents apiece. Otherwise they would destroy them.

I bought them and when a truck delivered a thousand books to my door I almost died! I stacked them away in our storeroom after dislodging the plaster casts and molds that occupied it. At first, no bookstore would buy them, and then when they finally did they didn't sell them and I'd buy them back. I had no luck until I found I could sell them to schools, libraries, museums and colleges throughout the country by writing letters. I'm not a businessman; the institutions drove me crazy wanting invoices in triplicate and bills in triplicate and receipts. I sold a lot to just ordinary people. Everyone who saw the book seemed to want it—except the people who inhabit bookshops. Finally I sold them all; now I buy them back from the Art Students League, where they still have a few odd copies.

From this I learned one important thing. As long as I was active the books sold. As soon as I got bored and neglected them nothing happened, and I am afraid this is true of any profession or activity in life.

When Tom Benton was teaching at the Arts Students League, he found the questions the students asked him so repetitious that he decided to write a book and then refer them to the book. I felt much the same way but sculpture presented another problem. It was very difficult for the student to get adequate information on the things related to sculpture. I had to find things out the hard way—not only by talking to other sculptors, but by looking up tombstone cutters and tool men, by hanging around machine shops and bronze foundries. I had to study the ancient sculptures of the world, not just to enjoy their beauty but to find out how sculpture was done. This I did from reproductions and from the works in museums and the Museum of Natural History. You have no idea how difficult it is to find out some bit of essential knowledge. When I began carving directly in stone, almost all sculptors modeled in clay and then had it cast in plaster and eventually turned it over to a professional stone-carver to point up and copy in stone. There was almost no one I could ask about carving direct—about how stone behaved and how to handle it; about tools for marbles and limestone and granites, where to buy them, how to temper them, how to use them; or about how to polish stone and the succession of carborundums and hones necessary. Today, again, sculptors have almost given up carving directly in stone or even wood. It takes too long; they can't bear to spend so much time on one work of art and there are so many easier and more intriguing ways of doing things, not to mention the effort. Stone-carving is work.

To me nothing approaches the beauty and satisfaction of a work carved directly in stone. Each piece is unique, and he who owns one by a real artist possesses a bit of eternity.

There were endless books on painting but almost none on sculpture—certainly none you could recommend to a serious young student eager to learn. I decided to write one myself. I wanted not only to give young sculptors complete information on actually doing sculpture; I included information as to where materials could be found and purchased as well as information on what books would be useful and on related subjects. I even made diagrams of how to make a strong box and how to crate sculpture. I included chapters analyzing the great sculpture of the world, of all ages and all people, and there was a section devoted to contemporary sculptors and sculpture. Every page was carefully laid out and planned and the illustrations were all related to the pages. It was a very comprehensive and beautiful book and should be invaluable to students. But students still call me up and ask the same old questions.

I say, "Do you have my book?"

"Oh yes," they say, "but that isn't in it."

I say, "Look on page so and so and you will find a complete answer."

I am beginning to think nobody reads a book. They just skim through it.

The book was in my mind, but I might never have written it if it hadn't been for Sam Golden, who had published a set of small books on artists of today and their work. Sam saw some pamphlets I had done for a teaching project that fell through for lack of funds. He suggested I do a book and gave me a five-hundred-dollar advance. That is how I actually got down to writing the book. When it was done, Sam Golden looked at it and, like too many publishers, he considered my manuscript just a starting point; he was now going to rewrite it himself. First we sat down and he started from the beginning with the acknowledgments. He objected to this one and that one, saying, "Why, why?" I explained why but he couldn't see it. We fought over that for two days and then got involved with the question of a title. After that, he was so exhausted he didn't care much what was in the book. I don't think he ever read it.

Manuel Komroff was editor for Sam Golden at that time and he was to check and edit my manuscript. After glancing over it he said, "What the hell, Bill; you know so much more about sculpture than I do. How can I edit this?" and he turned it in as is.

There was still the question of a title.

My son, Tessim, said, "After all, you want to sell the book. I've got just the title for you. I've even got two titles for you to choose from—"The Art of Chiseling" or "How to Make a Model." Finally we came up with *Zorach Explains Sculpture: What It Means and How It Is Made*. Naturally it was never a best-seller, but it is in libraries and schools and available to students and people interested in sculpture wherever they are. Sam Golden lost interest, but the Tudor Publishing Company brought out a second edition at a slightly lower price so that it is still possible for people to find it.

In 1959, the Whitney Museum gave me a retrospective show. They went to great trouble and expense to bring my big stone sculptures from West Palm Beach and from the Metropolitan Museum as well as from my studio—even borrowing the large aluminum of the "Spirit of the Dance" from Radio City. Some pieces were unavailable and were exhibited in plaster patined to look like bronze or stone. To me it was a most comprehensive and impressive show. I could not ask any more adequate presentation of my lifework in sculpture.

The catalogue of the exhibition was in itself a beautiful and impressive work of art. And in addition the Museum published it enlarged into book form with additional plates, some in color, and with a fine article and analysis of my work by John I. H. Baur, Associate Director of the Whitney Museum of American Art. It is a serious study and evaluation of my art from the beginning to the present.

We have lived in Robinhood on Georgetown Island not far from the city of Bath for over forty years. Six months of the year we spend in New York, but we are legal residents of Maine. The Bath Garden Club asked my advice about a fountain for the city. I gave it serious thought. There was a small, irregular pool in the city park with a jet of water in the center. The Garden Club wished to have something there that would be an attraction and enhance the city. They had collected a small amount of money and were considering three disks in the pool with water spouting from each, but they weren't quite happy with the idea so they consulted me. I wrote them that I would contribute my services and create a fountain that would be a work of art that the city and future generations would be proud of, if they could raise the money to cover the costs. I wanted no compensation for my part in it, which would be creating the model, designing the fountain, and supervising the project from beginning to end. I wanted this to be my gift to the city of Bath—as a thing to be enjoyed for all time. They would have to raise the money to have the model cast in bronze, to have a suitable basin made, and to have it set up in working order.

The estimated cost was somewhat startling to them, but I knew I had to allow for the unforeseen contingencies that always arise. I am happy to say that I was able to keep the whole thing within my original figure. The Garden Club selected a magnificent dark granite for the basin. This was quarried, carved, and finished in Finland and shipped here. I made a three-foot model which was displayed in the public library for everyone to consider—a kneeling figure, rising, with arms uplifted, called the "Spirit of the Sea" in deference to Bath's maritime and shipbuilding past. Water splashes in delicate streams over the bronze woman and falls into the pond over the lip of the basin. It is an impressive thing, and I think Bath, a small city, is fortunate to have a real work of art that anyone could be proud of in its public park. I, too, am proud of it and proud of Bath for having it.

The ladies of the Garden Club, under the leadership of Mrs. Arthur M. Bowker and Mrs. Arthur Sewell were wonderful. They set out to raise the money by contributions, sales, teas, and various projects, until they collected the full amount. Barbara Sargent, the wife of the Congregational minister and an artist in her own right, was an enthusiastic and determined supporter. She was extraordinary in her efforts and understanding.

Then one day in New York, where I was peacefully working on the project, I had a letter from Barbara Sargent telling me that all hell had broken loose in Bath. My enemies had caught up with me—the old discredited Communist bugaboo. While it might be discredited in New York and Washington and Texas, it was all new to Bath. The Bath City Council and the Garden Club were sent the same old unverified and scandalous charges against me. I am proud of the civic-minded ladies of the Garden Club. In spite of the charges, they gave me a vote of confidence and recommended we go ahead with the fountain. But the town was torn apart and horrified; the papers were full of it. This time I followed my own judgment and decided not to ignore the charges as I had during the Texas fiasco. This was my country, where I lived. I could not let it pass unanswered, no matter what any lawyer said. I sent a long statement to the Bath paper:

> . . . These accusations are an old story to me, and I would be inclined to ignore the whole business as ridiculous; but out of respect for my friends in Bath and Maine and because I have made this part of the country my home, I feel it necessary to answer this attack as concisely as possible.
>
> Let me say in the first place I am not a Communist, have never been a Communist, and have never had any dealings with the Communist party, nor have I supported any causes that I suspected of being Communist. In fact I am not and have never been politically minded. I am art minded; art is my life, and all my contacts with

> people are in relation to art. I came to this country at the age of four and have been a loyal citizen all my life. . . .
>
> . . . The attacks are by innuendo only. I also suggest that if they find my name on any petition let them look carefully at the other prominent names on the petition and also consider the political atmosphere at the time. . . .
>
> . . . As to my gift of the fountain, in the end the decision rests with the citizens of Bath. They will have to think this over seriously, and they will have to decide whether they will accept these accusations as the ultimate truth or William Zorach as a sincere upright citizen as well as a fine artist. I will be happy to answer any questions anyone may wish to ask or have any of you write to anyone whose opinions you would value.

It was given front page attention in Bath and also in Portland, and some very intelligent editorials were written that I was very proud to read. In Bath two men who had spread this scandal appeared in the open. Before, it had always been underhanded and no matter what I knew, I could not prove it. I immediately got in touch with Arnold Weissberger of Weissberger and Frosch, attorneys. I suggested that they write to this leading person who was spreading these accusations, telling him that I was suing him for one hundred thousand dollars for slander. This shut him up. He and his friends made no further effort to stop the fountain. The City Council voted me support and I went ahead with the project.

The granite basin arrived from Finland and an enormous derrick came down from Portland to set up the fountain. They handled the sixteen tons of stone as delicately as if it were a feather and set it on its foundations. They picked up the over-life-sized bronze figure and set it in place with the most subtle assurance while the crowd held its breath. The plumber handled the water outlets with great skill and, when certain pieces didn't fit, he rushed back to his shop and came back in a few minutes with something that did. Plumbing is always a mystery to me. I couldn't believe it would work but it did. I held my breath while the streams were adjusted. It was beautiful. There was a ceremony in the city park with the band playing, and civic leaders making speeches. Professor Phillip Beam of Bowdoin made a fine and learned speech. I said a few words and the water sprayed perfectly.

I think that almost everyone in Bath was proud and happy.

CHAPTER EIGHTEEN

MY CHILDREN play a very important part in my life. I loved them dearly. I had great pleasure watching them grow and develop. Tessim and Dahlov and Marguerite are in all my sculpture, for my sculpture is based upon my life and the people and things around me that I loved. They were my life. Through them I came near to all other human beings. I realized my art through them.

We feel we know our children as we know ourselves. It is a shock when we come to realize how little parents really know of the lives of their children. Every child has a secret life where no grownup may enter. It is an early attempt to establish identity. Tessim had a life of his own from seven on. He was not communicative with his parents. He would get up early in the morning, get his own breakfast, and be off to school often before we were up. One day we got a telephone call from the school. "Will you please keep Tessim home until the janitor gets here. We always find him waiting at the door." He was a natural-born visitor. He knew everybody; he visited all our friends, his school friends, people he picked up on the streets, all ages, all kinds. His visits were short, he never stayed long at any one place. He never mentioned to us where he had been or what was said, and if we ever asked we found out absolutely nothing.

One day in Provincetown a stranger stopped me. She said, "It is so wonderful you have taught Tessim all those beautiful songs you learned in Russia. He was telling me all about it. I stopped him one day in the street, he was singing such a lovely song."

I was stunned. I did not remember a word of Russian or a Russian song. I did not disillusion her or let Tessim down. I am sure it was a lovely song that he made up.

As I mentioned earlier both of our children went to the City and Country School. One day a devastating and terrible problem arose and lasted for several weeks. Sprague's family supported the school financially; four of their children were in it. Sprague was in Tessim's class. He was very conscious of the role that his parents played in the school—and so were the teachers. One day, in great excitement, we were called in. Tessim was accused of having cut a hole in Sprague's new sweater. Another classmate said that he had seen Tessim cut it with scissors. Tessim, enraged, was in tears. He shouted it was a lie. It was a most painful and difficult situation. Should we support Tessim against the teachers, Sprague's family, and the school, realizing there are circumstances under which any child will lie. No one doubted the crime, and how could we know the truth? How could we possibly find out the truth? We realized what a devastating thing it would be to Tessim if he were innocent and we, his parents, didn't believe him. The school was furious with us, "for not getting the truth out of him." Tessim stayed home for a week or so. Would he ever go back to school? Then one day I went to school and asked to see the sweater. I said immediately, "This was not cut by a scissor—this sweater was ripped." Sprague was called in and confessed that he had ripped the material on a nail. Tessim came out from under a black cloud. He was joyous. Now Sprague would be punished; now the teachers would tell him how sorry they were that they had accused him unjustly. The whole thing was dropped. Sprague was not punished; no teacher ever said she was sorry. For Tessim, it was an illuminating experience in the ways of the world.

Tessim was not a progressive-school child by nature. He was fascinated by the projects but bored by the laissez-faire and the cult of self-expression. He detested "rhythms" and the lack of discipline. Tessim liked work and tasks to be accomplished. He didn't like being left at loose ends or having learning disguised as play. He had a terrific drive and, when absorbed in some enterprise, he was at it night and day and could not be pried loose. The year they had a printing press, he worked day and night and almost ruined his eyes.

We bought the place in Maine when the children were very young, and they spent wonderful, healthy summers in the country. Tessim sailed and fished and put out lobster traps. The yield was small but there was always hope. The little girls had to fish bait for him; they wanted to play but Tessim said, "You've got to fish bait," and they did. One summer he picked blueberries—over a hundred crates of blueberries. At first he received five dollars per crate from the Boston Commission Merchants. When they sent him an invoice for railway express on the "spoiled" crates he shipped them, we all quit. He drove us crazy getting him crates, getting him boxes, taking them to town to the express office. Tessim flourished but the wear and tear on us was terrific.

When Tessim was thirteen we let him go to Europe with two school teachers and three girls his own age or a bit younger. They toured France in an old Ford. In Switzerland the teachers left the children in a camp and went on to Paris. Tessim was to bring the girls to Paris a week later, which he did. The teachers were having such a good time and Tessim had proved so efficient that they asked him to take the three girls to Brittany for two weeks with a French teacher from

Rosemary Hall. I gather that Tessim had no sympathy with their lack of interest in Brittany. The girls were content to stay put in the hotel reading Tauchnitz editions while Tessim wanted to see and explore Brittany. Finally he decided to leave them and the French teacher alone in the hotel. He went off to see Finistère and spent the nights alone in little Brittany inns. For years afterwards he went sailing out in the Sheepscot Bay in the red Breton sailor's jacket he'd brought back from France.

Tessim was a brilliant boy and had great talent for writing, but luck was not with him and luck or chance plays a great role in all our lives. He wrote a fine story about Maine and slavery in the early days. Several publishers seemed ready to publish it but changed their minds at the last minute. One of his children's books was "adapted" by a leading children's book publisher—they finally compromised a plagiarism suit in his favor. He couldn't break through in writing. Tessim went to Johns Hopkins University and then to American University and Harvard to do postgraduate work. He met Peggy Harris, who was in Radcliffe, and a year later they were married. He got a job in the Labor Department under Francis Perkins and later in the Treasury under Morgenthau. When he was a little boy, people would ask him, "I suppose you will be an artist like your father when you grow up?"

Tessim would say, "No indeed. I don't want to starve to death."

Now he is a food-broker, dealing with Alaska King Crab for the most part. Peggy, now that their boys are in college, is librarian at the Brooklyn Museum, which she enjoys as it is both art, activity, and life.

My daughter Dahlov grew up painting. When people asked her if she was going to be an artist when she grew up she said, "Certainly."

The Museum of Modern Art gave her a one-man show when they opened their educational department under Victor D'Amico. She was eighteen years old at the time. Lincoln School suggested that the Museum look over the work of various children for a possible exhibition. When they saw all the mass of work Dahlov had done, they were interested and gave her the show. Dahlov did not like the idea. She felt that she was being promoted as a child prodigy. I had saved everything she had ever done because I thought it was unusual. I had had so much experience with children's art in progressive schools that I knew just how unusual it was. She did creative sculpture, especially tiny animals in ceramics and painted endless pictures, mostly of animals. She always had the ability to draw any animal doing anything; certain children have this thing about animals. It came as naturally to Dahlov as breathing. She loved all animals and knew them in all their ways and movements—how they felt and how they thought. I used to be furious when I had to drive to Maine with a car full of cats and dogs and mice and guinea pigs and birds. But I am weak when it comes to crossing the young in the things that mean so much to them. It hurts me less to suffer than it does to see them suffer.

Life was not all art for Dahlov when she was in school. She was the child that progressive education was made for. She was endlessly creative. She never asked "What shall I do?" or, "What can I do next?" She was completely absorbed in the school projects.

Even as a child Dahlov never needed many people; perhaps that is why she can live year round in a farm in the country. She has always been devoted to just a few special friends. As a child she had two deep friendships—Faith Reyher, whom she found in Provincetown at the age of four and they are still warm friends, and Joan Michelson, who has been living in Denmark for some years. Joan's mother moved up to Harlem to work among the Negroes. Clarina was a dedicated person who wanted to better the world and raise the standards of the underdog. Dahlov would visit Joan, go to meetings and parties, and come back through Harlem at midnight alone. No one ever bothered her. We hadn't the least idea of this until long afterwards. At certain points we just didn't touch the lives of our children.

Dahlov never studied art nor did either of us teach her, but she was exposed to art every day of her life because she lived with two artists. She does not paint like either one of us. She does not need models; she has the kind of visual memory her mother has and the creative vision to see what others do not see and to treasure it. I remember seeing her in front of a canvas empty except for a beautifully executed bit of detail in one spot.

I said, "Do you know what you are going to do?"

She pointed to her forehead. "It's all in my head," she said.

Dahlov writes and illustrates children's books, even making the separations herself. She has published over twenty and continues to enjoy writing. She understands the minds of children without playing down to them. Children love these books and almost any adult can enjoy their imagination and beauty. She lives on the Baker farm in Maine, helps with the activities and farm work, takes care of her house, and finds time for everything. She made a magnificent collage of the Garden of Eden, which her family won't let her part with. She makes stuffed animals of cloth that are delightful in their sculptural forms and in their color patterns. These she first made for her own children and as gifts for her friends' children.

When Dahlov was eighteen she married a young man, Adolph Ipcar, about ten years older than herself. I was one of those fathers who thought no one was good enough for his very special daughter and I was desperate about it, but I was wrong. It has been a successful and happy marriage. I will add that I had liked my son-in-law before I found out he was going to marry my daughter. At the time they were married, Adolph was teaching in the government experimental project at Reedsville, West Virginia. Just before the new term opened, the funds were cut off and the school folded. They decided it was an opportunity to try a year

72. The artist's studio in Brooklyn, New York. 1960.

73. *Choun.* (Inca Sun God) 1960. Pink Maine boulder. 5½″ high. The Downtown Gallery, New York City.

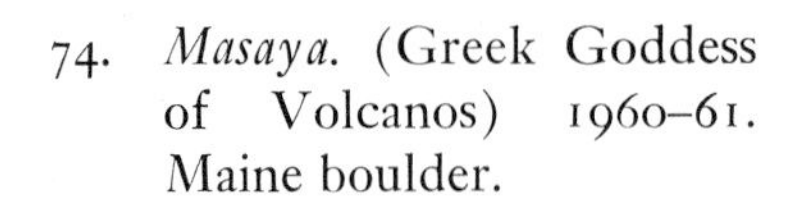

74. *Masaya.* (Greek Goddess of Volcanos) 1960–61. Maine boulder.

75. *Constance*. 1960. Spotted Maine granite. 6″ high. The Downtown Gallery, New York City.

76. *Plum Tree in Winter*. 1960. Watercolor. 5″ x 7¼″. The collection of the Zorach children.

77. *Sea Pigeon.* 1960. Maine granite. 7¾″ long.

78. *The Mermaid.* 1960. Maine glacial boulder. 12″ high. The Downtown Gallery, New York City.

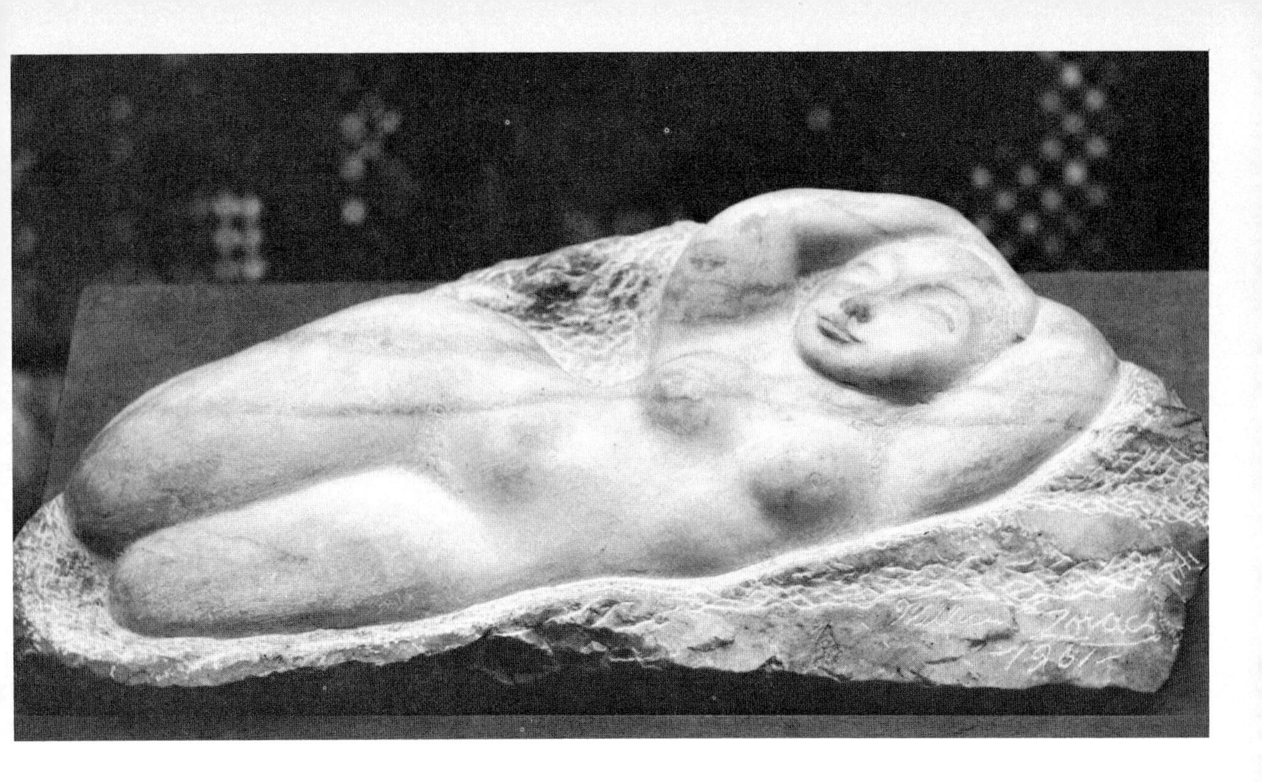

79. *Odalisk*. 1961. Yellow marble. 22½″ long. Collection of Mrs. John Hay Whitney.

80. *Sleeping Puppy*. 1962. Maine glacial boulder. Collection of Tessim Zorach.

81. *Singing Bird*. 1963. Spotted granite. 12″ long. Collection of the Zorach children.

82. *Olympic Runner*. 1965. Bronze. 14′ high. Kiener Memorial, St. Louis, Missouri.

83. *Eulogy*. 1966. Bronze. 81″ high. Des Moines Art Center, Des Moines, Iowa.

84. *Cat with Long Whiskers*. 1966. Maine granite. 18″ long. Collection of Mrs. Adolf Berle.

85. *Wisdom of Solomon.* 1966. Casota limestone. 39½″ high. The artist completed this just before he died. Collection of Mr. and Mrs. Lester Avnet.

of life on a Maine farm. Dahlov loved farm life; I'm afraid it came a little hard to Adolph at first, being a New York city boy, but they are still running the farm, a small dairy farm next to our place in Maine. They'll never make much money but it is a wonderful way of life and companionship for them.

Dahlov and Adolph have two boys and Tessim and Peggy have three. Boys are fine but I wish someone had managed a granddaughter or two. I dearly love little girl children. But one by one the grandsons are graduating from college, so maybe I can look forward to a great-granddaughter one of these days. I have already acquired my first granddaughter by marriage. We are all delighted to have a girl in the family and this girl especially.

For years our New York grandsons spent their summers with us in Maine. We had a hundred acres of woods and shore and fields and a big house with lots of room. We couldn't have three small grandsons spend the summer in the grime and heat of New York nor would it have seemed right for them to find another place for the summer. Of course their mother was there to look after them and we had no responsibility. But when three city grandsons in the house with us and two more grandsons in the house above us on the hill were added, the peace of Robinhood was shattered. They tore through my deepest concentration. They raged and ravaged through the farm and the woods and the shore. I was ready for murder and it was a four-year-old grandson who all but triggered my thoughts into action. I was sitting on the lawn chipping a dog out of a magnificent boulder, the one Janet and Joe Bosse have in their garden in Greenwich Village, when two young men aged four and five appeared, each carrying a big rock.

"Let's get rid of Bill," they said. Peter threw the rock at my head. Charlie's rock was too heavy for him to throw or I'd have been hit a second time. I never got a chance at murder. Peggy rushed to their protection like a mother hen with chicks. And she was right; they were in real danger.

That was a red-letter day. Charlie and Peter had imaginations that were alert and complementary. Early in the morning they decided to look in the beehives and see what the bees were doing. Fortunately the bees were too busy to bother with two small boys and a few well placed stings settled that. Next they visited our attic, where one of our students worked. The student, at that time Harold, had no money and what paints and canvas he possessed were all his capital. The two small villains emptied every bit of his paint out of every tube, smeared up all his canvases, covered themselves with paint from head to toe, and put the rest on their clothes in a multicolored goo. We couldn't believe our eyes when two animated fauve paintings appeared on the lawn. We simply didn't know what to do. I don't even know what we did; but during that day they found time to pour sand in my gasoline engine, with shocking results. Then they went down to the shore, got into the boat, untied it, and set out to sea. Unfortunately, they were rescued!

Life in Robinhood wasn't exactly conducive to concentration and creative thought those summers but I admit that was an exceptional day. Later on, the older ones went off to camps and eventually the younger ones as well. But believe it or not, I missed them. I was always delighted to see them whenever they returned to the farm.

My youngest grandson, Jonny, never seemed to want to do much art work but he was apparently more interested than the others. He asked me questions.

When I was carving a duck in white marble he said, "What would you do, Grandpa, if the head fell off?"

I said, "Jonny, it would break my heart."

Just then off it came.

Jonny said, "Grandpa, what will you do about your heart?"

I said, "I'll have to put it together again."

The duck slowly became a sea gull with its head tucked under its wing and my heart was mended. Jonny had wise thoughts for a little boy of ten. I took him to the Museum of Modern Art.

He looked at the pictures very carefully and said, "Do you know what is next, Grandpa? People are going to go into a room with nothing but empty walls and imagine pictures."

Another time he said, at a Picasso exhibition, "Do you know what's going to happen, Grandpa? People are going to start looking like these pictures."

When my grandson Charlie was very young he wanted to work with me in the studio, chipping stone and squeezing clay. He liked to use a big brush and red chalk water and paint abstractions on newspaper. Swish, swish.

After he'd done a few strokes he'd say, "Where are the thumb tacks?"

He couldn't get his masterpiece up on the wall fast enough. I thought he might turn out to be an avant-garde painter, but it was only a phase. The need for self-expression through art has skipped this generation, but not art appreciation an understanding. That they have.

My children were wonderful at posing for me for drawings and even for sculpture on occasion. I guess they were brought up to accept it as a way of life. But not my grandchildren. If they saw me get out a pencil and a piece of paper they'd duck, or even a certain look in the eye would send them kiting. One day I caught Charlie sitting on the back steps.

I immediately yelled, "Hold that pose."

He did but he said sadly, "Why did I have to sit here in the first place?"

Marguerite said to me, "Do you mean to say you have written an autobiography and not a word about your love life? If anyone has read this far, you can't let them down."

"I thought that was strictly personal," I said.

"You can't have an autobiography and leave out the strictly personal side of life."

"I can't be specific," I said.

She replied, "Go as far as you can."

Maybe Marguerite was right when she said the first time she saw me, "A ladies' man."

I don't like the sound of it, but I have never been a man's man. I enjoy men and my contact with men. But it is almost wholly with men who are artists, writers, musicians, and professional men; last of all with businessmen. Theirs is a different world. But with women it is another story. All my life I have been very susceptible to the female sex. They excite me and I enjoy them. From men I ask an intellectual give and take. With woman I am happy; I enjoy them to look at, to be with, to love. And yet I am a one-woman man. I have been married to one woman for over fifty years. To me Marguerite is the most wonderful woman in the world. I can be exasperated and fed up, but I love her and I have the greatest appreciation for her as an artist and as a person.

During my life many women have fascinated me and I have dreamed of what life might be like with each of them. I have been terribly emotionally involved at times. But I have never done more than contemplate a change. I have never taken any steps to bring it about. And when, years afterwards, I met these girls that I had thought so marvelous, I was certainly glad I had done nothing about it. I am sure they were too. Marguerite was never a jealous woman but she used to be annoyed at the women who "understood" me and told me what a great artist I would be if I could only shake off her influence–for theirs–then the world would be mine. They felt so badly at seeing me hamstrung and led astray when I could be wandering free and untrammeled in their companionship.

Marguerite used to be amused at the girls who were enamored and brought her flowers. She always said then she knew they had serious intentions and she wasn't sure I had not given them cause. I was always so intrigued by new and fascinating females that I would go to see them, listen with deep sympathy to their life stories and the shortcomings of their husbands, comfort them the best I could, and wish there was some way I could solve their problems. Apart from the glamor girls there were others. I remember one girl back in the early days, one who almost moved in on us. She was so fascinated that she would arrive in the early morning with her little boy and a raw cauliflower or such item for their lunch and settle down for the day. She didn't believe in cooked food and only ate raw vegetables. She was pretty and interesting and deadly serious and adoring. I soon got so fed up I would walk out on her and leave her to Marguerite–who didn't appreciate this one bit. She considered Marguerite very selfish in not offering to take her in and share me with her. I painted a large picture of her and the boy in the kitchen of their cold-water flat, in greens and grays, with all the interesting kitchen forms and details. Marguerite thought it was a wonderful picture but I wasn't satisfied with it and kept repainting it until I destroyed it.

There were the girls who wanted to show me their work and have me encourage and promote them, who took me to their bosom if I was sympathetic or appreciative and who dropped me like a hot brick if I didn't respond to their genius as well as their charms.

I was running up the stairs to see a friend next door on Tenth Street when I bumped into a young woman. We stood on the stairs and talked. I asked her what she was doing and where she came from. She said she was a dancer studying dancing with Martha Graham and had come to New York from the West. I was always interested in the dance and dancers. She fascinated me. She was vivacious and full of movement and young life. She had no inhibitions, she was completely amoral and unscrupulous, but she had gay and tender impulses. She didn't hesitate to lie and steal and use people. She haunted me for a number of years. She went through the whole gamut of life that is offered to a young girl living in Greenwich Village. She fell in love with a young kid who had poetic potentials and had been thrown out of college because of his affairs with girls. She thought he was wonderful, a genius. She lived with him in disreputable squalor in Patchin Place. She danced, she wrote, she stole from stores—not just little items but big things such as a fur coat. She was arrested for shoplifting but the Judge fell for her line and let her off. She thought it was a joke but she was more careful after that. She stole beautiful art books and wanted to give them to me. I gave her a lecture and told her to take them back and never to do such a thing again. She just looked at me with those sweet kitten eyes and walked away.

Finally I took her to the Jonases. They liked to do things for young people. They took an interest in her for a while, but they were not her kind of people and also they became fed up and disillusioned with her way of life and worried about her association with their children. I gave her some money to go out West, where she was supposed to have had a job offered to her. She did teach in dancing schools out West for a while and finally married a writer, had a child, and was divorced. Many years later I met her in a gallery in New York. She looked so old.

I said, "My god, your hair is gray!"

"Well," she said, "I'm fifty years old. You don't look so young yourself!"

After that I never saw her again. I can seldom retrieve lost relationships; the illusion remains too real to me and that makes it impossible to go through the reconstruction that is necessary.

My life has been spent as an observer and an artist. My eyes have been trained to see the beauty in this world and life around me and trained to see not only visually but with love.

The basis of my life is love. I love people, especially young people and children. My approach to human beings is simple and direct because I am sympathetic and genuinely interested in their lives and their ideas about life. I have lengthy conversations with tramps who come to the door, with men I meet on the road or in trains or on farms. Perhaps I go too far; Marguerite has always said that, if I were left alone with a woman, by the time we parted she would have told me her whole life, even whom she had slept with last night and whom she hoped she might sleep with tomorrow.

The war with its suspicions and intrigues and false interpretations of values drove me somewhat into myself. I became less outgoing and retired more into myself.

I have known all kinds of people, from Republicans and Democrats to anarchists to those I felt were communists. But my contact with them has always been art—not politics. I have always been a liberal-minded person but I have never been politically minded. I have never belonged to any organizations except art organizations.

When I was very young I thought socialism might lead to a better world, but I was disillusioned a long time ago about the state taking over and regulating our lives. I could never see dictatorship or regimentation. I realize that when a person is dedicated to a political idea, he must devote his life to fighting for that idea and even be willing to go to jail if necessary. My dedication has always been to art and no one ever asks us to go to jail for art. No one ever asks an artist to die for art—starve, maybe—but not die. An artist owes it to himself and to the world to live for art.

When I am up in a plane flying ten thousand feet above the earth, I'm thrilled by the sun over the far horizon, the night drawing swiftly on. And I look down upon the world. The cities are like clusters of tiny pebbles on a wide stretch of sand, and the roads are delicate silken threads weaving across the far stretches of the plains. A car or truck moving along looks like a little red ant crawling along the crevices of a sunlit rock. And I wonder what all this struggle of people and all this fear and hatred and worry is about. This may be a feeling of futility or pessimism or frustration—or it may be maturity. And then again I think, everything must have a purpose in the larger cosmic sense. There must be a reason for all these conflicts of races and masses of human beings—to keep a balance in the rhythm of the whole because the balance of the universe is rhythm. Rhythm is the basis that keeps the universe from falling apart. Rhythm is what keeps a work of art from falling apart. Rhythm must be the ebb and flow that controls the heavens. I find it hard to accept that conflict—war—has value in that it prevents stagnation; it keeps life in constant flux and turmoil.

I have always suffered from periods of depression when the problems of life got me down. At these times I sleep; sleep is a life-saver for me, a release from tensions, a retreat, a rejuvenation.

I would like to read, but nothing has such a soporific effect on me as the printed word. A chapter in a novel is more effective than any sleeping pill. A few lines fire my imagination and I am off on my own into another world. When I emerge I have completely lost track of the point at which I took off. I hate books that are drowned in words. The one novel I have ever read from beginning to end and that held me every word of the way was Tolstoy's *War and Peace*. To me, that was a marvelous book.

I love the early history books of this country. I buy them in junk shops and from discarded libraries and read them all—they are so live and personal. They take you right into the early life of this country as nothing else does. There are plenty of broad and comprehensive books on history. I enjoy these fresh and intimate pictures of life that bring you people as human beings. Otherwise only art books, biographies, and explorations can hold me.

Our house in Maine had a wonderful collection of books on explorations. I have penetrated the jungles of Africa with Stanley and Livingstone and traced the Nile with Baker. I have followed the caribou and sneaked up on seals on the ice with Stefansson; I have starved with Kane and Greeley and Nansen, and frozen and suffered. I have been shipwrecked in the Antarctic, and lost in jungles. But for Marguerite to actually get me to Guatemala or Mexico is a major and soul-rending operation. Not that I do not enjoy it when I am there—it's just that I never want to go anywhere. Not even from New York to our home in Maine.

I buy art books endlessly, of today and yesterday and the day before yesterday, most of them in languages I can't read. And the ones I can read I find have little to say about art and little to do with art except from an art historian's viewpoint. I don't say this facetiously. Most writers on art are composing literary essays on art, using art only as material to start their literary imaginations soaring. Art is primarily visual, not literary. I buy art books for the reproductions. Beautiful art of all times is available in our museums but it is another thing to sit home and explore the art of the world, mull over it, enjoy certain aspects of it today and something else tomorrow. To see what Picasso is doing today and what the Sardinian craftsmen were doing before history. To realize the exquisite restraint and perfection of the delicately trivial things of life that the Japanese thought worthy of perpetuating. And the raucous bid for attention of this eager, impatient "today," denying time and permanence but dynamic with effort.

In school I never went past the seventh grade. I have acquired an academic education the easy way—by degrees. In 1958, I was given an honorary Master of Arts degree at Bowdoin College and the same year received a Citation at Bates College, and in 1961, I received a Doctor's degree at Colby College; in 1964, both Marguerite and I were given Doctor's degrees at Bates. I appreciate these honors and it gives me a certain pleasure when I remember that my formal education ended before high school and what a mysterious struggle it was to get that far.

I have never been one to pretend to knowledge that I did not possess or to be embarrassed by my ignorance. If I do not understand a word I never hesitate to say so or to ask for the meaning. Like all self-educated men, my knowledge is great in certain areas, yet many things about people and events that a school child would know I have never even encountered. I am interested in knowledge—

I love to be introduced to new phases of the world which I have never been conscious of before. But unless these things are integrated into my life, I am apt to set them aside and forget them. Each time the forgotten knowledge turns up it is new to me and I am again entranced.

Because of my compulsion to work and my absorption in it, I am a poor visitor—unless I have watercolors along and can sketch. I am a poor traveler for the same reason. I am glad my wife persuaded me to go to Mexico and Guatemala and the Caribbean, but I hope she doesn't persuade me to go anywhere else. I realize that from actual contact with a country and its people you get something that no book or photograph can give you. But I have a terrible resistance to the mechanics of travel, deadlines, tickets, the endless waits, the frantic rush, customs, shots, the barrier of language. I just don't want to go places. It destroys all the continuity of creation and yet I know it has an inestimable value. I come back fresh to my stones and to my problem, and some way the problem has been solved and the stone is a new and exciting challenge.

CHAPTER NINETEEN

MY PLACE in the art world did not come easily to me. Success did not just fall into my lap. It was my innate belief in myself and in the importance of art in life that sustained me through the long years of struggle. It never occurred to me to give up or to seek some other, perhaps easier, way of life. I have said that luck plays an important part in our lives. Neither Marguerite nor myself were lucky, and I want to say this clearly; so many times we did not quite get the prize and we did not quite make the sale. We could never slip by a jury of any kind for an exhibition anywhere. Perhaps it was just as well. Too much luck, too much success too quickly, can be fatal. The heartbreak and the ever-recurring disappointments made us tough. It might have destroyed us but thank God it never made us feel our work was no good, although it certainly made us feel it was unwanted and unappreciated. We long ago gave up sending our work to juries. We exhibited only when invited. This is still true today—only today we are invited.

In the beginning we had exhibition after exhibition and sold nothing—not one little thing—and yet we had wonderful publicity. Over and over a sale seemed assured right up to the final moment and then nothing happened. Either the customer vanished or he bought some other man's work. There is always some of this in every artist's life, but for us it was a consistent pattern. The same thing happened with commissions. There was enthusiasm right up to the last minute and then, finally, nothing. Now and then a commission or a sale would slip through to us. We did not need much nor did we want much, just money for living and art materials and freedom to work. The big collectors never could quite buy my work. Even today very few of them own any of it beyond token pieces. My work is mostly owned by "people" and by museums, whose collections it will always enhance. And I would rather have it that way. My art is not a stock-market item to be bought and sold and manipulated. The people who think of art in that way do not want my work. I am not insulted, I am flattered.

People knowing my reputation and my success will find this hard to believe, but it is so essentially true that I must include it, for it can have great meaning and encouragement to young artists. I am not complaining. I have had all the success I could want and all the recognition I could want, have sold as much work as I have needed to and received all the honors I could wish for. I have never been greedy for fame or money or honors; yet I appreciate what has come to me. I am happiest to see my work where it can be enjoyed by people—in their homes and in museums and public places, for there is a permanency in this and it will live for humanity. Even if forgotten at times, it will return and be seen afresh.

Between Marguerite and myself there was never any conflict over art. There were plenty of arguments, and I hate arguments but Marguerite loves to argue and discuss things; and again, I hate discussions. But we never argued about recognition, appreciation, or fame. In each of us there was an inner feeling that the acclaim of the world had nothing to do with the value and meaning of a work of art. We each did what we could to the best of our ability. Marguerite has an extraordinary sense of design and of form and color. She often helped me work out the design relationships in sculpture. She always said that I had a depth of feeling and an original creativeness that was beyond hers. The realization of these qualities was of value to both of us. It has been a lifetime of collaboration without ever subordinating individuality. We have found each other's ideas and criticisms bracing, even when unwelcome. We have never had any conflict about money. It belonged equally to both of us, no matter who made it. Marguerite likes to live in sympathetic and beautiful surroundings. She likes order and beauty and, no matter where we have lived, she has made it attractive and livable. I have great resistance to possessions. It is painful to me to replace worn-out autos, refrigerators, suits, rugs, furniture, shoes, anything. Only desperation or my wife's insistence makes it possible. It is ridiculous, but the resistance persists.

There is a tendency among men to transform the loved one into a mother image, or at least to seek to identify the two. I had that tendency but Marguerite would have none of it. She was not going to be any man's mother. To her, marriage was a partnership; share and share alike, the good, the bad, the difficult, the joys—all of life and living. If one partner possessed a particular quality or ability, he should use it for the common good. Work, ideas, accomplishments were to be shared. She was happy to do the cooking, to make her clothes and the children's, and in the very early days she made my shirts out of pongee silk. But she felt that the care of the house and children was the responsibility of both of us. I evidently had sewed on buttons and darned my own socks when I was a boy at home. These jobs she never took over nor did she ever look after my personal belongings.

All my life I have asked her, "Where did you put my shirts, my ties, my shoes?" And the answer was, "They are just where they always are unless you've done something else with them."

My mother would have rushed and laid out my shirt and ties and socks but not Marguerite. She took care of her personal belongings and it was up to me to take care of mine. Since we both worked at home in the same studio with two children under our feet, we both took care of the house and children.

The last word my father uttered on his dying bed was "Hor-a-vana," which means life has been a drudgery and a struggle. I graduated from the drudgery long ago. I do not think that I even found life a drudgery, because no matter what the odds against recognition and acceptance in the art world, no matter how hard it was to find money for even the barest living in the beginning, I was leading the life I wanted to lead, doing the work I wanted to do and was best equipped to do. What more can any man ask than that? I had everything, my wife, my two children, and always, my work. My life has been a struggle but fundamentally I believe the struggle is good for the soul, forges character, and deepens the power of expression. I do not regret any of it. I would go through it all again, gladly.

One day my grandson Jonny said, "How does it feel to be a famous artist, Grandpa?"

Actually, to this day I cannot believe I am a famous artist and I told Jonny, "It doesn't feel any different from anything else. Only sometimes you feel sort of sick, like butterflies in your stomach."

"I know," said Jonny.

At best fame is illusive. Fame today does not mean fame tomorrow. When there were enthusiastic articles on my work spread across the art pages, I thought I had arrived. At least I had reached a certain standing and place of prominence in the world of art. I didn't realize that every dog has his day, that this was my day, that tomorrow there would be a new man at the top, and that, even if you were not forgotten, the excitement of discovery was gone. No one knows who of the artists working today will be the famous ones tomorrow or two hundred years from tomorrow. The important thing is to work and do as fine and as creative work as is possible for you. We all have limits beyond which we cannot go and illusions about ourselves we cannot realize. Looking over old magazines of eighty years ago which we found in our house in Maine, we saw articles and reproductions of the famous and successful artists of that day. Pictures of them in their grandiose studios, draped in fishnets from the ceilings and decorated with embroidered Spanish shawls. And the astonishing sales and prices of this period. And yet not one of these artists is remembered or valued today. But there are artists of that same period who are still known and treasured by the contemporary art world.

Most people do not buy art, they buy illusion. The power of self-deception in human beings is astonishing. But that too is all right. It establishes a contact which may greatly enrich their lives and eventually lead to a development of understanding. When you come right down to it, the collections that enrich our Museums and our lives were not bought for the most part by men who loved and understood art.

One does not seem to make close friendships with people in later life. It is only in one's youth that one makes close friends. I realized this most keenly when I became a member of the National Institute of Arts and Letters. All these people had arrived, they were involved with their own lives and were interested in themselves. Everyone was very friendly and happy to meet another personally at meetings of the Institute and at dinners. We all enjoyed each other but that was the end. We all went on our way—I, too, like the rest of them. A number of times I tried to call up a member I had become friendly with and would like to see more of, but I could never find him so I just forgot about it and gave up. I'd send them invitations to my exhibitions and to Marguerite's shows but I never saw any of them at our openings. That seemed to be the way of life. Close and lasting friendships seem only to be made in one's youth. And as we grow old these too drop away. Our friends move to the far corners of the earth; they die and, of course, when they do that is final. But sometimes life just involves them, as a cocoon is wrapped in threads of silk and closed in upon itself.

I find as we go on in life we become advisors, father confessors, analysts. People come to us for advice and for recommendations for jobs. People timid at facing the world, indecisive people, people troubled in mind and in soul and in heart, restless people—all want help and advice. One tries to straighten them out. One should sit in a shrine with a cup in one hand and hand out words of wisdom, which they like the sound of and then usually forget.

I think back over the rare and special talents I have come across in my life—the very, very special ones who had something in art that others seemed to lack, and a degree of talent that was more expressive and powerful and original than anyone around them. To these I can only say: live art, sleep art, think art, talk art, write art, in other words marry art. If you are to be an artist, set yourself an ideal and keep in mind always your aim to do what you have set out to do to the utmost of your ability. Treasure talent in yourself and allow nothing to degrade it. Recognize your own talent; do not confuse it with the talent of another. Allow every man his own without envy. Do not defeat yourself.

All these things I tried to convey to the students I worked with and to all young artists I came in contact with. Some took my advice to heart, others didn't. But I have the feeling that most of them understood what I was saying and didn't resent it.

I cannot name all those who studied or worked with me and later went on to become fine artists in their own right—among them are Rhoda Sherbell, Helaire Blum, Margo Harris, Nat Kaz. I know I am unintentionally omitting some others, for the list is long.

There is very little to distract me in Maine, except the mosquitoes. The air is delicious, the rocks and the sea a pleasure. There are the exciting days when the wind is out of the northeast and the sea is like indigo laced with white. The landscape is crisp and deep and edged with black pines and golden cedars. There are also the wild days when the whole world is in turmoil. Then the fog will sit all day above the line of trees on the far shore and suddenly drift in on the turn of the tide and close us into our own niche in the clearing. In times of drought the dust rests on the leaves and the heat presses like it does in California and for a time you are no longer in Maine. I can paint watercolors of the world in front of our house and they are always new and exciting. The scene is inexhaustible.

There is the glory of the Maine autumn with cerise laid over vermilion on the maples, and pale yellows under chartreuse, and the rich heavy reds, oranges, and purples of oaks, becoming a wall of blackness in the deepening evening. The long, beautiful black shadows reach across the green meadow from the woods even before the fall sun has reached its zenith and is slipping behind the tall pines and below them the lavenders of alders. Red apples cling to the leafless branches through ice and snow. I stand at the window looking out into the cold, set up my watercolors, and paint the apple tree.

We are near our daughter Dahlov and her family and we see and enjoy our few neighbors. We engage in the local art activities, for Maine is quite an art-conscious state with good local exhibitions and many fine artists living and summering there, scattered all over the state. Artists like to live and work in a place that has a special beauty—preferably an unspoiled and uncommercialized beauty—where there is a real life among the people and the activities of work and living. The art school of Skowhegan, Maine, is one of the finest schools I know of in this country. There young people can develop freely and get the best instruction in the best surroundings. It is run by my friend, Willard Cummings, who will tell you that it functions independently, but to me it is his creation, and his sense of art values and organization have made it the great school it is. Bill is that rare person who can take care of every detail, keep a complicated project running smoothly, and yet remain an artist. We go up there at least once a summer and visit the students and the family and hold a seminar. It is always a pleasure.

There are endless beautiful glacial boulders on the shore across from our place. That is where I got the porphyritic diabase from which I carved the head of Christ and my two black cats.

There are all the rocks I could ever use right on my doorstep. But up at Cape Split in northern Maine, where John Marin painted, there are more rocks, perhaps not so different except that all rocks, like snowflakes, are different. Young John once took us out to the offshore islands. One island was so beautiful it reminded me of the high Sierras. Piled in wild abandon all around the shore there was a world of magnificent glacial boulders. There wasn't any rock formation—just boulders of every size and color. I wanted to pitch a tent there and move over with my chisel and hammer. I could hardly tear myself away from the place. We took back all the boat would hold. I just couldn't bear to leave such a wealth of stones, and yet I can never carve all I brought back. It is pleasant to be surrounded by such potential in shape, color, and size. To contemplate them and suddenly see possibilities, to pass by them and get a vision of something that was not there for you yesterday.

I have no artistic creed or formula. I have no fixed point to which I am bending every energy. I have made no wonderful or new artistic discovery. Perhaps I have not even had a new vision. There inevitably comes a time when every work of art must stand alone, apart from time, apart from the newness of its vision or the temporary importance of the scientific discoveries that attended its birth. Perhaps I am expecting too much when I send my work forth naked in the very day of its creation. But I cannot do otherwise.

There are things one does for the pure love of form and color, in the easy abandonment to the moods and the fancies of the moment. These are my watercolors. Then there are the visions imprisoned in the rock and the visions deep in one's soul—the things one does in seeking for the inner rhythm of nature and life, in the journeys into an unknown region where one can grasp only mystic fragments from the great subconscious that surrounds us. There is much of pain and exaltation in creative work. A resistless, relentless power that makes one ever create. This is my sculpture.

All these things have their place and their value.

ACKNOWLEDGMENTS

The following photographs appear through the courtesy of Peter A. Juley & Sons: *Figure of a Child;* Marguerite Zorach in front of *Land and Development of New England; Interior and Exterior; Spring;* William Zorach; *Floating Figure; Two Children; Artist's Daughter—Dahlov; Bathing Girl; Cat; Child on Pony; Mother and Child* (detail of early stage of roughing); *Mother and Child* (Spanish florida rosa marble); *The Artist's Daughter; Spirit of the Dance* (plaster); *Lenin Memorial; Seated Cat; Builders of the Future* (back view); *Faith of This Nation; Seated Nude; Awakening.*

The following photographs appear through the courtesy of Oliver Baker: *Summer; Football Player; Dahlov; Black Cat; Victory; Mask; Memorial to Six Million Jews;* Zorach Exhibition at The Downtown Gallery; *Mother and Child* sculpture for the Mayo Clinic Relief; *Head of Moses; The Family; Love; Plum Tree in Winter.*

The following photographs appear through the courtesy of Geoffrey Clements: *Two Figures; Nimbus; Tree into Woman; New Horizons* (plaster); *Man and Work; Reclining Figure; John the Baptist; Lovers; Eulogy.*

Acknowledgment is also made to the following individuals for the photographs named: Paul Hansen for *Artist's Daughter;* Einars J. Mengis for *New Horizons* (bronze); Harold Ferman for *Olympic Runner.*

Index